The Practices and Training Sessions of the World's Top Teams and Coaches

Library of Congress Cataloging - in - Publication Data

Saif, Mike (Edited by)
   The Practices and Training Sessions of the World's Top Teams and Coaches

ISBN No. 1-890946-34-6
Library of Congress Catalog Number 99-069771
COPYRIGHT © January 2000
Second edition June 2000

This book was originally published as newsletters in the USA, Australia and the UK.

Editor
Mike Saif

Art Direction
Kimberly N. Bender

Line Editing
Bryan R. Beaver

WORLD CLASS COACHING would like to thank
WorldofSoccer.com for the use of graphics.

REEDSWAIN INC
612 Pughtown Road
Spring City, Pennsylvania 19475
1-800-331-5191
www.reedswain.com

The Practices and Training Sessions of the World's Top Teams and Coaches

Second Edition

Edited by
Mike Saif

published by
REEDSWAIN INC

Table of Contents

Table of Contents

Table of Contents by Practice

Table of Contents by Teams

Table of Contents by Teams

February 1998 Issue

Flank Play - MLS Style

By Ed Puskarich - Chief Scout and Assistant Coach of the Dallas Burn

The Dallas Burn incorporate a 3-5-2 formation. This necessitates plenty of practice of flank play, especially from the outside midfielders. Dallas often work on flank play and use the following two practices regularly during the season.

The drill in diagram 1 starts with one of the defenders playing the ball back to the attacking midfielder, A1. A1 has a choice to play the ball directly to A2 or to play a give-and-go with one of the two forwards, A3 or A4, and then play the ball wide to A2. A2 should receive the ball about 30 yards out. A2 can either play the ball first-touch into the penalty area or he can touch the ball forward and attack the end line before crossing. A3 and A4 alternate runs to the near and far post. A5, the weak side midfielder, runs to support the far post. An important factor of this drill is that everything should be played with one-touch.

Coaching Points

- Everything one-touch.
- If forwards can't finish with one-touch then the ball is laid back one-touch to the attacking midfielder.
- Strong driven crosses.
- Forwards must continue runs.
- Wide player to be aware of the forwards' runs before crossing.

Variations

- Drill can start without defenders.
- Add defenders according to success of drill.
- Add a tracking defender to chase the wide player.
- Alternate left and right flank crosses.

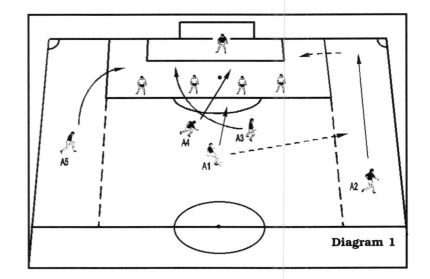

Diagram 1

Diagram 2 is a progression from the drill in diagram 1. This time the ball is played in by A1 from the center circle to A2. A2 plays the ball out wide to A3. As before, A3 can either cross first-touch or attack the end line before crossing. This drill changes to a more game-like situation when the attacking team has to make X number of passes before they are allowed to play the ball to the wide player.

Variations

- The game can be played with a goal at each end with each team attacking and defending. In this case the wide players play for both teams.
- Tracking defenders can be added for the wide players.

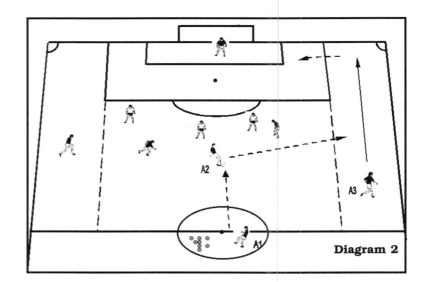

Diagram 2

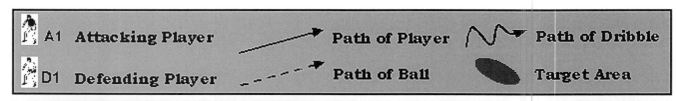

A1 Attacking Player	Path of Player	Path of Dribble
D1 Defending Player	Path of Ball	Target Area

Flank Play - English Style

By Michael Hennigan - First Team Coach of Blackpool Town F.C., England

Michael Hennigan started playing professional soccer in England in 1963 followed by spells playing in South Africa and Australia before returning to England to pursue a coaching career. In 1984, he joined Howard Wilkinson at Sheffield Wednesday F.C. as the club's Youth Development Coach. When Howard Wilkinson moved to Leeds United F.C. in 1988, he took Hennigan with him, this time as Assistant Manager/First Team Coach. In 1992, Leeds United F.C. won the English Championship and during his eight years there, Hennigan coached world-class players such as Eric Cantona, Thomas Brolin, Anthony Yeboah, Ian Rush, Gary McCallister, Gordon Strachan plus many others international players. In July 1997, Hennigan was offered the position as First Team Coach at Blackpool Town F.C. by one of his former players, Nigel Worthington.

A staple of the training sessions at Leeds United and now at Blackpool Town are based on flank play, crossing and finishing. In fact, these kind of practices are typically conducted at least once a week during the season. In diagram 3, the players are lined up in groups of three about 30 yards out. On the flank a server or coach plays balls toward the end line. A1, A2 and A3 take turns to chase the ball and cross into the penalty box. The server varies the pace of the passes to give A1, A2 and A3 different looks and options of crosses. The three forward players make runs to the far post, near post and center of the penalty area. The forwards are coached to finish in as few touches as possible. They are not allowed to score if they are closer than the six-yard line. An important part of this drill is the desired area for the wide players to aim their crosses. As you can see in diagram 3, there is a 'Second Six Yard Box' coned or marked out. The wide players must direct their crosses to this area.

Coaching Points

- Aim crosses to 'Second Six-Yard Box'
- Vary types of crosses.
- Finish in as few touches as possible.
- Time runs into penalty area.
- Don't 'kill the space' by running into penalty area too quickly.
- Communication between forward.

Variations

- Low driven or high crosses.
- Can only score on first-touch.
- Can only score from headers.
- Add defender(s) in penalty area.
- Add tracking defender for wide players

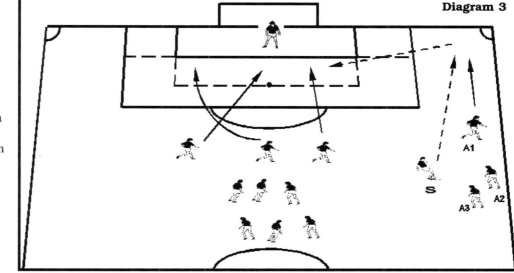

Diagram 3

Editor's note... It is interesting to see how similar the drills are to the ones that the Dallas Burn use in their practices. Even though the teams are a continent apart, and their styles of play are quite different, each team emphasizes wide play in their practices and coach finishing with the first-touch whenever possible. One difference, however, is that both Leeds United and Blackpool spend a specific amount of time concentrating purely on headers from their crosses. This follows the typical pattern of English soccer teams who are well known for being strong headers of the ball.

Flank Play - English Style

In diagram 4, the field is set up a little larger than half of the field. The size of the field depends on the number of players. In this case, the field is set up for 11 v 11 with the six-yard line extended. The game is basically a scrimmage between the two teams. The objective is to score goals directly from crosses. Therefore, the ball needs to be played wide, early and often. No goals can be scored inside of six yards. Again this encourages players to target their crosses to the 'Second Six-Yard Box.'

Coaching Points
- Encourage quality crosses away from the goalkeeper
- Pass the ball wide, early and often
- Time runs for headers
- Quick strikes at goal
- Shoot one-touch from knock down headers

Variations
- Use 'Floaters' depending on level of players.
- Score only directly or indirectly from headers.
- Score only directly from volleys.

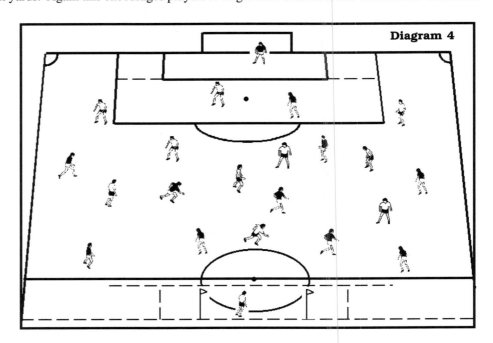

Diagram 4

In Diagram 5, the field is set up the same size as the previous drill. However, this time the object of the game is getting the ball out wide and keeping it out wide. Therefore, two small goals are set up for each team to attack. No goalkeepers or goal-tending is permitted. Players are not allowed to score inside five yards of the goals. Again, this field is set up for 11 v 11. This drill is usually played as a two-touch game.

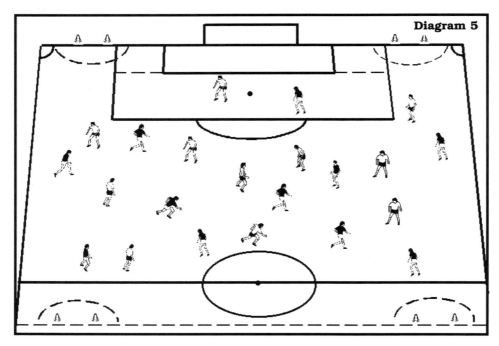

Diagram 5

Coaching Points
- Play ball wide, early and often
- Keep ball wide.
- Look for give-and-go's and overlaps.
- Switch play
- Keep head up for vision and awareness.

Variations
- Use 'Floaters" depending of level of players.
- Unlimited touches.
- 'Floaters" to have unlimited or only one touch.

The Competitive Cauldron

Have you wondered what makes the University of North Carolina Women's team so special? Why have they won 15 of the last 17 National Championships? Ever wondered what Anson Dorrance does at practice that makes his teams so competitive? One of the things that he attributes North Carolina's success to is something he learned from watching the legendary basketball coach, Dean Smith. Coach Dean Smith assesses every player in practice, keeping a record of every shot made or missed and every small-sided game won or lost. Anson took that idea and formulated his own method for his soccer teams. The following article is an excerpt from his book 'Training Soccer Champions' by Anson Dorrance and Tim Nash.

We give our players the best outside competition available. But I also firmly believe in setting up a competitive cauldron in practice because outside competition, no matter how challenging, cannot be the only environment where players are pushed. No matter how often you play, you will spend more time in practice. And that is where your players always get their edge. Our practice environment is competitive because we keep score in everything we can. Every player is assessed in every aspect of the game in practice – and we end up with her overall practice performance for the year. I can look at the charts and see that there is a direct correlation between the best players on the team and their rank on these charts. It doesn't always end up pure. But the order of the rank is always very, very close to being the way I would rank my players subjectively. We use the rank within the team as a reference point as opposed to a decathlon point system because practice competition within the team is always going to be the crucial factor in match playing time. And it all gets back to the core principal of the competitive team cauldron. Also, with the evolution of the matrix, player-v-player ranking is the simplest way to generate positive competition in practice sessions, creating the intensity necessary for optimum player development. In the player matrix, we don't give equal weight to every competition. We consider speed, one-v-one ability and a player's impact in all small-sided games to carry the greatest weight.

Areas of competition used throughout the year include both anaerobic and aerobic fitness work such as distance runs and sprints, speed tests, different kinds of one-v-ones, shooting, heading and passing drills. Goalkeepers are also included in the matrix. (Anson explains all of the drills and the matrix in greater detail in his book.)

As often as possible, our strikers are playing with regulation goals and active goalkeepers. Finishing against goalkeepers into regulation goals puts positive pressure on everyone in the exercise – the players trying to finish, the defender and the keeper. This is why we always try to carry four goalkeepers on our roster. We try to recruit two and encourage two to walk on from campus population. That way we can use many games with live keepers. It's an excellent environment.

We try to create a competitive cauldron in all the training environments, which is also what we try to create with our schedule. We try to create as much competition as possible in the four-v-fours, five-v-fives, three-v-threes and even in the eleven-v-eleven, starters-v-reserves scrimmage at the end of training. All the games are recorded and posted on the wall. They see it every day – wins, losses and ties. All the categories are reworked after every practice by the manager who rearranges the rankings. At the end of the season, it's all tabulated.

There are practices, however, where we don't do everything on the matrix. We want to make some practices recreational, like a pre-game day where we might not do anything that is recorded. In these situations, we do low-energy, non-competitive, team building exercises that still require focus and technique. However, these exercises don't knock them around physically or psychologically. We want to taper them physically and emotionally going into a game. The coaches don't talk about the charts too much because we don't want everything to be oppressive. We try to be relaxed and laid back about everything, except when training begins. Then there is a fury of intensity. We just put the charts on the wall. The kind of player who wants to be a champion will fight to the top of that ladder. If she doesn't want to be a champion, her ranking will not affect her. You are just not going to motivate them to move up the ladder unless they want to compete. What players basically need is a challenge, and the charts are another challenge for them. It will also objectively showcase their weaker areas. If they have a lot of pride and competitive spirit, they will fight to the top of the ladder or spend more time in the areas that need work. The only time we talk about the charts is in our player conferences. We look at the areas where they can improve and ask them if they would like to be more competitive in that particular area. If they say they would, then it's their goal to improve. Not ours. We will share everything we can to help them get better. The desire to be the best should always be present, and the charts are a reminder. That's why they stay on the wall year-round.

Excerpted with permission of the publisher from the book 'Training Soccer Champions' by Anson Dorrance and Tim Nash. For ordering information call 1-800-331-5191.

Passing and Possession for the Youth Player

By Sam Saif - Coach of the U16 youth team, Sheffield United F.C., England

Sam first took part in the F.A. coaching schools at the age of 21. After attaining the FA preliminary award, Sam went on to coach teams at the youth and semi-pro level. Always looking to improve, Sam continued his soccer education with the F.A. coaching schools and received the prestigious F.A. Full Badge a few years later. In 1989, Sam became part of the coaching staff at the Center of Excellence for Sheffield United F.C. In 1995, Sam joined the coaching staff at the Center of Excellence for Leeds United F.C. as the coach of the U14 team. He returned to Sheffield United F.C. in 1997 to coach the U16 youth team.

Many of the training sessions done with the youth players at both Leeds United and Sheffield United are spent teaching the players how to take care of the ball. Coaches encourage having a good first controlling touch, quality passes and movement to receive the pass, good body position to receive the pass and protect the ball, and creating space with and without the ball. Almost every training session involves some type of small-sided game, 3v3 or 4v4, where the players have a chance to devel-

op these skills. When in possession of the ball, quality of possession is encouraged as well as movement in advance of the ball to create goalscoring opportunities. When not in possession of the ball, correct individual defending techniques are stressed and players learn how to provide cover and balance. Depending on the age and ability of the players, games are sometimes limited to three, two or in some cases just one touch at a time. The following two practices are used extensively throughout the season.

The first drill is designed to improve the quality of the controlling touch and the quality/weight of passes. It also promotes awareness, vision and constant thought of where to position oneself to be of help, and what the best options are when in possession of the ball. **Effective screening (controlling the ball away from the pressure of an opponent) of the ball in all areas of the field is an important technique in modern soccer. It is especially important in that it facilitates maintaining possession of the ball.**

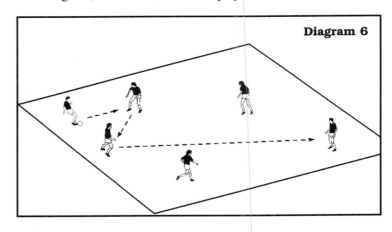

Diagram 6

The drill is set up in a square about 30 x 30 yards (diagram 6). Six players are constantly moving inside the square. The players are asked to pass the ball in a short-short-long sequence. Movement of the players should be to support close by the ball when a short pass is on and have players creating space for the long pass. The player receiving the long pass receives it with the outside of the foot keeping himself between the ball and an imaginary opponent. He then alters direction and starts the sequence with a short pass again. When players receive the ball, they should do so in a fashion in which they would be able to shield and protect the ball from any opponents. In other words, they should control away from pressure using their body as a barrier between the ball and an opponent. Players are encouraged to use one touch whenever possible. This drill quickly teaches the players the importance of keeping their head up and moving into correct supporting positions. **It is extremely important that this drill is played at a realistic game pace.**

Coaching Points

- Receiver of the long pass creates space by moving away but then quickly checks back to the ball.
- Weight and quality of passes.
- Keep possession of the ball on outside of foot and protect from imaginary defender until supporting player is close by.
- Sometimes fake to pass to supporting player then turn the other way.
- Use fakes by controlling the ball in one direction and moving the other direction.
- The closest two players to the ball offer support.

Variations

- Long passer must follow the ball to support the receiver.
- Limit number of touches to one or two depending on age and ability.
- Long passer must follow ball and passively pressure the receiver.
- Long passes must be high.
- Long passes must be driven low.

Passing and Possession for the Youth Player

Small side games are used frequently not only with our youth players but with the pro's as well. They are a valuable tool for teaching players the skills and techniques required for the modern game. Small sided games, (3v3 or 4v4) give the players far more touches of the ball and puts them in game-like situations many more times than a full-sided game does. Just about all our practices include small-sided games no matter what the technique or skill is being taught. However, I must stress that the games are played at a realistic game pace to ensure the players are able to duplicate in games what they do during practice.

The next drill in diagram 7 is a small-sided game which I use on a regular basis with the youth players, usually 3v3 or 4v4 if goalkeepers are available. The emphasis is on passing, movement and support when in possession of the ball; and pressure, cover and balance when defending. Again, it is important that these small-sided games are played at a realistic game pace. Therefore, each game should be two to three minutes duration with a rest period of no less than the game time. The size of the field depends on the age of the players, i.e. U16's 40 x 30, U12's 25 x 20. In diagram 7, the field is set up with cones as small goals. Goals can be scored only inside a marked out five yard area. If goalkeepers are available, larger goals can be used and the goal scoring area can be enlarged. To score a goal, a team must have all it's players in the attacking half. This eliminates too many long balls and encourages close support play. There are no corner kicks. If the ball goes out of play, it is passed back in from the lines. In this drill, scoring is not as important as passing and movement. In fact, a common condition of this game is that the player must move after making a pass, otherwise the ball is given to the other team. Offside is also in play with this particular game.

It is extremely important to let the players play without stopping the game to give instruction. The coach should offer encouragement and positive advice from the sideline. Use the rest period to give instruction and make your coaching points and then let the players play again. Look for improvement after each rest period.

Coaching Points - Offensive
- Pass and move to support in advance of the ball.
- Keep head up to improve scanning ability.
- Quality passes and controlling touches.
- Run at defenders; if the forward pass is not on, turn and shield the ball and pass to a supporting player.
- Receive the ball with an open body position.

Coaching Points - Defensive
- Encourage defending goal side of the ball.
- Try to force lateral and backward passes.
- Communicate, especially the defender furthest back.
- Pressure the person with the ball; force him into quick decisions.
- Stress correct individual defending techniques.

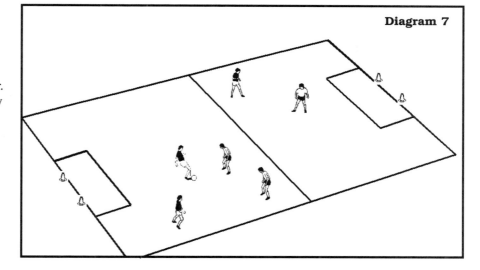

Diagram 7

Variations
There are literally hundreds of variations for these types of small-sided games, depending on whether you want to concentrate on the offensive or defensive side of the ball. Offensively, touches could be limited; goals can only be scored after a give-and-go, an overlap or a one-touch pass, etc. Defensively, you could try to win the ball back within a certain number of passes; a goal could be given to your opponents if they make X number of forward passes; or the defensive team scores points if they steal the ball from an opponent's forward pass, etc.

Mid-Season Practices - MLS Style

Practices of the Kansas City Wizards

Ron Newman was a former professional player in England. He started coaching in the United States in the old NASL. When the NASL folded, Ron continued coaching, this time in the MSL and the indoor game. Ron's record speaks for itself. He has won more games and more national championships in the professional game than any other coach in American history. When the MLS was formed, Ron was heavily recruited and it was Lamar Hunt that persuaded Ron to take the Head Coach's position at the Kansas City Wizards. During his two seasons at Kansas City, and with the help of his son and Assistant Coach, Guy Newman, Ron has continued his success. The Wizards have made the playoffs in both seasons and combining the two seasons, the Wizards have won more regular season games than any other MLS team.

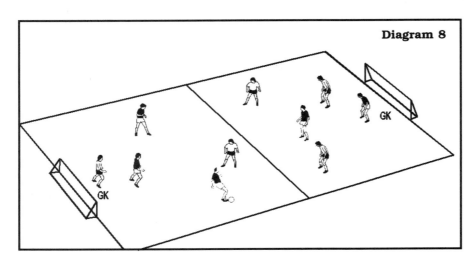

Diagram 8

In the middle of a hectic season, when the team is playing two or more games a week, Ron keeps his players ticking over without over-exerting them and risking fatigue or injury. A typical practice during the season includes the following two drills. The players are split into four teams and two separate games are played simultaneously for about ten minutes each. After each game and rest period, the teams rotate, giving each team time on each game and against different opposition. It is important to note that all facets of the game are covered by these two simple small-sided games. The goalkeepers are involved and passing, shooting and defending are all components used in the practice.

Diagram 8 is a small-sided shooting game. It is played with 3 v 1 in each half. The players must stay in their half. The size of the field is about 40 x 30 yards. The objective is for the three players to pass the ball and create opportunities for shots. The single defender works at closing down space and denying those opportunities. The three players in the opposing half look to block shots if possible. The lone forward in the opposing half looks for rebounds and to pounce on any loose balls.

Possible Variations are to play 2 v 1, or before taking a shot, players must pass to the lone forward in the opposing half who acts as a target man and lays the ball back to any of his teammates to shoot. Players could also be made to shoot before reaching a set number of passes to encourage taking quick early shooting opportunities, or players could be encouraged to shoot with only one touch.

In diagram 9, the field is set up about 30 x 30 depending on the number of players. Small goals or cones are used. This is just a straight forward small-sided game in which the players are encouraged to maintain possession, look for quick passes, give-and-go's, etc.

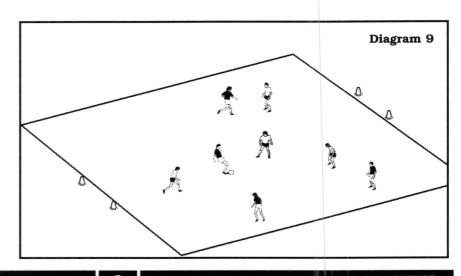

Diagram 9

Possible Variations
- Play with a "floater".
- Only score after a one-touch pass.
- Only score after a give-and-go or overlap.
- Limit number of touches.

Preparing Your Team for a Major Tournament

The Tahuichi Academy is probably the most successful youth soccer club in the world today. The Tahuichi Academy was formally organized on May 1st 1978 and before long, over 200 students attended the academy. In it's first year, Tahuichi won the U14 Bolivian National Championship. They were then invited to the first-ever South American U14 Championship in Buenos Aires, Argentina where it defeated the mighty Independiente of Argentina 4-1 in the final before 50,000 spectators.

Since then, Tahuichi teams have been represented in 72 top international tournaments in the U.S., Asia, Europe and Latin America. Their record has been nothing short of phenomenal. From the 72 tournaments entered, Tahuichi has won 49 and placed second 9 times. In over 300 games, they have lost only 25 - and in the process, they have scored more than 1,600 goals and conceded only 180. Currently, over 60 Tahuichi graduates have signed professional contracts including Marcos Etcheverry and Jaime Moreno (D.C. United). Eleven members of the Bolivian National Team are current or ex-Tahuichi graduates. Over 25 more have received full college scholarships in the U.S.

WORLD CLASS COACHING asked Tahuichi to share it's methods on preparing their youth teams for major tournaments. The following is Tahuichi's preparation for their U15 team in readiness for the 'Mundialito', the U15 World Youth Club Championship held in January.

Tahuichi's preparation for the Mundialito or any major tournament is a three-month program which leads up to the competition. Each month is broken down into specific soccer components. The first month is dedicated to physical fitness, the second month to technical training and the third to tactical training and competition.

Twenty-two players are selected to live and train together for the three months. However, only 18 players will travel to compete. This brings an element of competition to the training sessions. Before training begins, each player has a thorough medical check-up. Many Tahuichi students arrive at the academy suffering from malnutrition and sickness. While they are training, they will eat three meals a day plus vitamins, minerals, amino acids and other nutritional supplements. For these players, it is a chance of a lifetime to carry on the honor and tradition of Tahuichi.

The first month of training is unbearable. It is six-days-a-week of physical conditioning. Each day consists of two three-hour sessions in heat that can sometimes reach 115 degrees and 90% humidity. For the whole month, a soccer ball is not used during the training sessions.

Coach Ciro Medrano, or "El Loco" to his players, pushes them through each training session with his own unique style. He says, "To truly be alive, a human being must be challenged beyond their imagination. To truly appreciate life you must suffer. To truly be a champion you must sacrifice and suffer."

The first day of each week, the players are tested to see if they have improved over the previous week. The test is fairly simple. They are timed for a two-mile run, 1,500m, 800m, 400m, 200m, and 100m. Also checked are the players weight, and measurements of the waist, thighs, calves, chest, neck, height and body fat.

Weight training is three times a week. Sessions consist of light weights with high reps of thirty different stations. Each station is done for thirty seconds with thirty seconds rest. Three to four sets of all thirty stations are done each session.

Everything the players do is measured and timed. Every week, training is increased and the challenge for the players is to do better than the week before.

Typical training days might include the weekly fitness tests in the morning. In the afternoon, they will be driven 14 miles out of town and timed on their run back to the academy. The next day might consist of weight training in the morning followed by more running in the afternoon. This time the running would be four miles cross-country through rivers and over dirt and rocky terrain to arrive at a place with 100 foot-high sand dunes. Multiple sprints are done up and down the sand dunes followed by a three mile run through the sand and finally a four mile run back to the bus. Sundays are rest days and the players are treated to a sauna and massage.

Next issue we will focus on Month Two - technical Training.

For further information on the Tahuichi Soccer Academy please call 1-770-986-3692 or visit them online at: http://tahuichi.home.mindspring.com.

Improve Your One-Touch Finishing

By Howard Wilkinson - Technical Director of the English Football Association

Howard Wilkinson is the Technical Director of Coaching for the English F.A. Howard has previously coached the U21 England National Team, Notts County, Sheffield Wednesday and at Leeds United where he took them to the League Championship in 1992. Howard has achieved success at every club he has coached. He guided Notts County from Division Two to Division One, and later repeated that success gaining promotion to Division One with Sheffield Wednesday. He later left Sheffield Wednesday to join Leeds United who at that time were struggling in the lower reaches of Division Two. In his first full season, Leeds gained promotion, winning the Division Two Championship. Two seasons later, Leeds United won the English Championship beating out Manchester United into second place.

Analysis tells us that approximately 72% of goals are scored with one-touch finishing. This obviously makes practicing one-touch shooting/finishing extremely worthwhile. The following drills are all for one-touch finishing. When conducting these practices the following needs to be stressed.

Session

- If you don't shoot, you don't score.
- It is where it finishes, not how it gets there.
- Low shots are more difficult to deal with than high ones.
- Accuracy is more important than power.
- Follow everything in.
- Being there to finish frequently enough is crucial.

Shooter

- Needs to be alert and a quick thinker.
- A quick mover - reactions.
- Be persistent - willing to keep missing.
- Be brave - physically and mentally.
- Be composed.
- Needs a wide range of techniques.

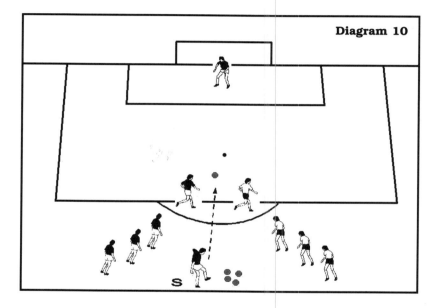

Diagram 10

The first drill in diagram 10 is designed to practice the technique with the ball going away from the shooter. Players are lined up in two teams either side of the server. One player from each team steps forward, facing the goal. The server plays the ball between the two players who compete as to who gets the one-touch shot. Either player competes for rebounds from the goalkeeper. **Service variations** include on the ground between the two players, on the ground between the players - favoring one player, in the air over the players and in the air favoring one player.

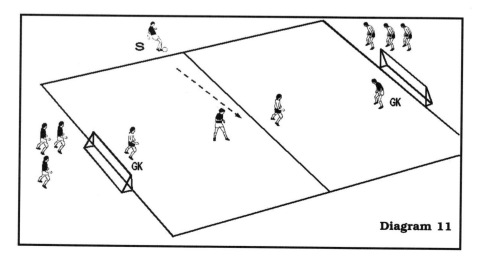

Diagram 11

Diagram 11 shows a drill for the ball going across the shooter. The field is 30 yards long and 40 yards wide. Two players stand with their backs to the server. The server passes the ball between the two players. They react to the server's command of 'TURN'. The players compete as to who gets the one-touch shot. Again, each player competes for rebounds. **Service variations** include on the ground fast, on the ground slower, in the air to bounce slower and in the air to pitch fast.

Improve Your One-Touch Finishing

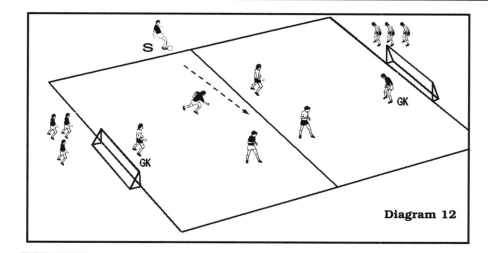

Diagram 12 is a progression of diagram 11. This time it is 2 v 2. The players have the option of shooting or setting up their partner. Again, look for rebounds from the goalkeeper.

Diagram 12

Diagram 13 illustrates a practice for volleys, overhead kicks and setting-up play. The field is 36 yards long and 44 yards wide. The server floats long diagonal passes to the runner (A1), into the area of the far post, around 12 yards out. A1 practices volleys across his body, bicycle and overhead kicks.

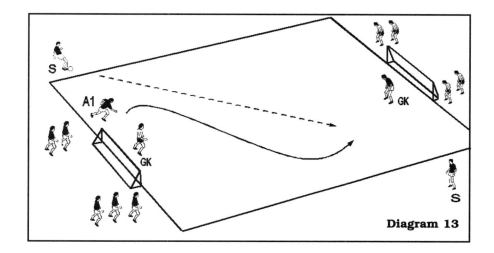

Diagram 13

Diagram 14 is a progression of the drill in diagram 13. A1 is now joined by A2. This time A1 attempts to head the ball down to A2 who finishes early and with his first touch.

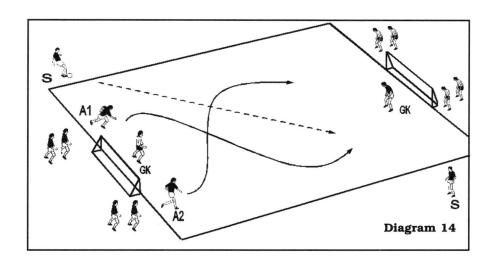

Diagram 14

Coaching Points for diagrams 13 and 14

- The angle of attacking run and body position should set the player up to hit the ball with the foot furthest from the goal.
- Adjust body position to ensure the ball is struck through its top half.
- If the ball is high, the player is required to perform an over head or bicycle kick.

More One-Touch Finishing

I first saw this drill in 1991 at an F.A. coaching seminar in my home town of Sheffield, England. Chris McMenemy, then the Manager of Chesterfield Town F.C., was conducting a session on finishing. Now on the coaching staff at Newcastle United F.C., England, Chris continues to use this drill often during the season. He also did a very interesting session on the different styles of play of some of England's top clubs and the reasons certain types of players fit into those styles. I hope to bring you this excellent session sometime in the future.

The drill should be done at a fast pace. Initially, it might seem that players are moving all over the field in a somewhat chaotic manner. However, after a short time, the drill should start taking shape. This is an excellent finishing drill. All the players involved are actively moving, making it a very game-like situation.

In diagram 15, players are lined up about 25 yards from goal. A1 passes to A2. A2 lays the ball off to the coach, C. After passing, A1 quickly runs around A2 to receive the pass from the coach, C. A1 then crosses the ball low and hard into the penalty area. After passing to the coach, A2 runs around the cone into the penalty area to receive the cross from A1. A3 is waiting in the penalty area giving A1 a far post and a near post option to cross to. On completion of the shot, A1 takes A2's position, A2 takes A3's position. A3 joins the line.

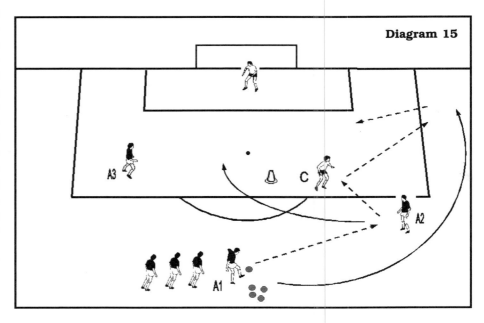

Coaching Points
- Play at a realistic game pace.
- Finish one-touch whenever possible.
- Stress quality crosses.
- Shots must be on target.

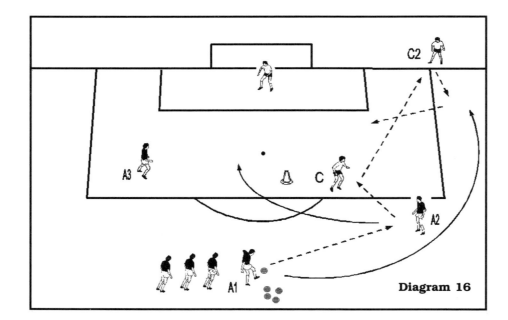

Variations
- Change sides
- If player scores, he stays in the penalty area
- Low crosses
- High crosses
- Score from headers, volleys, knock-downs, etc.

Diagram 15 is set up to give the players practice with the ball going away from the crosser. Diagram 16 is a slight variation. This time the coach passes the ball to C2 who plays the ball back to A1, giving him practice of the ball coming at him.

March 1998 Issue

Improve Your One-Touch Finishing

By Howard Wilkinson - Technical Director of the English Football Association. This article is a continuation of last issue's excellent One-Youch Finishing drills.

Squad Practice

Diagram 1 shows a field 36 yards long and 44 yards wide (two 18 yard penalty boxes). Initially, one attacker from each end attacks each goal simultaneously, e.g. S1 serves to A1 and S4 serves to A4. A1 then joins the A4 line and A4 joins the A1 line.

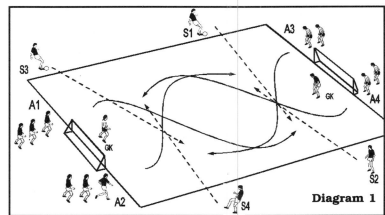

Service Variations

- Driven low across the '2nd six-yard box'. Slide to finish if necessary.
- Driven diagonally towards the far post.
- Pulled back - short, sharp, late.
- Ball pitches to come up just in front of attacker.
- Driven below chest height for diving headers.

Progression

Progress to attacking in pairs to produce knock-down headers for partner to volley or half-volley and look for rebounds from the goalkeeper.

Diagram 1

Diamond Shooting

The field in diagram 2 is 36 x 44 yards, as above. However, the sidelines are now tapered in toward each goal giving a diamond-type shape. This stops the players from taking the ball out wide and taking shots from difficult angles.

Balls are placed in each goal with a player at each side of the goal to retrieve balls. Players are organized into 4 v 2 in each half. Players can only stay in their own half of the field. The four players can only score from their own half of the field. The two forwards can follow in for rebounds. Goalkeepers can only play the ball in their own half. Defenders are limited to two-touch and any player that shoots the ball over the crossbar is replaced by one of the fielders.

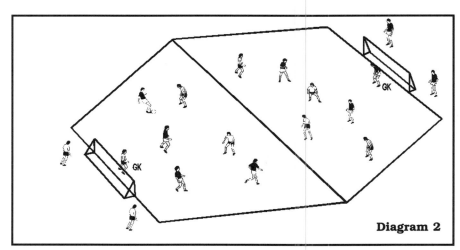

Coaching Points

- Take the first shooting opportunity.
- Attempt to shoot on the first-touch whenever possible.
- Follow shots in for rebounds.

Possible Variations

- Use one of the two forwards as a target man.
- One of the four players can join the attacking half with the ball.

Diagram 2

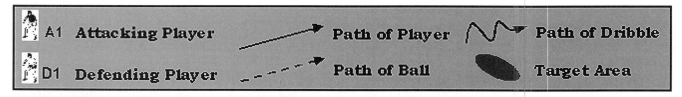

A1	**Attacking Player**	➔ **Path of Player**	⌇➔ **Path of Dribble**	
D1	**Defending Player**	⇢ **Path of Ball**	● **Target Area**	

NY/NJ MetroStars

Team Defending by Alfonso Mondelo with the NY/NJ MetroStars. Observed in Orlando, Florida - Pre-season 1998.

Stage One

In diagram 3, A1 passes to A2. The defensive team reacts by D3 pressuring the player with the ball, A2. D2 slides to his left to cover D3. D1 slides to his left to guard A4. The ball is passed constantly from A1 to A2 and to A3. This forces D1, D2 and D3 to constantly slide from side to side as a unit. This is done for almost 10 minutes until the defenders are comfortable with their responsibilities. Then for a further five minutes, the wide players, A2 and A3, have the option of playing the ball into the target player A4. A4 holds the ball and then plays it back to A1 to start over.

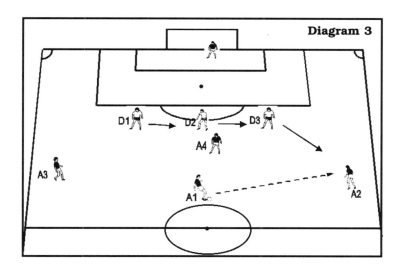

Stage Two

D4 and D5 are added in diagram 4. Their responsibility is to cut off any attempted pass by A2 or A3 to A4. Again, the ball is passed from one side of the field to the other by the offensive team for 5-10 minutes, allowing the defensive team to become familiar with their responsibilities.

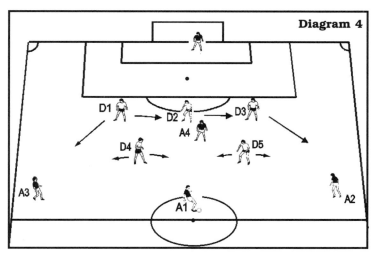

Stage Three

A5 and A6 are added in diagram 5. The ball is again passed amongst the offensive team including A5 and A6 for 5-10 minutes. This time D4 and D5 have the extra responsibility of pressuring A1, A5 and A6 and to cut off any passes through the middle to A4. This is followed with 10 minutes of free-play with the offensive team attempting to score.

Stage Four

This time the goalkeeper starts with the ball and plays it wide to D1 or D3. The defending team attempts to play the ball out of the defensive half. Again for 5-10 minutes.

Stage Five

Develops into a 9 v 9. The defending team is encouraged to pressure the ball, try to intercept passes and look to force passes wide or back rather than commit themselves with tackles.

Chicago Fire

A complete 90 minute practice by Bob Bradley and Chicago Fire. As observed at Orlando, Florida - Pre-season 1998.

Warm-up

This drill in diagram 9 was used as the initial warm-up. Half the players formed a circle roughly 30 yards in diameter, and stood bouncing on the balls of their feet. The other half of the players, each with a ball, dribble inside the circle and play give-and-go's with the outside players. After two minutes, change positions and repeat, then stretch. Then repeat again a second time with further stretches.

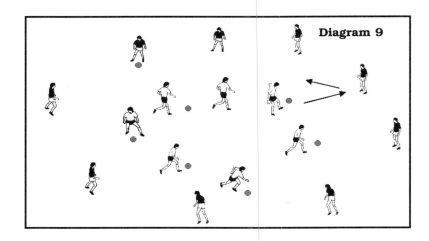

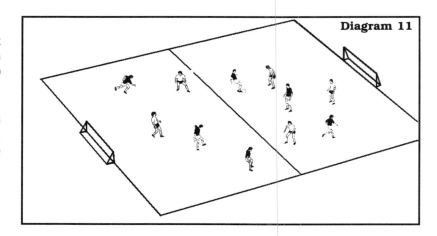

Warm-up

A similar drill, shown in diagram 10, was used for a further warm-up. Again, half the players formed a 30-yard circle with the other half inside. This time roughly two-thirds of the outside players had a ball. The players in the middle moved around and checked towards a player with a ball to receive a pass and then passed to an outside player without a ball. A variety of options were stressed when receiving the pass, such as, play a return pass back, hold and shield, fake one way and turn the other way. Also, as shown, A1 checks toward D1 and receives the ball with an open body position allowing him to turn and play the ball to D2. As before, two minutes, then change, then stretch. Repeat again a second time with further stretches.

The squad was then split into two groups of 11. While one group worked on a small-sided game the other group worked on shooting. After 20 minutes the groups alternated. The session ended with a cool down and stretches.

Small-Sided Game

In diagram 11 the small-sided game was set up as 5 v 5 + 1 with the floater playing for the team in possession. The field was 30 x 30 yards with small goals and no goalkeepers.

A restriction of two-touch was in place. The emphasis was an extension of the warm-up, crisp passing, a good first touch, head-up to see the field and plenty of movement.

Chicago Fire

The shooting session started with players 40 yards out then running with the ball and shooting long range shots from approximately 25 yards. This lasted 5 minutes.

Stage One

The group was then split into forwards and defenders. In diagram 12, the forwards start with the ball at the half-line and play a give-and-go with the coach. The defenders start on the edge of the field, 15 yards from the goal-line. As the forward, A1 plays the give-and-go, the defender, D1, enters the field. A1 can either shoot before D1 engages him or he can dribble around D1 to shoot. The players then join the opposite line.

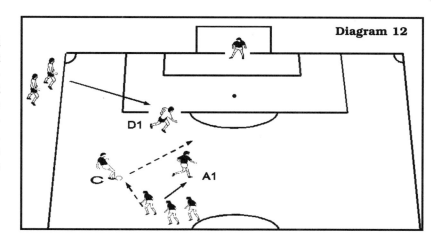

Diagram 12

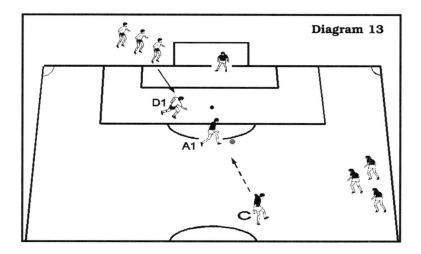

Diagram 13

Stage Two

As shown in diagram 13, the defenders moved behind the goal and the forwards moved to approximately 25-30 yards out. The forward, A1, checks to receive a ball from the coach and attempts to beat the oncoming defender, D1 by turning and shooting. The players then join the opposite line.

Stage Three

The final progression was 2 v 2 from 25 yards in (diagram 14). The coach plays the ball in from 40 yards out to one of the two forwards. The forwards move and make check-runs to receive the ball. Once in possession, the forwards are encouraged to develop a quick shooting opportunity by passing to each other, or if no shooting opportunity develops, they can trail back to the coach who is limited to one touch.

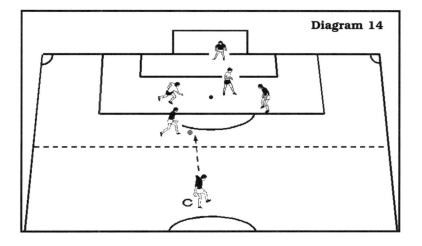

Diagram 14

Anson Dorrance - Off-Season

Anson Dorrance continues from last month's article on 'Competitive Practices' and gives his views on the 'Off-season'

The entire fall is about developing the team to the maximum extent. The off-season, however, is dedicated to individual growth and individual development.

For the entire off-season, all we do is play. We don't want the players to get bored yet we believe year-round play is crucial, and making sure each part of the year has nothing to do with any other part assures that players don't get bored. The second reason is that we want to have fun, so we just play. We devote the whole off-season to playing whatever games we can. The ultimate game that you can play, in my opinion, is five v five – four field players and a goalkeeper. It gives you the basic elements of the game. It gives you enough players for fundamental attacking shape – penetration, width and support. The numbers also allow for classical defensive shape – pressure, cover and balance. Five v five requires consistent involvement by all the players in every attack and in every defense. You can't hide or hangout in this game, or your teammates will get shredded. It permits players a lot of time on the ball. It has every dimension, so much so that the Dutch – who on the men's side might produce the highest number of quality players per capita in the world – make a religion out of it. Five v five is an excellent compromise between the eleven v eleven game – where the ball-to-player ratio is miserable (22-to-1) and ball touches are at a minimum but has the gamut of tactical choices – and the one v one game where ball touches are frequent, the ball-to-player ratio is excellent (2-to-1) but has little tactical complexity or variety. And since we always play with goalkeepers in this environment, we are practicing finishing all the time. One more thing: It's fun to play.

One additional day a week, we go into racquetball courts and play three different games. We start out with one v one, which in my opinion is the cornerstone of the game. We set up a cone at each end of the racquetball court as goals, and now you can do anything to beat the other player. You can play it off walls or just take on the other player one v one. It's the ultimate duel. You against your opponent. No one is going to interfere. Each player plays three different games against three different opponents, and each game lasts four straight minutes. Then as a rest – because one v one is exhausting – we play soccer squash with a size five tennis ball. You're allowed one bounce and two touches to get it back to the front wall. It's basically just a shooting game. We do that for about twenty minutes, and for the last twenty minutes we play two v two on the racquetball court. We encourage the players to get in the right shape – one up high and one back – and they are encouraged to use the walls. The game is basically about combinations. You want them to pass and move, pass and move. We use a size three ball here, but now it is a regu-

lation size three. It's a tremendous game for movement. It's also a great game for learning how to set up your opponent because, in a way, it's six against two if you count the four walls you have available to combine with. At the end of the session in the racquetball courts, we have the players shoot for twelve minutes, using a regulation ball. We vary it a bit with one-touch, first-time shots, or two-touch preparations and quick shots to get them to develop some power and a better strike.

It's important to let the players know what each game is designed to develop. Before all these games, I bring the whole group together and make one coaching point – whichever coaching point that particular game is designed to bring out. Then, I stand on the sideline and encourage that point. Obviously, I point out good things that aren't related to that one point we are working on, but I try to get the players to concentrate on the one thing that each game is designed to encourage. I don't want to cloud their brains with a thousand different pieces of information. Our off-season games are different activities which will develop a certain aspect of play. For example, on the Astroturf all we talk about is attacking and defensive transition and shooting at every opportunity because that game caters to those aspects. In the Tin Can with a size five tennis ball on a thin Astroturf field, we talk about speed of play and running with the ball. So we encourage the players to be running with the ball as much as possible. This will develop their aptitude on the run, when the ball is never static and they're always active. Then in Carmichael with the size three ball, we encourage them to never panic, solve problems technically, weave in and out of traffic with possession, and develop individual confidence with the ball in a crowd. There is nothing soccer-specific about our off-season facilities. We just took what we could find and created different games based on what was available. We made a soccer facility out of everything we could.

Before all these events, we do a Coerver warm-up – changing direction with the ball and changing pace. Let's face it, the whole game is about your capacity to change speed and direction with a soccer ball. So everything in the off-season – although all we're doing is playing games – is a constant review of some aspect of the game. Each game is entirely different from the other, and you can't get burned out easily. Each one helps you become a better soccer player, but they are all entirely different. As a result, players in our program have a year-round enthusiasm for the game, which is rare. I'm not saying we can't get burned out, but we try to stay plugged into our kids. If one of my off-season captains comes up to me and says the team is burning out a little bit, then instead of playing more five v fives, we might have a one v one tournament and the next

Anson Dorrance - continued

day we might have an eleven v eleven tournament to mix it up a little bit and make it more fun. And it doesn't have to be some form of soccer. At one point during the 1996 off-season, we were in Carmichael playing mini-soccer, and Nel Fettig suggested we play basketball. So after twenty-five minutes of soccer, we played twenty-five minutes of basketball.

All those five v five games are a review of five weeks of our winter training. After spring break, all we really do is go outside and play forty-five straight minutes of eleven v eleven. It all gets back to the core principle of player development, which has never been very complicated: Play as often as you can and keep score in every game you play.

Excerpted with permission of the publisher from the book 'Training Soccer Champions' by Anson Dorrance and Tim Nash. For ordering information call 1-800-331-5191.

MLS Warm-ups

Kansas City Wizards

One of the warm-ups used most often by the Wizards is a game of 'Walking Soccer'. The players are split into two teams and play on a smaller than usual field size. For instance, 11 v 11 would play on a field slightly smaller than a half-size regulation field. Ron often starts practice with one-touch soccer, his belief is that if players can play one-touch soccer than they are certainly capable of playing regular soccer. After five minutes, stretch. Play for another five minutes and stretch. Progress on to jogging-soccer or walking-two-touch soccer for five minutes and stretch. Finish warm-up with five minutes of free-play followed by a final stretch.

New England Revolution

Thomas Rongen believes in warm-ups that incorporate soccer related conditioning and uses a ball whenever possible. With the aid of conditioning expert, Vern Gambetta, New England has altered their warm-ups from the traditional jog and stretch routines. Early on in a training session players will do dynamic-active work as opposed to the static stretching. As Thomas says, "The game is dynamic so the warm-ups should be similar to prepare you for the game." Static stretches are done at the end of practice.

Dallas Burn

Every session begins with a 20-minute warm-up. because of the warm climate in Dallas, the players do not require a lot of running to get the blood circulating. This allows them to combine a great deal of ball work into the warm-up. Start in groups of 2-3 players with one ball, juggling. A team favorite is 5-6 players in a circle playing one-touch keep-away from two players. Stretching is done during and after all warm-ups, focusing on the four major muscle groups, quads, hamstrings, groin and calves. The players are always allowed a few extra minutes on their own to stretch any specific muscle they need.

Colorado Rapids - Goalkeepers

Start with a seven-minute jog followed by the light stretches. then, in a 10-yard square with 3-4 goalkeepers, dribbling a ball and on command from the coach, the players flick the ball above their head and jump up to catch the ball as high as possible (five minutes). Next, dribble, and on command, pick up the ball of another player (five minutes) Then progress to dribble, and on command, touch the ball away and dive on another's ball. Stretches are done between each of the three dribbling drills and at the end.

Tahuichi - Technical Training

In the last issue, Tahuichi focused on Month One - Fitness, the first of a three-month preparation program used for major tournaments. This issue, Tahuichi focuses on Month Two which is dedicated to technical training. Outlined below are two of the technical drills Tahuichi uses on a regular basis.

Technical Session

A typical example of a technical training session is to have the players work in an area of 10 x 35 yards. In this area, half the players have a ball at their feet and are standing approximately one yard apart. The other half of the players are laying face down approximately one yard in front of a standing player. Approximately four yards behind the face-down player is a two foot high hurdle and then a further four yards behind the hurdle is a cone. When the coach blows his whistle, the face-down players quickly get up and receive a pass to their right foot from the standing player. They quickly return the pass, then turn and sprint, jumping over the hurdle and around the cone, do a tuck and roll and then sprint back to a face-down position. The sequence is then repeated but this time the ball is passed to the left foot.

The players will do as many repetitions as they can in 45 seconds and then switch places with the standing player and repeat. This will be done a second time for one minute, a third time for one minute, 15 seconds and a fourth time for one minute and 30 seconds.

Immediately following the passing drill, the same drill will be used for heading, volleys, dribbling, or a combination of trapping with the chest or thigh followed by a pass. During this session the players must be intense, technically precise and be given an opportunity to recover so they can have the energy to repeat the intensity and technical precision over and over.

Technical and Psychological Drill

In diagram 15, players form a circle approximately 30 yards in diameter. Start off with one ball. The player passing the ball always follows his pass and takes the place of the player receiving the ball. The player receiving the ball calls out the name of the person he is going to pass to before he receives the ball. Once the players have acheived a good rhythm, add another ball. Continue adding balls depending on the number of players and the success of the drill. This drill not only refines the quality of passing and control but also encourages the players to think ahead.

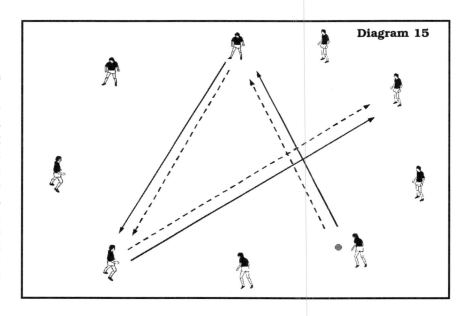

Diagram 15

Coaching Points
- Start off dribbling if necessary.
- Encourage one-touch whenever possible.
- Stay alert and evaluate options.
- Control the ball to the direction of the next pass.

In the next issue Tahuichi will focus on Month Three - Tactical Training and Competition.

For Further information on the Tahuichi Soccer Academy please call 1-770-986-3692 or visit them online at: http//tahuichi.home.mindspring.com

Glasgow Rangers F. C.

Glasgow Rangers F.C., one of Europe's top clubs and winners of 10 of the last 11 Scottish Premier League Championships share some of their coaching routines.

Passing Routine

In diagram 16, A plays a long pass to B who plays a give-and-go with C and then plays a long pass to D who plays a give-and-go with A. Once this has occurred, C & B and A & D should change positions after the long pass. The player receiving the short pass dictates whether it is on his left or right side.

Coaching Points

• Angle made to receive the short pass.
• Driven or chipped pass.
• Alter the side of which you play the give-and-go.

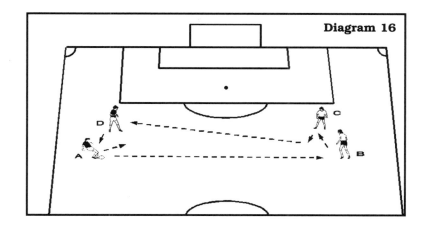

Diagram 16

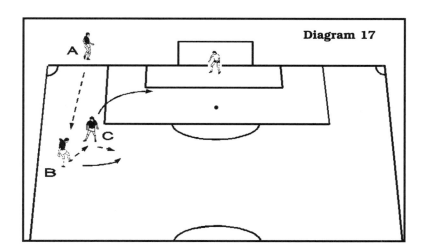

Diagram 17

Shooting Drill

The ball is played in by A to B (diagram 17). B controls and passes to C who lays a one-touch pass to B who shoots at the goal. After making his pass, C turns and runs in toward the goal for any rebounds.

Coaching Points

• Driven or chipped pass from A.
• Quality first-touch from B.
• The angle of pass back to B should be inside and away from the goal.
• Use both sides of the field.

Variations

• When B passes to C, C turns and shoots. A follows in for rebounds
• When B receives the pass from A, C becomes a defender
• In diagram 18, C starts the drill by checking toward A who passes it to C.
  C returns the pass one-touch to A who plays it to B. B then looks to shoot.
  After his pass, C turns inside and becomes a defender.

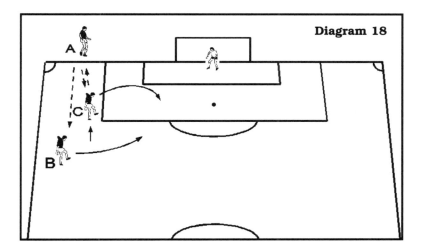

Diagram 18

Glasgow Rangers F. C.

Crossing and Finishing With Extra Attacker

In diagram 19, the ball is played from A1 to A2 who lays it off to A3. A3 plays the ball into the path of A4. A4 attacks the end line and crosses into the goal box. After making their passes, A2 and A3 become attackers and make runs into the goal box. D1 and D2 are defenders and pick up A2 and A3 as they make their runs into the box. A1 becomes an extra attacker at the far post.

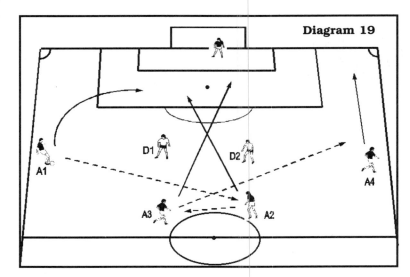

Diagram 19

Coaching Points - Offensive

- Chipped or driven long passes.
- Angle to receive pass - first touch.
- Timing of runs into the box.
- Get across the defenders when attacking front post.
- Extra attacker at far post to time run so he doesn't arrive too early.

Coaching Points - Defensive

- Pick up the attackers' runs early - outside the goal box.
- Cover front post run by staying goal-side of the attacker.
- Pick up and clear any rebounds.

Javanon - National U17 Champions

Tim Chastony has enjoyed remarkable success as the coach of the Javanon U17 boys. Under Tim's guidance, Javanon have amassed an incredible 52-1 record. Over the last 12 months, Javanon has also won the National Snickers U17 Championships as well as major tournaments such as the Tampa Sun Bowl, Ohio Buckeye Invitational and the inaugural Superclubs National Championship. Tim shared with WORLD CLASS COACHING one of his favorite practices.

The field is set up 40 yards wide and 60 yards long separated into two 25-yard end zones and a 10-yard center neutral zone (see diagram 20). A1 and A2 maintain possession in their zone until they create an opportunity to play the ball to A3 in the offensive zone. As soon as A3 receives the ball, N1 or N2 can enter the offensive zone, in this example N1. N2 stays in the neutral zone and supports for a trail pass. A3 can either turn and play 2 v 2 with the supporting N1 or pass back to N2 in the neutral zone and play 2 v 2 with him. If option two is used, N1 must return to the neutral zone. N1 and N2 play for both teams on offense.

Coaching Points

- Accurately driven passes to target player.
- Target player to create space to receive pass by making check-runs.
- Straight back support in neutral zone.
- Look to receive lay-offs from target player.
- Quality finishing.
- Individual and support defending.

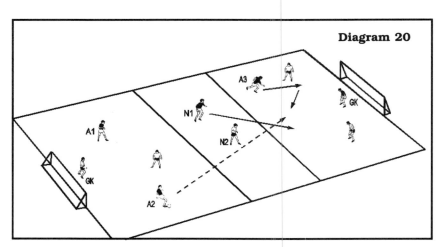

Diagram 20

Variations

- Both N1 and N2 can enter offensive zone to create 3 v 2.
- Target player can lay ball back to N1 or N2 into neutral zone for a one-touch shot.
- Limit defenders to two-touch.

April 1998 Issue

Nottingham Forest

During my visit with Nottingham Forest I was fortunate enough to spend time observing both the First Team and the Youth Team during practice. Look for some of these excellent sessions in upcoming issues. Below are some Dutch - Style passing drills from Youth Team Coach, Paul Hart.

In diagram 1, all players step away from the ball before checking back to receive the pass.

A passes to incoming B.
B passes wide to incoming A.
A passes to incoming C.
C passes wide to incoming B.
B passes to incoming D.
D passes wide to incoming C.
C passes to incoming E.
E passes wide to incoming D.
D passes in front of running E.
E crosses to incoming F.
F finishes.

A becomes B.
B becomes C.
C becomes D.
D becomes E.
E becomes F.
F collects the ball and becomes A.

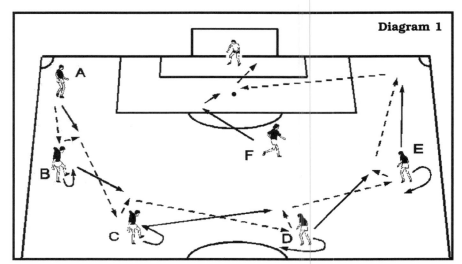

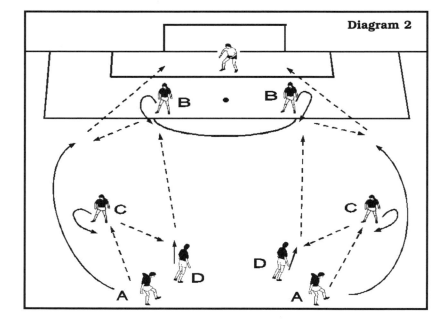

In diagram 2, both lines play simultaneously. C and B step away from the ball before checking back to
receive the pass.

A passes to incoming C then makes an overlap run past C.
C passes to incoming D.
D passes to incoming B.
B passes wide to overlapping A.
A shoots.

A becomes B.
B collects the ball and becomes A.
C and D stay in their positions.

A and B switch with C and D every few minutes.

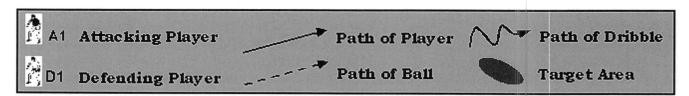

A1 **Attacking Player**	➤ **Path of Player**	〜➤ **Path of Dribble**
D1 **Defending Player**	⇢ **Path of Ball**	⬭ **Target Area**

Nottingham Forest

In diagram 3, B starts the drill by stepping away from A and then checking back to receive the pass.

A passes to incoming B and follows his pass.
B passes back to A, turns and runs around cone.
A passes the ball in front of running B.
B passes directly to C.
The drill continues with C and D.

A becomes B.
B becomes C.
C becomes D.
D becomes A

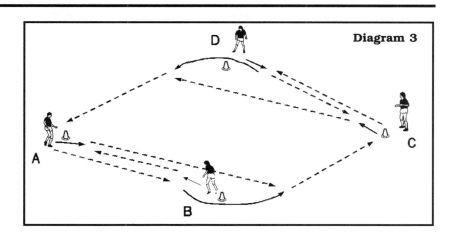

Diagram 3

In diagram 4, B starts the drill by stepping away and then checking back to receive the pass from A.

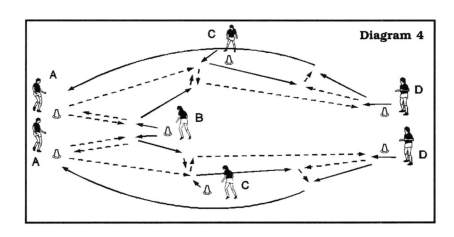

Diagram 4

Work on one side at a time.
A passes to incoming B.
B passes back to A, then turns and runs towards C.
A passes to incoming C.
C passes first-touch to incoming B.
B passes to incoming D.
D plays a give-and-go with incoming C.
D collects the ball and runs around the cone to starting position A.

A becomes B.
B becomes C.
C becomes D.
D becomes A.

In diagram 5, B starts the drill by stepping away then checking back to receive the pass.

A passes to incoming B.
B passes directly to incoming C then turns and run towards D.
C passes in front of deep running B.
B passes to incoming D.
D passes back to incoming B then turns and runs towards the spare cone.
B passes in front of deep running D.
D collects the ball and runs around the empty cone to A.

A becomes C.
C becomes B.
B becomes D.
D becomes A.

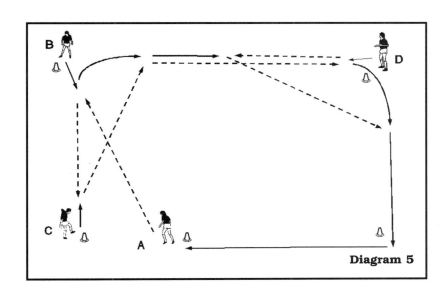

Diagram 5

Nottingham Forest

In diagram 6, B starts the drill by stepping away from A, then checking back to receive the pass.

A passes to incoming B.
B lays off a one-touch pass to incoming A then turns and runs towards C.
A passes to incoming C.
C receives the ball, turns and runs with the ball around the cone to D.
D passes to incoming E.
E lays off a one-touch pass to incoming D then turns and runs towards F.
D passes to incoming F.
F receives the ball turns and runs with the ball around the cone to A.

A becomes B.
B becomes C.
C becomes D.
D becomes E.
E becomes F
F becomes A

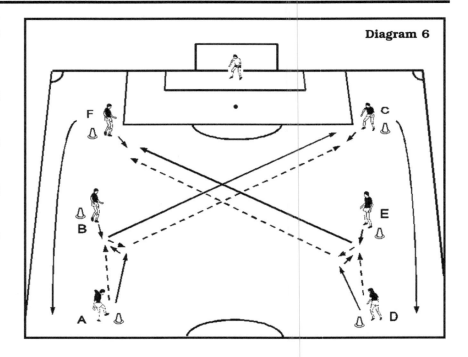

Diagram 6

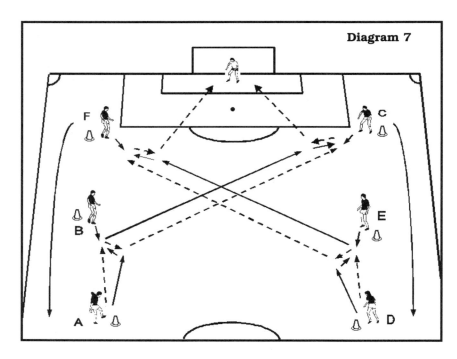

Diagram 7

In diagram 7, B starts the drill by stepping away from A, then checking back to receive the pass.

A passes to incoming B.
B lays off a one-touch pass to incoming A then turns and runs towards C.
A passes to incoming C.
C lays off a one-touch pass to incoming B.
B shoots.

A becomes B.
B becomes C after shooting.
C becomes D.

Repeat from other side starting with D. Alternate sides.

During my visit with Nottingham Forest I had the pleasure of spending some time with goalkeeper coach Mike Kelly. Mike is one of the most respected goalkeeper coaches in the world. He has been goalkeeper coach to the England National Team for the last three World Cups and two European Championships. Look for some of his goalkeeper sessions in upcoming issues.

Anson Dorrance - Fitness

Anson Dorrance completes the third of a three part series. In the previous two issues Anson Focused on 'Competitive Practices' and the 'Off-Season'. This month he shares his thoughts on "Fitness".

One thing I learned very quickly is that if you want your teams to be successful – since you only meet them for short periods before competition – the players have to be responsible for their own fitness training. So we established very early that the players had to come in fit. We sent all of them letters with the skeleton of a fitness program that has evolved into a self-coaching program we now send to our UNC team in the early summer to prepare the varsity-eligible players for the fall.

In my experience with the state and regional team, and even in my first stint with the Sports festival teams, I learned that it was impossible for me to get players fit in the short period of time I had them before a competition. So I developed an attitude among all the teams I trained that the players knew they had to come in fit. At first, the pre-camp fitness was on the honor system, and the novelty of the experience created a positive enthusiasm for what were obviously grueling expectations. This eventually evolved into fitness testing. I don't care how responsible your players are, if they know they have to take a fitness test on the first day of practice and they know they have to do well on it to be considered in the future, it puts a wonderful kind of pressure on everyone for performance. It also puts positive pressure on them to do some work before they get to camp.

After China, I implemented a sprint-training regimen that I got from Michelle Akers. She came into a camp a heck of a lot quicker and faster and with more explosion than she ever had before. I really liked how fast she was and how anaerobically fit she was, so I asked her what she had done. She shared with me something that she got from the Olympic Training Center about doing twenty-yard sprints, and forties, and sixties, and eighties and hundreds. Because I was so frustrated with the lack of strength in our legs in the World Cup final, I stole this stuff from Michelle, introduced it to our college kids at UNC and named it in Michelle's honor.

This concept of training on their own evolved over time, and it's continuing to evolve. For the first time ever, we extended this philosophy to include training our players on how to stay fit year-round. And it was serious. We talk about how to maintain your anaerobic fitness by doing at least one of these anaerobic sessions per week. To maintain their aerobic base, they have to do two bouts per week, and at least one of them should be interval training, like cones or one-twenties. The other should be a hard twenty- to thirty-minute run. Not a run where they are out for recreation, but one where they feel like throwing up when they're done. We tell them, "If you are running to get fit, it shouldn't get easier the more you run. If it gets easier, you should run harder. And if you run hard enough, you should feel wasted after every run. As you get fitter, just run harder." The idea is to deepen fitness-basing, and obviously, throwing up is an exaggeration, but the point is made. In 1995, for the first time, we made it mandatory to maintain fitness on a twelve-month basis to see if we could survive the fall with a young, inexperienced team. Also for the first time, we ran two Cooper Tests. One in the fall and one in the spring. I was amazed that we had as many people pass our fitness test in the spring as we did coming into the previous season. That showed me we have educated the players on having greater personal responsibility in fitness training. Now when our season ends, they don't go into total remission like a lot of players do. When the season is over, everyone encourages players to rest. Well, the rest you should take is from soccer. That's where you are burned out. You should never rest from personal fitness training. If you have developed a deep fitness-base, the worst thing you can do is go through Yo-Yo fitness-basing, which is where you kick back, eat Bon-Bons and don't do a thing, and all of a sudden you have to get fit again. Now, you've lost the investment you've made in developing your fitness base by taking time off. Then you have a grueling fight to get fit again. Why ever do that to yourself? It doesn't take that much to maintain fitness, but it takes an excruciating amount of work to regain fitness or get fit. Our philosophy is never to get out of shape.

These fitness ideas started as an experiment by telling kids to come in and pass fitness tests. It evolved into a culture that the players have maintained and we have encouraged. We tell them, "Listen, if you want to play at the highest level, you can never lose fitness." The rationale we use is that a marathon runner doesn't win an Olympic Gold medal at age fifteen, sixteen or seventeen like a gymnast. And the reason is that fitness-basing takes time. It takes a long-term investment. Marathon runners don't go through periods of the year when they're inactive. They are always in incredible shape, and the peak for certain events. But their philosophy is to be constantly deepening their base. Our philosophy is to pour time and effort into developing a very deep anaerobic and aerobic fitness base. Soccer played at its highest level requires this, and that's what we require of these young women.

Excerpted with permission of the publisher from the book 'Training Soccer Champions' by Anson Dorrance and Tim Nash. For ordering information call 1-800-331-5191.

Interview with Thomas Rongen

Thomas Rongen, Head Coach of the New England Revolution, shares his thoughts followed by a complete pre-season practice observed in Orlando, February 1998.

What do you believe are the key aspects in team success?

I believe there are four components a modern player needs. It is important that all players are technically sound; that is the foundation of a team. You need players that tactically are capable of problem solving and making decisions in the course of a game that we as coaches do not really control. It is also important that in the modern game that players need to be strong, fast and fit enough to play for a full 90 minutes. Mentally players need to have the desire and willingness to succeed and have a commitment to excellence.

What is your preferred playing style?

My preferred playing style is not necessarily the way the team is going to play, the players available will ultimately dictate that. The MLS is unique in that coaches are not fully responsible for signing their own players, therefore the team doesn't always reflect the philosophy of the coach. I would like to play a 4 – 3 – 3 or a 3 – 4 – 3 but the U.S. hasn't really produced any good wing players over the last 20 years, so if I can't play with three up front then I have to decide what is the next best way of playing. We will probably play a 4 – 4 – 2 and attempt to build out of the back as much as we can whilst also playing direct if possible and maintain quick ball circulation. If there is a style that I would try to model it would be the 'Total Football' of the Dutch and especially Ajax way of playing.

Do you ever change your style or formation depending on who your opposition is?

Yes and no, I prefer not to. I think it is hard enough to get a team to play in one particular formation. I think that some coaches talk about changing in the course of a game from a 4 – 4 – 2 to a 3 – 5 – 2 or a 3 – 4 – 3. Well, I think that is virtually impossible. Any of those systems just require so many tactical components and so much work during the week that you really need to look at your players during the pre-season and design a system that suits them. Then, within that system, make some adjustments depending on who you play, where you play and the desired result of the game.

Do you utilize videotape sessions with your players?

Yes, but not a lot. I was a player myself, and in an hour or two video session, most players are asleep. So we keep them short just to get the point across to the team. We also do them individually with players sometimes. We do game analysis but we break the game down and do 20 minutes or at the most, 30 minute sessions.

How often do you work on shooting and finishing?

During the season almost daily. We put a lot emphasis on finishing and shooting. During pre-season however, we have to concentrate on everything - tactics, fitness and technical training, but we do try to incorporate as much shooting and finishing as we can within those sessions. Working on finishing is vitally important, it is something that we here in the U.S. still don't do very well. Playing in the final third is the hardest part of the game. Even the best in the world have a tough time with it. Look at the Brazilians in their loss to the U.S., they certainly could have and should have scored, but didn't.

How often do you work on set-plays?

I don't think enough, which in part is due to the MLS hectic scheduling of travel and playing twice a week. You end up in a regeneration mode rather than a teaching mode. However, if you look at the last World Cup and even over the last decade you will see that a lot of goals are scored from dead-ball situations, so that is something we will have to emphasize a little more this year, both defending and attacking at set-plays.

How do you structure a typical practice?

If I just go through a typical 90 minute session, we start with a warm-up which includes a lot of soccer related conditioning. We have conditioning specialist Vern Gambetta with us who has introduced a lot of very dynamic work early on as opposed to the typical static stretch type of warm-up. Then we go into a technical training phase where we might work on something we saw in the last game, because we want the game to be an indicator as to what we need to work on, or it might depend on who we are playing next. We also do a lot of possession games followed by games with certain conditions and we usually end up with some finishing.

What practices do you do regularly with your players?

We work a lot on possession. We have a wide variety of possession games using small fields or larger areas and altering the number of players to create different situations. Players are encouraged to maintain possession, sometimes attacking one goal or two goals and against zonal defending or when the other team is matched up man for man. We play a lot of 6 v 6 + 2 floaters all the way up to 8 v 8 where they are in match pressure situations.

New England Revolution

Pre-season practice observed at Orlando, Florida 1998.

After a 25 minute warm-up and stretching routine with conditioning specialist, Vern Gambetta, the players are split into four groups of four. Each group does five minutes of work at a station followed by a three minute rest period. The groups then move to the next station until they complete all four stations. The teams' results are recorded to keep the practice competitive.

Shooting

Diagram 8, is 2 v 2 shooting in a field the size of two goal boxes (36 yards long x 44 yards wide). Full size goals and goalkeepers are used. Players are encouraged to take early shooting opportunities.

Diagram 8

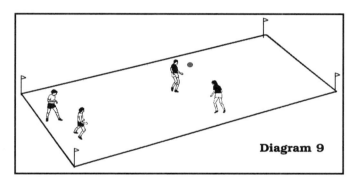

Diagram 9

Heading

In diagram 9, the field is 15 x 5 yards with flags marking out the goals. The defending team retreats back to their own goal but are not allowed to use their hands. The attacking team has to progress to the opponent's goal using headers and attempt to score with a header. If a team scores, the ball goes out of bounds or touches the ground, the defending team then becomes the attacking team.

Soccer Volleyball

In diagram 10, the field is 15 x 5 yards. A net is set up in the center about chest height. The players have no more than four touches to get the ball over the net. The ball is allowed one bounce on the ground.

Diagram 10

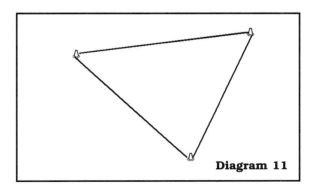

Diagram 11

Running

In diagram 11, the players do a series of sprints, jogs, sideways running, walks and jumps round a 40-yard triangle.

Tahuichi - Tactical Training

This is the third of a three part series. Tahuichi prepares for a major tournament using a three month program. Each month is broken down into specific soccer components. In the two previous issues, Tahuichi focused on Month One - Physical Fitness and Month Two - Technical Training. This Month the focus is on Month Three - Tactical Training and Competition.

The third and final month of preparation is dedicated to tactics and competition. During this month coach Ciro will work on their swarming style of defense and their relentless attacking style of offense, free kicks and corner kicks both offensively and defensively, and penalty kicks.

A typical week of tactical and competitive preparation starts on Monday with a one-hour tactical lecture in the morning and a two-hour tactical training session in the afternoon. Tuesday and Thursday they'll do two two-hour tactical sessions. On Wednesday morning, they'll have a fitness session with and without the ball and in the afternoon session they'll play a game. The Friday morning session would be a tactical lecture and in the afternoon they would have a light tactical session. Finally, on Saturday and Sunday, they would play two or three games.

Coach Ciro prepares the team competitively by arranging most of their games with Bolivian 1st and 2nd division professional clubs. He also takes the players to Brazil for four or five days to play matches against 2nd and 3rd division professional clubs. These games are super intense and in many of the matches, Tahuichi has beaten these clubs. Even though the players from the pro clubs are usually 6 to 14 years older than the Tahuichi players, coach Ciro firmly believes that if you want your players to excel competitively, they must be challenged by opponents who are superior. That is the reason why coach Ciro has the Tahuichi players compete against older, stronger, faster, and experienced players.

Throughout the three months, Tahuichi also emphasizes stretching, sports psychology, nutrition, self-reflection, and continues some physical fitness without the use of a ball during the second and third month through a maintenance program.

There is no exact secret to learning soccer. Tahuichi trains as if they are about to go to war because most of the Tahuichi players are physiologically smaller in size in comparison to the rest of the world. Being smaller in size is due to lack of nutrition, sleep deprivation, and extreme poverty. When you put all of these things together you have future athletes who are weak, unhealthy and spiritually broken. So, Tahuichi rebuilds the player from inside out with loving care, nutrition, spiritualism and a lot of hard work. Coach Vince Lombardi once said, "The harder you work, the harder it is to surrender."

Tahuichi's record can speak for itself.

What is truly amazing is not their record, but how Tahuichi, with very little resources and so much poverty, can still attain their yin and yang.

A Partial List of Accomplishments

South American U13 Champions	Argentina	1996
South American U15 Club Champions	Bolivia	1995
South American U15 Club Champions	Chile	1992
European Tour (Germany & Holland - 13 Games)	Undefeated	1994
Tahuichi 1 v 0 Feyernood (Holland)	Holland	1994
Tahuichi 3 v 1 Boca Juniors (Argentina)	Bolivia	1996
Tahuichi 1 v 0 Necaxa (Mexico)	Bolivia	1997
Tahuichi 2 v 0 Nacional (Uruguay)	USA	1995

Tahuichi - Tactical Training

Diagram 12 is a tactical session incorporating overlaps, crossing and finishing. On the half-line there are four lines of players. The drill is started by A1 passing to A2 and then making an overlap run down the flank. A2 passes to A3 who then passes in front of overlapping A1. A1 attacks the end line and crosses. After making their passes, A2 makes a far post run and A3 runs to the edge of the goal box. A4 attacks the near post.

Work the right flank for 10-15 minutes then the left flank.

Coaching Points
- Play at a quick pace.
- Stress the quality of passes.
- One-touch whenever possible.
- Crosses should be away from the goalkeeper
- Time runs into the goal box (don't get there too early).
- Finish with one-touch whenever possible.

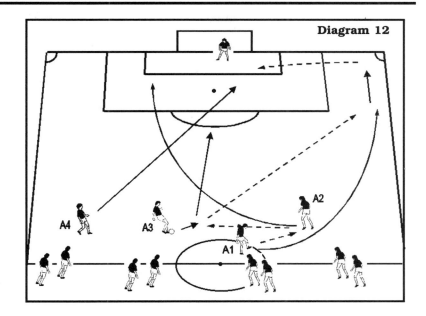

Diagram 13 is a full field drill incorporating defensive clearances, attacking full-backs, midfield runs, crossing and finishing. The drill is set up with goalkeepers and three lines of players on the half-line. Players in lines A and C are midfielders and in line B are forwards. The drill is started by midfielder A playing a high pass into the goal box and then running wide to support D2. The central defender, D1, clears the ball out with his first touch attempting to get the ball wide. D2, the full-back, runs wide, collects the ball and runs up the field and plays two give-and-go's with A. A's final ball is played in front of the running D2, who attacks the end-line and crosses. After making his final pass, A then makes a run to the far post. The forward, B, makes a near post run. E1 and E2 defend the cross.

Midfielder C then starts the drill going in the other direction passing a high ball to E1.

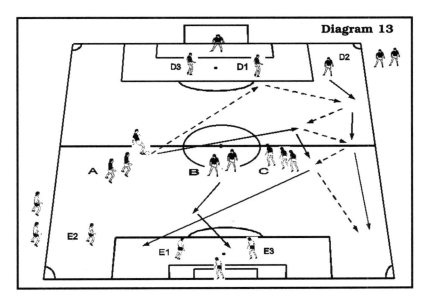

Note
This is an extremely physically demanding drill. Many of the players are making 40-80 yard runs. It is important that the drill is played at a game realistic pace. Therefore, with the exception of the central defenders, the players need to be in lines of three to allow for adequate rest so they can go full pace each time.

Youth Player Development - The Dutch Way

Youth Player Development – The Dutch Way - By Jack Detchon.

During our trip to the two Soccer Conferences in the USA at Boston and Santa Clara, Graham Morgan, Rob Littleford and I were most fortunate to spend considerable time with Bert Van Lingen the Netherlands' Assistant National Coach, also Jan Derks and Vera Pauw. All the coaches were stimulating and far-seeing and very good teacher coaches. The basis of the Dutch F.A.'s scheme of work is as follows:

AGE	AIM	CONTENTS
5 years (Perliminary stage)	Ball-feeling • To master the ball. • The ball and me.	Skills games: • direction • speed • accuracy
6 - 11 years	Basic game Maturity	Development of insight & technical skills by playing simplified game situations (basic forms)
11 - 16 years	Match (11-11) Maturity	Team requirements:Development of requirements of each line and positions by smaller and bigger sided games (and simplified
16 - 18 years	Competition Maturity	To learn to perform in service of the coach's ideas.
18 years	Optional Maturity	Specialization of multi-functional influencing. To cope with the stress of the game.

The age group which this article deals with is from 6-11 years. The basis of the work with young players throughout Holland is the group of eight players, which they use in 4 v 4 games and 5 v 3 and 6 v 2 practices. Why 4 v 4 and not 3 v 3 or 5 v 5? A game of 4 v 4 is the minimum number of players per side that will give both width and length to the game.

There are no F.I.F.A. rules to 4 v 4, there are no throw-ins, corners or leagues. The players spread wide and long, support the ball and the importance of BALL POSSESSION is inculcated together with the maxim "Position Keeps Possession".

If the players find keeping possession difficult then the game is changed to a 6 v 2 possession practice, which progresses to 5 v 3. Great stress is placed on control to pass, the quality of the first touch maximizing the chances of a good pass following.

In order to encourage specific skills, the 4 v 4 format is put into different shaped pitches.

These games with different organizations, different sizes and different demands require from players intelligent responses, different technical behavior and different physical behavior. As Bert Van Lingen says, they allow "The game to be the Teacher" but at the same time it was noticeable that both Bert and Jan Derks were at great pains to use the question and answer technique to ensure (a) that the child tended to solve its own problems and (b) having done so really understood the game.

This article is reprinted with the kind consent of Catalyst the official journal of AFCAT.

Youth Player Development - The Dutch Way

The four main field sizes and game organizations used to create different demands for the youth player.

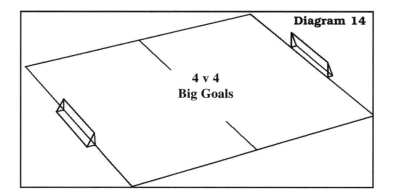

Field One

Diagram 14 is 20 yds long x 30 yds wide, big goals. This obviously is the shooting game (but emphasis can be placed on good defending).

Field Two

Diagram 15 is 30 yds long x 35 yds wide. The four goals encourage switch play, crosses and headers and the value of playing with the "head up" (counter-balance by balancing defensive positions).

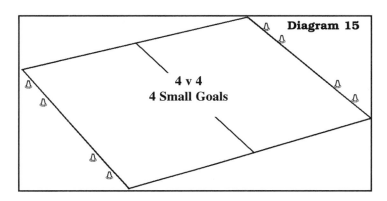

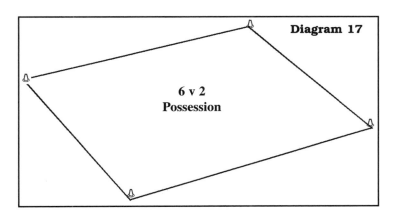

Field Three

Diagram 16 is 20 yds long x 25 yds wide. Dribbling and wall passing (counter-balanced by pressuring and tracking players). Goals are scored by crossing end lines A or B with the ball under control.

Field Four

Diagram 17 is 25 yds long x 18 yds wide. 6 v 2 or 5 v 3 possession play (counter-balanced by defensive challenging).

NY/NJ MetroStars

Observed in Orlando, Florida - Pre-season 1998

This was the last 60 minutes of a training session. The players were split into three groups of seven players. Two groups played a small-sided game in the goal box while the other group worked on shooting and crossing. The teams rotated every 15 minutes until all three teams had played against each other in the small-sided games. The score of the games were recorded to promote friendly competition.

7 v 7 Small-Sided Game

In diagram 18, two teams of seven inside the goal box with small goals and no goal-keepers. The players are encouraged to work on keeping possession, quality of passing, and concentrating on a good first-touch so that the body position is open when receiving the ball.

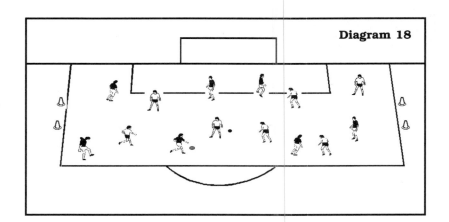

Diagram 18

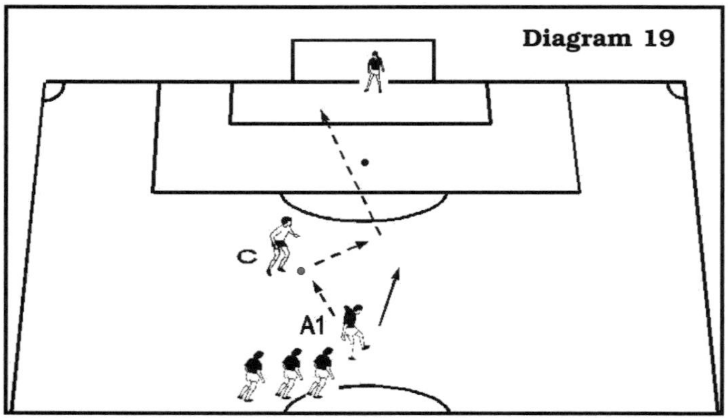

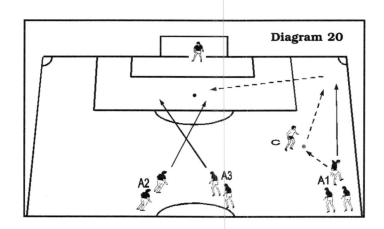

Diagram 19

Unopposed Long Range Shooting

In diagram 19, the players line up 40 yards from the goal. A1 passes to the coach who lays off a first-time pass back into the path of A1 who shoots with his first touch.

Coaching Points

- The pass into the coach needs to be firm.
- The coach lays the ball off creating an angle.
- A1 shoots low to the far post.

Crossing and Finishing

Diagram 20 shows A1 passing to the coach who lays off a first-time pass into the path of A1. A1 either crosses with his first-touch or attacks the end line and crosses. A2 and A3 make crossover runs into the goal box.

Coaching Points

- Vary the crosses - low and hard, driven high, etc.
- A2 and A3 time their runs into the goal box.

Diagram 20

May/June 1998 Issue

San Jose Clash

Pre-season practice observed at Orlando, Florida 1998

A 15 minute warm-up and stretching routine was followed by 15-20 minutes of short sprints, fast footwork and speed drills. The remainder of the session was spent on finishing and shooting with five drills, working 15-20 minutes on each.

The drill in diagram 1 is set up with two 18 yard goal boxes marked out with a five yard wide channel down each side. Full size goals and goal-keepers are used. The drill is designed to teach the forwards how to pressure the ball and once posses-sion is gained convert them quickly into goal chances. Goalkeepers also benefit from practicing receiving and distributing the ball with their feet.

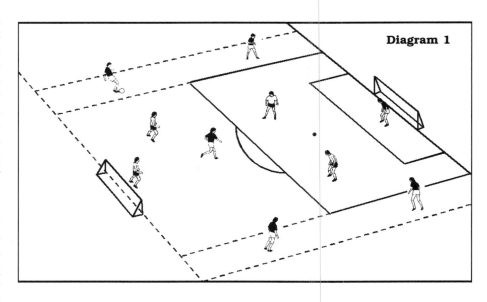

The game is played with five play-ers, two in each channel and one on the field playing keep-away from three forwards. The four channel players are limited to one touch and are not allowed to pass the ball to each other. However, they can pass to the goalkeepers. The object of the game is for the three forwards to pressure, force mistakes and gain possession. Once in possession the attempt is made to score quickly and in either goal. To make it a competitive situation the five players scored a goal if they made 10 consecutive passes.

Diagram 2 is a one-touch shooting drill. As in diagram 1, the field is two adjoining 18 yard goal boxes. Players are lined up on the four corners. Full size goals and goalkeepers are used.

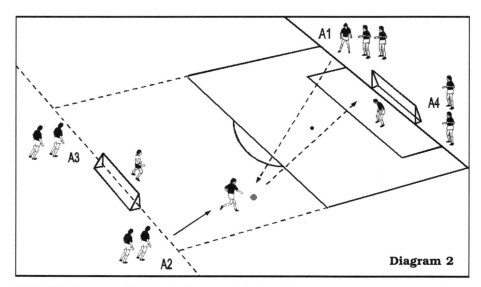

A1 serves to incoming A2.
A2 shoots one touch.
A1 joins the A2 line.
A2 joins the A1 line.
A3 serves to incoming A4.
A4 shoots one touch.
A3 joins the A4 line.
A4 joins the A3 line.
The drill continues with each line taking turns to serve to the shooter.

Coaching Points

*   Keep shots low
*   Aim to the far post
*   Follow shots for rebounds
*   Quality service

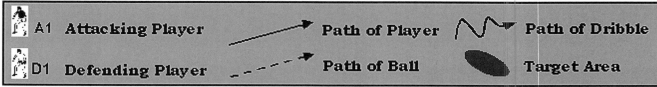

A1	**Attacking Player**	→ **Path of Player**	∿ **Path of Dribble**
D1	**Defending Player**	⇢ **Path of Ball**	⬤ **Target Area**

San Jose Clash

The drill in diagram 3 is a progression of diagram 2. The set up and organization are the same. This time the service is in the air and the lay-offs are with the head or chest.

A1 serves to incoming A2.
A2 lays off a one-touch pass back to incoming A1.
A1 shoots one touch.
A1 joins the A2 line.
A2 joins the A1 line.
A3 serves to incoming A4.
A4 lays off a one-touch pass back to incoming A3.
A3 shoots one touch.
A3 joins the A4 line.
A4 joins the A3 line.
The drill continues with each

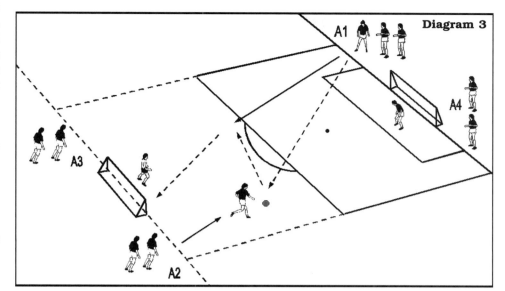

The drill in diagram 4 is set up keeping the same field size as the previous drills. This time the players are lined up on the sides of the field and the service is in the air for practice of volleys and half volleys.

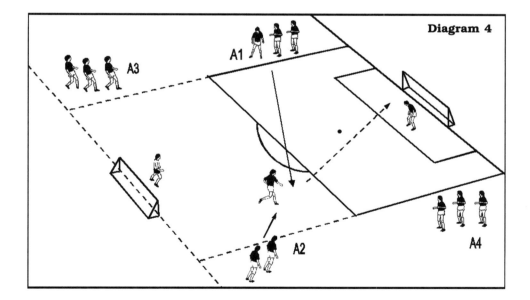

A1 serves to incoming A2.
A2 times his run to volley or half volley a shot on goal.
A1 joins the A2 line.
A2 joins the A1 line.
A3 serves to incoming A4.
A4 times his run to volley or half volley a shot on goal.
A3 joins the A4 line.
A4 joins the A3 line.
The drill continues with each line taking turns to serve to the shooter.

Coaching Points
• Quality service
• Time runs - not too early
• Strike the upper half of the ball

The final 20 minutes of the practice was 4 v 4 using the same field set up. The players were split into three teams. Two played, the other team retrieved balls. The first team to score two goals or the team winning after four minutes stayed on the field to play the next team.

New England Revolution

Pre-season practice observed at Orlando, Florida 1998

After a 25 minute warm-up and stretching routine the shooting/finishing practice was set up with two groups - one at each end of the field. After 20-25 minutes the players alternated drills. Very noticeable was the high intensity of work done for short spells.

The drill in diagram 8 is played on half a field with an 18 yard goal box marked out on the half-line. Full size goals and goal-keepers are used. There are two forwards and two defenders in each goal box. The ball is served unopposed by a player from one goal box to a teammate in the other goal box - then play 2 v 2 looking for quick shots.

After a shot or loss of possession the ball is then served by the other team into the opposite goal box.

Coaching Points

- Low shots.
- Accuracy more important than power.
- Follow shots for rebounds.

The players are split into five groups of two. Four groups play while one rests. Play hard for two minutes followed by a one minute rest. Then rotate groups so that each group plays each other group. One group is always resting.

The drill in diagram 9 is played on half a field using one goal box. There are two forwards and two defenders in the goal box. The four servers take turns passing the ball to the forwards - then play 2 v 2 in the goal box looking for quick shots.

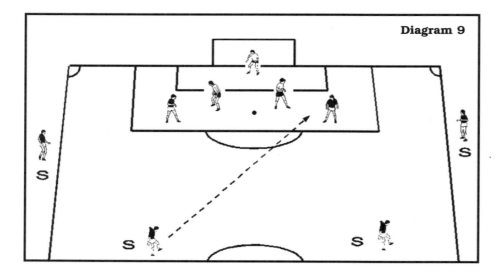

After a shot or loss of possession the forwards quickly look to receive a pass from the next server.

Coaching Points

- Low shots
- Accuracy more important than power
- Follow shots for rebounds
- Vary service - low or high

Play hard for two minutes followed by a one minute rest. Then rotate groups so that each group plays the other groups.

A Day at Manchester United

During my recent trip to England I was extremely fortunate to spend a day at one of the world's top clubs, Manchester United. My host for the day was youth team coach, David Williams. Over the years the youth system at Manchester United has been the envy of many of the world's leading clubs. Currently, Manchester United has a number of first team regulars that were developed through the youth system, including internationals David Beckham and Ryan Giggs. The youth team squad consists of players age 16 - 18. While I was observing the practice sessions, I was struck by the quality of their first-touch, the accuracy of their passing and most of all by the speed of their decision making.

The practice started with a 12 minute run followed by stretches. This was followed by a series of short sprints and quick foot movements done over a 15 yard distance. Included were turns, laterals, stop-start movements and various runs in and out of cones, etc. for a total of 15 minutes. The first warm-up game shown in diagram 10 was a simple possession game 6 v 6 + 1 floater. The game was played on a marked out field of approximately 60 x 40 yards with permanent small goals. However, the object of the game is to maintain possession so the goals were not used. The game was played for 15 minutes at a very quick pace with the coach stressing movement and quality of passes.

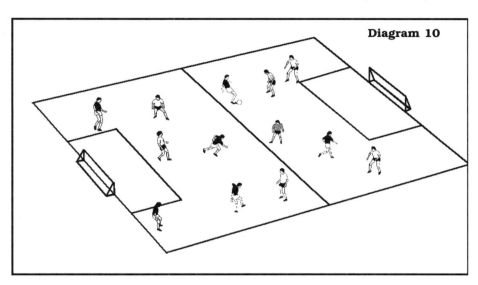

Diagram 10

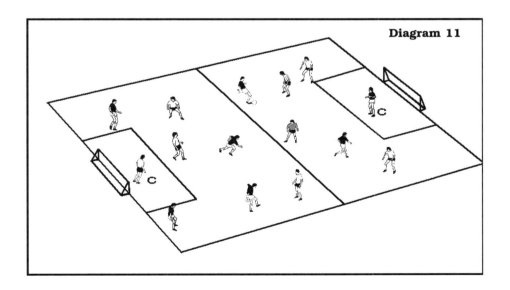

Diagram 11

Diagram 11 shows the progression. A coach stands in each goal box. A goal is scored by playing a ball from one half of the field to the coach in the other goal box. The pass should be in the air and the coach needs to be able to control the ball in the air. The coach can be used just like a goalkeeper for keeping possession. Each team can play any direction once they gain possession of the ball. Once a goal is scored, the coach plays the ball back to the scoring team. The coach stressed the same points as in the previous game with the added emphasis on quality lofted and driven passes over 30 - 50 yard distances. Defense was also stressed with players urged to close down quickly and prevent the team in possession from playing the long pass. Again, the game was played at a fast, energetic pace for 20 minutes.

The field in diagram 12 is 40 x 25 yards. Full size goals and goalkeepers are used. The game is 4 v 4 inside the field with four or six players on the sides. The side players play for the team in possession and have unlimited touches (but played mostly one and two-touch). The 4 v 4 players could not pass to each other - only to the side players. The goalkeepers could distribute to a field player or to a side player. The game was played for 20 minutes, and as in the previous games, the pace was very quick (game speed). The coach stressed creating and taking quick scoring opportunities that were created with fast goal-to-goal action. Again, defense was not forgotten, players were stressed the importance of tracking back with 'their player' during transition.

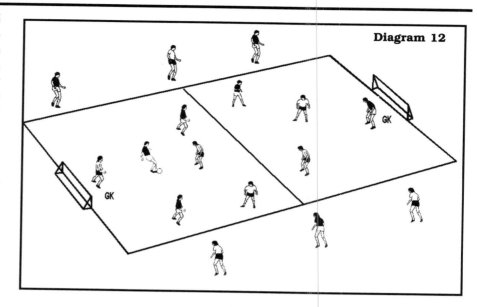

Diagram 12

Progression

The field was widened to 30 yards. The side players were limited to a maximum of two-touch. Goals could only be scored with a one-touch finish. Play for another 20 minutes.

At the end of the practice, the players that did not play in a game over the weekend did 10 - 15 minutes of running.

Some frequently used practices of the youth team:

- Many types of possession games such as three teams of three in a 40 x 30 yard field. Two teams keep possession from the other team. If a team loses possession they become the defending team.
- Games with 'floaters' who play for the team in possession.
- Games with players on the sidelines playing for the team in possession.
- Usually once a week they do a full 11 v 11 game to work on players learning their positional responsibilities. During these they may focus on one aspect of the game or they may cover all aspects.
- Shooting and finishing (shown in diagrams 13 and 14).

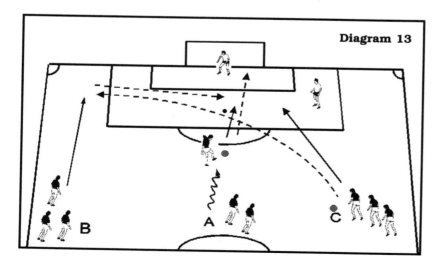

Diagram 13

Shooting and Finishing

The set up in diagram 13 is three lines of players about 40 yards from goal. Lines A and C have a supply of balls. A coach is inside the goal box with a supply of balls.

Line A starts the drill by dribbling and shooting.

C then switches the field with a pass to B who makes a run down the flank.

C follows his pass with a run into the goal box.

B crosses the ball to incoming A and C who finish with one touch.

A Day at Manchester United

The drill continues in diagram 14 with the same three players.

After B has crossed for A and C to finish, B runs into the goal box.

The coach passes a ball toward the end line.

A or C (in this example it is C) runs around the coach and crosses to incoming A and B to finish with one touch.

The drill continues with the next players in line.

Variation

Depending on the age or ability level, the cross field pass from C to B could be played in stages by C passing to A who then passes to B.

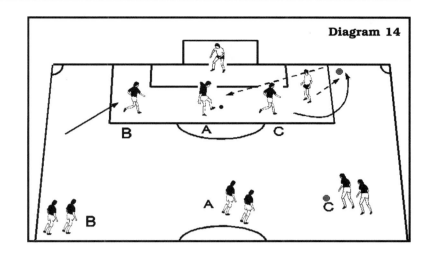

Bryan Hamilton

Bryan Hamilton's professional playing career lasted 15 years which included playing 50 games for his country, Northern Ireland. After being in charge at Wigan Athletic and Leicester City during the 80's and early 90's he was appointed as manager of the Northern Ireland National Team in 1994.

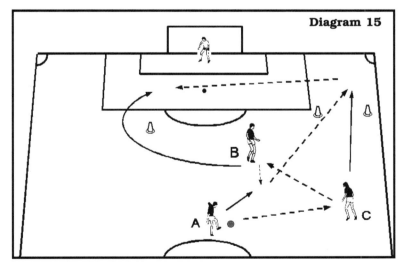

Finishing From Crosses

The drill starts when A passes to C and then runs towards B.

C passes to B and then makes a run between the cones.

B lays the ball off for incoming A and then makes a run around the cone.

A passes in front of running C and then runs to the near post.

Coaching Points

- Quality of passes.
- Quality of the crosses.
- Timing of runs.
- Angle of runs by A and B.
- Quality finishing.
- Follow for rebounds.
- The near post run by A is very important because it worries defenders.

Variations

- C can cross to the player at the near post, then the far post.
- Introduce a passive defender to clear any loose crosses.
- If the player at the far post cannot score he should head the ball back across the goal for A.
- Encourage the defender to play more realistically and have another player following up on the edge of the goal box.
- C can vary his options including pulling the ball back for the player on the edge of the box.

This article was reprinted with the kind permission of CATALYST, the official journal of AFCAT.

Mike Smith

Mike Smith is one of the world's most experienced international coaches. To date he has coached teams in 212 international games. From 1967 - 1980 he was the national coach for Wales. During this time he was in charge of the Welsh National amateur and professional U18 teams. In 1974 he was appointed the manager of the Welsh National Team, where he stayed until 1980. From 1985 - 1988 he was manager of the Egypt National team where he won the African Nations Cup and the African Olympics. Currently, Mike is at Wolverhampton Wanderers of the English First Division where he works with youth team players.

The Final Pass

Introduction

Statistics prove over any season or period that 50% of all goals scored are from restarts. Yes, we have seen great goals from corners, free kicks, penalties. Every team in the Premiership and the Football League spend hours on the practice ground working out ways of moving defenders at corners and free kicks in order to set up a chance to make contact and score, but only a few can produce the accuracy every time. It is the player who takes the corner kick or free kick who is worth his weight in gold.

Every time David Beckham runs up to take a free kick or corner for Manchester United you expect a goal. Zola at Chelsea has scored some superb goals from free kicks. Erratic free kicks are related to performance – so when we work on restarts, the player taking these all important kicks must be confident and must be on top of his game.

The same applies in free play – many games peter out because no player can unlock the opposing defense with a final pass that is timed to perfection. Teams that cannot get around the back of opponents hit aimless long balls into packed areas and hope for something to happen. Players become frustrated and stop thinking, it all adds up to a frenzy. We can all refer to the magic moments produced by the clever players across the world when a ball is played perfectly across or through a defense leaving a colleague with a great chance of scoring.

Once a team has players who work hard to produce a good final pass, then the rest of the team must accept the responsibility for getting into a position to receive and hopefully score.

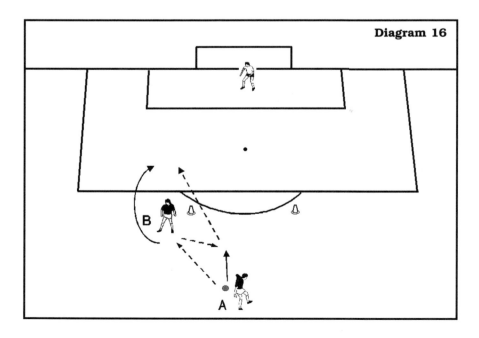

Diagram 16

Practice One

Diagram 16 starts off with an easy practice to develop the understanding of the weight and direction of the final pass.

A passes to B.
B lays off a pass to incoming A and then turns and runs into the goal box.
A passes with his first touch into the path of B.
B shoots to finish.

Coaching Points

- The lay-off pass needs to be correct - the right angle and the right pace to enable A to make the final pass with one touch.
- The final pass needs to be the correct weight - too soft and the ball will be behind B, too hard and the ball goes too far wide or to the goalkeeper.

Mike Smith

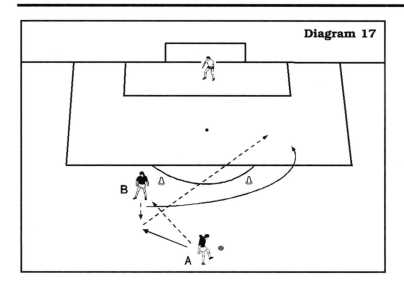

Diagram 17

Practice Two

Diagram 17 is a variation of Practice One with the same coaching points stressed.

A passes to B.
B lays off a pass to incoming A then turns and runs around cone into the goal box.
A passes with his first touch into the path of B.
B shoots to finish.

Practice Three

In diagram 18 we go from a wider position.

Option A

As the attacker runs at the cone on the corner of the penalty area, he has two choices, A and B. If he goes wide (option A), the two front players change position from near post to far post. As the ball is crossed in, each striker has one touch either to score or pass. A midfield player is also added but as soon as he is played in, he also has one touch to shoot or pass.

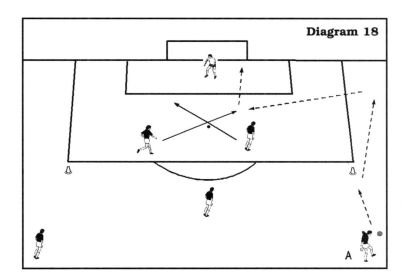

Diagram 18

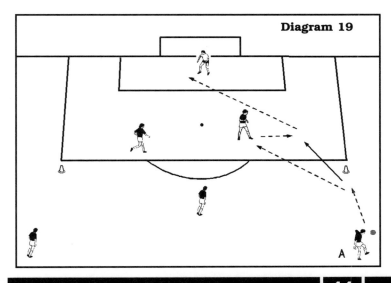

Diagram 19

Option B

Diagram 19 shows option B. If the attacker cuts inside, he can play off either striker and follows in playing one touch either to score or pass again.

Practice using both flanks.

Practice Four

This is a progression from Practice Three. Using half a field with coned corridors down each flank as shown, the ball is served into midfield. The center back has to mark one of the strikers.

Midfield players then work the ball into the corridors and the two attackers play against one defender – as they burst down the flank they have a choice as before, either A or B. So it is the same practice but one of the strikers is marked and so are the midfield players. All players have one touch in the box to either shoot or pass.

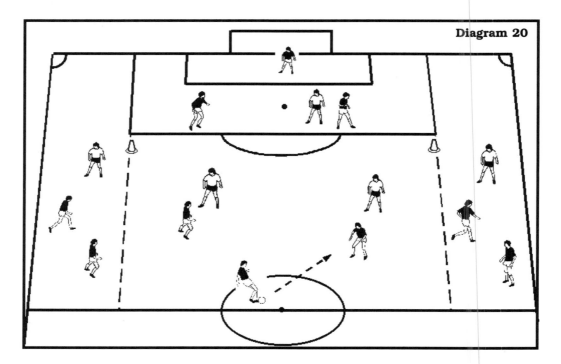

Diagram 20

Practice Five

Take away the cones and play free, but all the factors we have been working on come into play.

• Quality and accuracy of pass into the box.

• The selection of who to play in the box.

• The movement of players in the box to receive the ball.

• The quality of contact to score or set up pass for some other player to score.

• Cross passes are the most difficult, but any ball played in between defender and goalkeeper is a good ball. A ball sent in with pace is extremely difficult to defend against.

• Because only one of the strikers is marked, can any player produce a pass for the other striker? If he can, then that is vision and technique, this is what this session has been about.

July 1998 Issue

Leeds United

During my visit to England in March, I spent a day with the Leeds United youth team coaching staff. I was fortunate enough to watch the youth team play a league game against Sheffield Wednesday and later spend some time with Leeds youth team coach, John Dungworth, who shared some of his favorite practices with me.

Crossing and Finishing

A1 touches the ball toward the end-line, chases it and crosses into the goalbox. On A1's first touch, B1 and C1 make runs into the goalbox for a one-touch finish. After the shot, the players join the back of their respective lines. The drill continues from the other side with the next player in line C touching the ball toward the end-line for the players from lines B and A to finish.

After 5 - 10 minutes the lines rotate positions.

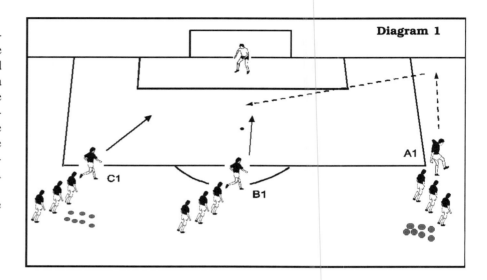

Diagram 1

Coaching Points

- The ball should be crossed outside the six yard box - away from the goalkeeper.
- Time the runs into the goalbox - don't get there too early.
- Accuracy of shot is more important than power.

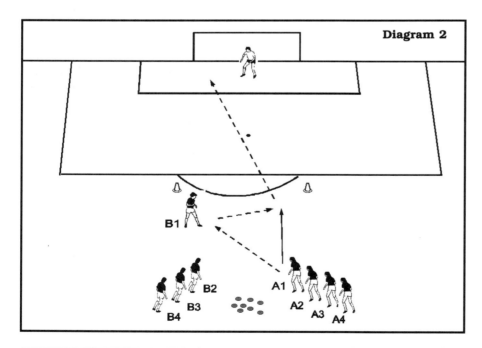

Diagram 2

Shooting

Two teams are lined up 28 yards from goal with a supply of balls.

B1 steps up to the edge of the goal-box.

A1 passes to B1.

B1 lays off a one-touch pass into the path of incoming A1.

A1 shoots one touch.

B1 joins the back of the B line.

A1 stays on at the edge of the goal-box to receive a pass from B2.

The drill continues.

A record is kept of the number of goals scored by each team to add an element of competition to the drill.

After 5 - 10 minutes the teams change positions.

A1	**Attacking Player**		**Path of Player**	**Path of Dribble**
D1	**Defending Player**		**Path of Ball**	**Target Area**

| A1 **Attacking Player** | → **Path of Player** | ⌇ **Path of Dribble** |
| D1 **Defending Player** | ⇢ **Path of Ball** | ⬤ **Target Area** |

Leeds United

Instant Shooting

Diagram 3 is 4 v 4 inside the goalbox. Both teams are attacking the goal. Players are spaced out around the outside of the goalbox and are used by the team in possession. The outside players can be limited to one or two touches.

To add an element of competition, the first team to score three goals wins and stays on the field to play the next four players. The losing team replaces the players on the outside of the goalbox.

Possession

In diagram 4, the drill is 4 v 4 or 5 v 5. The field is 40 yards x 30 yards. Players are placed on the perimeter of the field. Cones are placed two yards either side of the corners. Players are positioned behind the cones at each corner. To score a goal, the ball must be passed through the cones to the player in the corner who must then pass it back to the same player. The object is to maintain possession using the players on the outside of the field and create scoring chances.

Variations

- Outside players can be limited to one or two touches.

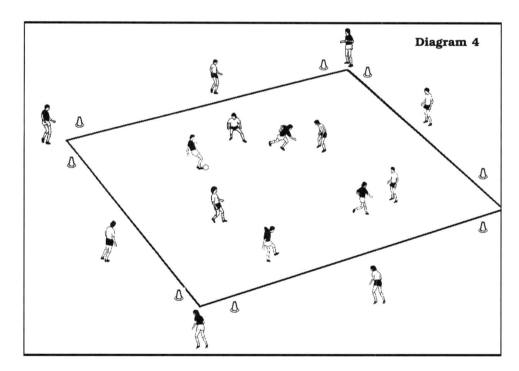

- Goals can be scored by passing the ball through the cones.

Coaching Points

- Encourage players to play with their head up.
- Try to maintain an open body position when receiving a pass.

Preki - Personal Fitness Routine

In his attempt to make the U.S. National Team, Preki undertook a rigorous personal fitness routine under the guidance of Misha Bacic, the Kansas City Wizards Assistant Coach responsible for conditioning.

Misha Bacic played professional soccer in Germany, France and his native country, Yugoslavia. Since coming to the United States in 1987 he has worked individually with several professional soccer players, most recently with MLS players Frank Klopas, Goran Hunjak and Preki. Previously he worked with the Houston Hotshots of the CISL and with the soccer team at Houston Community College where he earned a degree in physical fitness technology.

Before designing Preki's fitness routine Misha first conducted an evaluation and assessment of Preki's current physical condition and fitness. This included an aerobic test, strength test, speed test, plyometric test, determining the resting and maximum heart rate, body and limb measurements, flexibility test and body fat measurement.

Using a standard fitness formula, an elite soccer player is deemed to need a fitness level score of 58. Following Preki's evaluation his score was 38. It was also decided that Preki needed to lose 8-10 pounds and improve his flexibility. As an example of his improvement, during an evaluation plyometric test of knees to chest, Preki reached his maximum heart rate at 22 seconds. After working with Misha, Preki can now last two minutes before reaching his maximum heart rate.

The following fitness routines were used to improve Preki's fitness level from 38 to his current score of 58. However, due to Preki's work with the Kansas City Wizards and the U.S. National Team it was impossible to follow a strict day-to-day routine. Instead it was necessary to constantly evaluate Preki's workload and where he was fitness-wise before determining what kind of workout was needed.

The following components were defined and routines were designed to improve them. It is important to understand that the fitness routine is a step-by-step program. For instance, work on the anaerobic endurance isn't undertaken until the aerobic endurance fitness level is where it should be. And speed work isn't undertaken until the anaerobic endurance level is where it should be. And so on.

Preki - Personal Fitness Routine

1. Aerobic - Endurance	
2. Anaerobic - Endurance	
3. Speed - Decision making, starting, acceleration	
4. Agility	
5. Soccer specifics - Conditioning with a ball.	

Aerobic Endurance

This routine was followed until a fitness level of 57 was reached. (Approximately two weeks.)

Monday	Two-mile run followed by plyometrics with weights. (Knees to chest, bent knees with heels to behind and hopping on each leg.)
Tuesday	Three-mile run.
Wednesday	Four-mile run followed by plyometrics.
Thursday	Three-mile run
Friday	Four-mile run followed by plyometrics.
Saturday	Six-mile run
Sunday	Rest

Anaerobic Endurance

Workout 1

Run full speed for 30 seconds then rest for
30 seconds
Run full speed for 60 seconds then rest for
60 seconds
Run full speed for 90 seconds then rest for 90 seconds
Allow the heart rate return to 55% of maximum, (approximately 2-3 minutes) then repeat. Do three sets.

Workout 2

Run full speed for 30 yards then jog back. Repeat three times.
Run full speed for 30 yards then walk back. Repeat three times.
Allow heart rate to return to 55% of maximum. (approximately 2-3 minutes).
Run full speed for 40 yards then jog back. Repeat four times.
Run full speed for 40 yards then walk back. Repeat four times.
Allow heart rate to return to 55% of maximum (approximately 2-3 minutes).
Run full speed for 400 yards then walk back. Repeat.

Speed

Starting Speed - On command, sprint for 5-10 yards from various positions, standing still, walking, jogging, walking backwards, etc.
Acceleration Speed – Through observation, work on posture, hand and arm movement, frequency of steps and stride length.
Overspeed – Three 20-yard sprints down a hill. Walk back up the hill. Allow heart rate to return to 55% of maximum then repeat three times.
Overload Speed – Done during the anaerobic phase with weighted vest and/or ankle weights. More rest when using weights.

Agility

Various sprints weaving in and out of cones.

Soccer Specifics

Various drills with a soccer ball usually done with trainer and other players.
(See next page)

Preki - Personal Fitness Routine

The following are drills used by Preki to fine-tune his fitness routine. The drills were done at a fast pace and to exhaustion. All the drills can be done with the help of one other person but usually work better with with a small group of four or five players.

Shooting

Three servers are positioned as shown in diagram 11, all having a supply of balls. Preki positions himself in the middle. To start the drill, Preki receives a ball from S1, turns and quickly runs towards the goal and shoots. As soon as he shoots, S2 plays him a ball, Preki collects, shoots and turns to S3 to receive a pass and shoot. As soon as he shoots, S1 serves him another pass and the drill continues. It is important that the next server pass the ball as soon as Preki has taken his shot to keep him moving quickly.

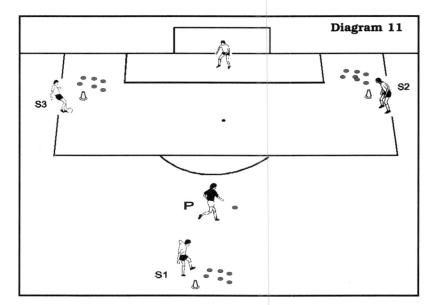

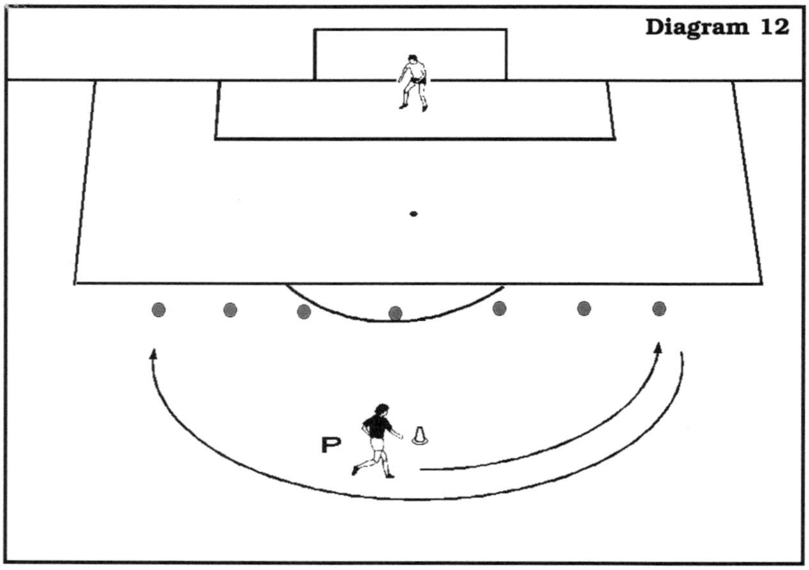

Diagram 11

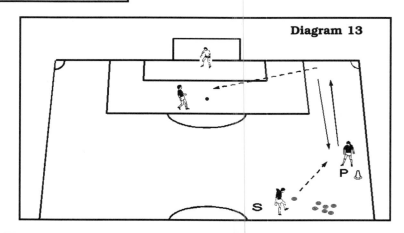

Diagram 12

Shooting

A number of balls are placed just outside the 18-yard line. A cone is placed 5 yards further away from the line of balls. Preki starts at the cone and then runs quickly to the ball furthest to his right and shoots. As soon as he shoots he sprints around the cone again to the ball furthest on his left and shoots that ball. As soon as he shoots he sprints around the cone to the ball that is remaining furthest on the right side and shoots. The drill continues until all the balls have been shot.

Crossing

A server with a supply of balls is positioned 40 - 50 yards from goal. Preki is positioned by a cone which is on the out-of-bounds line 35 yards from goal. The server starts the drill by passing a ball to Preki. Preki receives the ball, turns, sprints to the end line and crosses to a waiting teammate. As soon as he crosses he sprints back to the cone to receive another pass from the server and the drill continues.

Diagram 13

Brazil National Team

A practice observed in Florida during preparation for the Gold Cup 1998.

Crossing and Shooting

A1 serves to B1 then makes a run toward the far post.

B1 lays off one touch to incoming C.

C passes one touch toward the end-line for sprinting B1.

B1 crosses to incoming E and A1 for a one-touch finish.

After passing, C turns and runs towards D1 who is waiting for the next player in line A to start the sequence from the other side.

Change C when tired.

Variations

- Add defender to break up crosses.
- Vary service to wide players.
- Vary types of crosses.

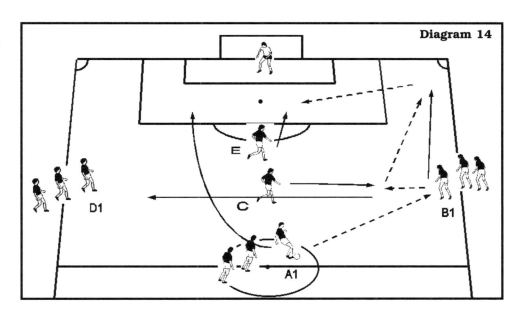

Diagram 14

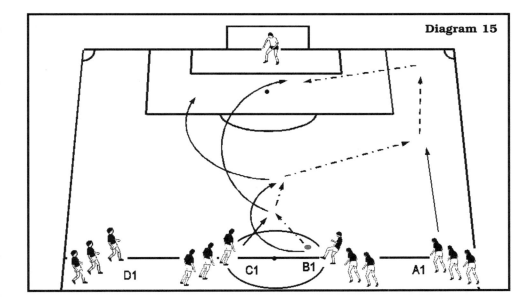

Diagram 15

Crossing and Shooting

B1 passes to C1.

B1 runs behind C1.

C1 passes in path of running B1.

C1 runs behind B1 and then to near post.

B1 passes in front of running A1.

B1 runs toward the far post.

A1 touches the ball toward the end-line and crosses for B1 and C1.

B1 and C1 finish with one touch.

Alternate to the other side with the next player in line C starting the sequence with a pass to the next player in line B.

Brazil National Team

Crossing and Shooting

B1 passes to C1.

B1 runs behind C1.

C1 passes into path of running B1.

C1 runs wide behind incoming A1.

B1 passes to incoming A1.

B1 runs toward the far post.

A1 passes into path of running C1.

A1 runs toward the near post.

C1 touches the ball toward the end-line and crosses for A1 and B1.

A1 and B1 finish with one touch.

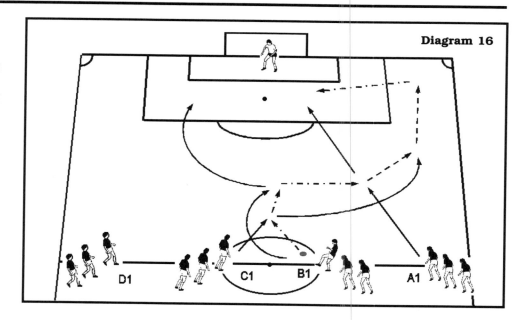

Diagram 16

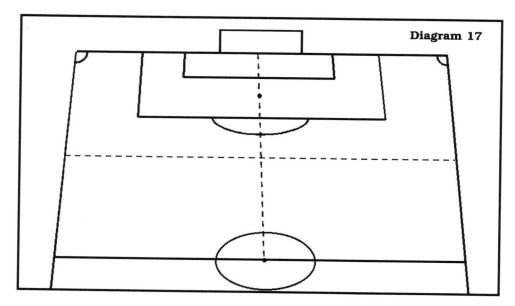

Diagram 17

Possession

Half of a regulation size field is lined into four equal quarters. Two teams of 9 v 9 play keep-away for 30 minutes using only one touch.

For the first ten minutes, play in only one quarter of the marked out field.

For the next ten minutes, play in only two quarters of the marked out field.

For the final ten minutes, use all four quarters (full half field).

San Jose Clash

A 75-minute practice observed in Orlando, Florida 1998.

This was a morning practice and was mostly a tune-up for a pre-season game scheduled for later that same day.

Keep-away

After a 15-minute warm-up and stretching routine, the players split into three groups of seven. All three groups play 5 v 2 keep-away in a circle of approximately 12 yards diameter for 15 minutes. The player that makes the mistake changes with a player in the middle.

Diagram 18

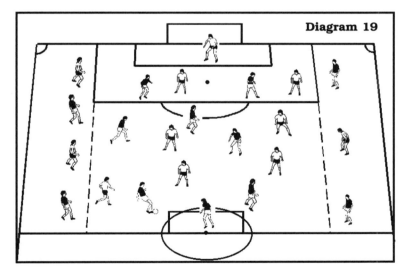

Diagram 19

Seven v Seven

Following the keep-away drill the same three teams play 7 v 7 for 20 minutes on half a field with out-of-bounds lines extending from the 18 yard box. Two teams play while the other team positions themselves around the perimeter to retrieve balls.

The games are played at a very fast pace and last only three minutes. The winning team stays on the field.

If the ball goes out-of-bounds, it is played back in with a kick-in.

Coaching Points

The players are constantly told to look for early shooting opportunities.

Practice ended with a 15-minute penalty kick competition followed by a 10 minute cool down.

Mike Kelly - Goalkeeping

In March I was fortunate to spend some time with Mike Kelly the First Team coach at Nottingham Forest. Mike is a goalkeeping specialist and has been the goalkeeper coach for the England National Team for three World Cups. Below are some of his goalkeeping practices.

After many years of study, including analyzing previous World Cup competitions, Mike came to the conclusion that most shots at goal came from the shaded areas (diagram 1). He also pointed out that almost 90% of a goalkeeper's saves are made in the marked-out triangle. Therefore, Mike structures his work so that 80% is done from the shaded areas to the triangle.

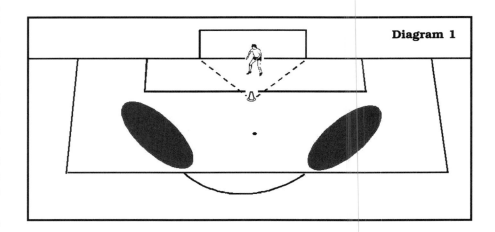

Mike has strong beliefs regarding coaching goalkeepers. He feels it is extremely important that when working on technique, practices should simulate game situations as much as possible. For instance, drills where the goalkeeper starts off on his knees or lying on the ground or when the ball is thrown for the goalkeeper to save are more fitness orientated and are not game realistic.

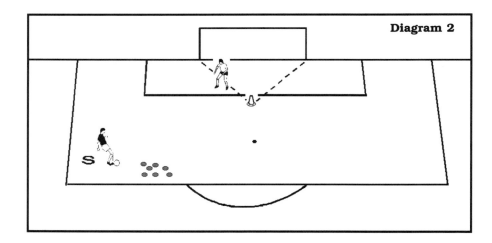

In diagram 2, the server shoots 8 - 10 balls each of low shots, chest high shots, and high shots. Repeat from other side. For the high shots, half volleys can be used.

Coaching Points
- Composure
- Focus on the ball
- Keep head still
- Strong stance
- Relax on feet
- Move into line of ball
- Mirror your hands

Mike Kelly - Goalkeeping

In diagram 3, the goalkeeper starts on the cone facing sideways. On the shout of "turn" the goalkeeper spins and makes the save from the servers shot.

Coaching Points
- Footwork - don't cross feet.
- Quick reaction time.
- Vary shots - low and high.

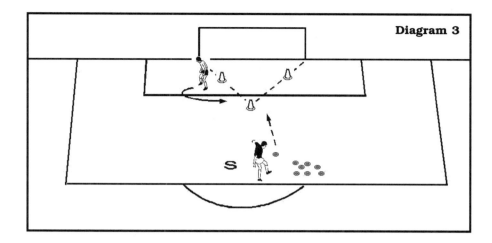

Diagram 3

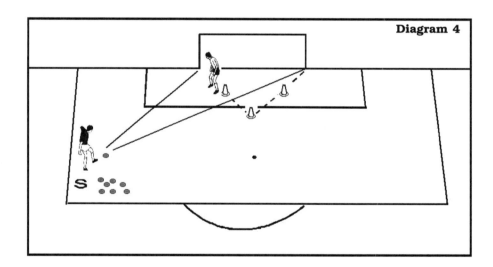

Diagram 4

In diagram 4, the server shoots from an angle. The goalkeeper should use the near post and cones to give him the correct angles.

Be careful of advancing off the 'triangle line' as this lessens the reaction time.

The goalkeeper should be within distance to save at his near post and cover his far post.

If the goalkeeper can't catch the ball he must deflect the shot.

Coaching Points
- Shorten the distance
- Keep hands low
- Good decisions

Diagram 5 is a shooting game inside the 18-yard box. The servers alternate playing balls into four attackers who play against three defenders.

This game is designed to test the goalkeepers' speed of reaction and his decision making.

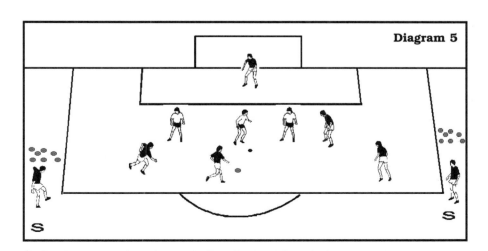

Diagram 5

Interview with Alfonso Mondelo

Alfonso Mondelo, now with the NY/NJ MetroStars, has enjoyed success throughout his coaching career. He began coaching with the New York Hota Bavarians, a semi-professional team in 1981 and led them to the national title in 1990. In 1994 he joined the Long Island Rough Riders and guided them to four consecutive North Atlantic Division titles. Mondelo also coached the national team of Puerto Rico through the qualifying stages of the 1994 World Cup.

What do you believe to be the key aspects in team success?

There are quite a few, but I think the most important aspects are chemistry, discipline, understanding of each other and a good work ethic.

What is your preferred playing style?

I think the best teams are the ones that can mix their game up. Teams that can play short quick passes, then go long and are unpredictable, are the toughest to play against. You never know what they are going to do.

Do you ever change your style or formation depending on who your opposition is?

Formations are as good as the players you have. I think your players dictate the formation you play. I prefer to play with a sweeper at the back because I think it gives us cover and depth to the defense. Other than that it depends on the players. If we have good wing players, we will play with wider players. If we have defensive orientated players, we might play with two defensive midfielders instead of one. It also depends on the opposition and what they bring to the table and how we match up against them.

Do you utilize videotape sessions with your players?

I think video is an important tool to have both as a learning tool to see what other teams are doing and also as a teaching aid to show players where the breakdowns are occurring. However, I don't think video sessions should be lengthy. I think they should be condensed where you can take five minutes and really point out the object of the session so the players don't get bored watching.

How often do you work on shooting and finishing?

I think that finishing is the key of the game. I think every practice should include finishing and working toward the goal. After all, finishing is the hardest part of the game so it really needs the most time.

How often do you work on set-plays?

During pre-season not much, but as the season goes on we will spend a lot of time on corner kicks and restarts near goal because they are direct scoring opportunities. After all, many goals in the World Cup and international competitions are scored from set-plays so you have to spend time on them.

> I think every practice should include finishing and working toward the goal. After all finishing is the hardest part of the game so it really needs the most time.

What kind of practice do you do regularly with your players?

Anything with the ball. We do a lot with the ball. We try to make sure the player's first touch is correct, after all, the key to the success of a team is how the ball is moved from player to player and the technical ability of the individual player. We will do a lot of the technical drills that involve passing and receiving the ball with any part of the body. Drills that include being able to take two touches without the ball hitting the ground, receiving the ball from different angles with the head, chest, thigh, etc. It is important that the players are comfortable with the ball. If we do a possession game or a shooting drill, the emphasis is always on the first-touch.

Team Defending from Alfonso Mondelo and the NY/NJ MetroStars appear in the March 1998 issue of WORLD CLASS COACHING.

Pre-Season practices observed in Orlando, Florida 1998.

Small-Sided Games

After a 20-minute warm-up and stretching routine the players are split into three groups of seven.

Half a field is marked out as shown in diagram 6. Each group of seven players play a small-sided game in one of the marked areas. Each game is 3 v 3 plus a floater who plays for whichever team has possession of the ball.

The scores of each game are noted. For the keep-away game, 15 consecutive passes = one goal.

The games last for 8 - 10 minutes followed by five minutes rest. The groups rotate fields until they play on all three fields. The practice ends with an eight-minute light jog followed by 10 minutes of stretching.

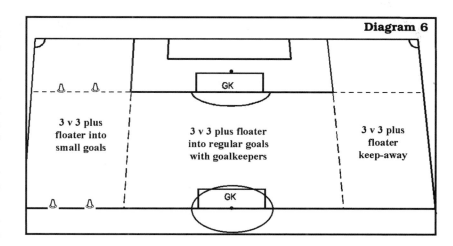

Diagram 6

3 v 3 plus floater into small goals

3 v 3 plus floater into regular goals with goalkeepers

3 v 3 plus floater keep-away

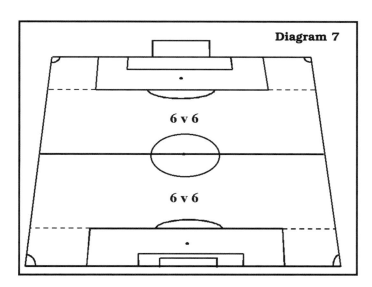

Diagram 7

6 v 6

6 v 6

Six v Six

The practice starts with a 10-minute warm-up of jogging and stretching. The players are then split into four teams of six. Two games of 6 v 6 keep-away are played using both halves of the field with the lines of the 18 yard goalbox extended as shown in diagram 7.

Play unlimited touches keep-away for four minutes.
Stretch for two minutes.
Play two-touch keep-away for four minutes.
Stretch for two minutes.

Six v Six – Progression

In diagram 8, the field is then reduced with lines extending from the sides of the 18 yard goalbox as shown.

Play unlimited touches keep-away for four minutes.
Stretch for two minutes.
Play two-touch keep-away for four minutes.
Stretch for two minutes.

The practice concludes with an 11 v 11 game using the full field for 40 minutes followed by a five minute light jog and stretches.

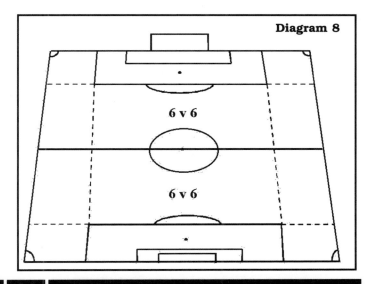

Diagram 8

6 v 6

6 v 6

Sheffield United - Youth Team Practices

During my visit to England I spent an evening with the Sheffield United Center of Excellence players aged U10 - U13. These players, as do all the players aged 9 - 15, are coached twice a week by the club's part-time coaches. This particular evening the four different age groups all practiced at the same time on an astroturf surface almost the size of two soccer fields. The weather was steady rain and around 45 degrees but it didn't seem to bother the players or coaches. The practice focused on passing, moving and receiving. Below are a sample of the drills.

Pass Control And Move

Four players start in the middle of a 40 x 40 yard square, each have a ball. Eight players position themselves around the perimeter of the square. All the players in the square dribble at the same time and then call to a player on the perimeter and pass him the ball.

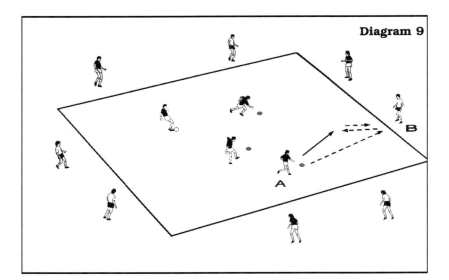

In diagram 9, A passes to B. As soon as A passes to B he points in the direction to where he would like the ball passed back to him.

B passes back to A with one touch.

A makes a short pass back to B and takes B's place on the perimeter.

B collects the ball and takes A's place inside the square.

Coaching Points

• Quality passes - correct weight.
• Be alert when on the perimeter.
• Keep your head up.

3 v 3 Plus Perimeter Players

Diagram 10 is a progression of the drill in diagram 9. In a grid 25 x 25 yards play 3 v 3 keep-away using outside players, if needed. The outside players can pass to each other if none of the middle players are available to pass to. This keeps the game moving. Initially, the team without possession of the ball should remain relatively passive. As the players start to achieve more success, the defending team can defend progressively stronger.

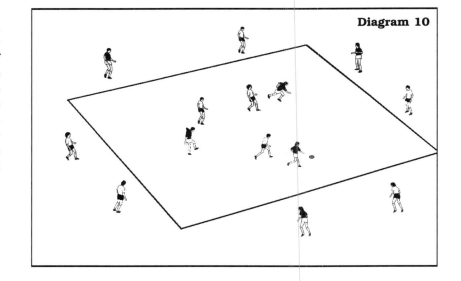

Coaching Points

• Quality passes - pass away from the defender.
• Receive passes with the foot furthest from the defender.
• Create space to receive a pass by moving away then 'checking' back.
• Promote fakes, moves and individual skills.

Progression

When you receive a pass from a perimeter player - return the pass and change places.

Sheffield United - Youth Team Practices

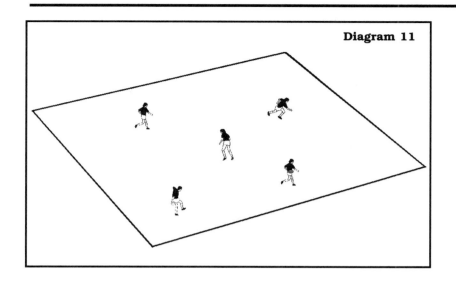

Diagram 11

Sequence Passing

Diagram 11 is an awareness drill. Five players are in a grid 25 x 25 yards. Each has a number, one through five. The players move around the grid and pass to each other in sequence, one passes to two, two passes to three, etc.

After making a pass, the player must move away from his space. When it is his turn to receive a pass, the player must call to the person with the ball.

Therefore, the players must be constantly thinking and always be aware of what is happening.

Variations

• Must take 2, 3 or 4 touches before passing.
• Receive with one foot and pass with the other.
• Fake one direction and receive the ball moving in the other direction.

Pass – Control – Turn – Pass

Four players to a 20 x 10-yard grid, each end player passes to the middle player at the same time. The middle players receive the pass with an open body position, turn toward the inside and pass to the opposite end player. The end players receive the pass with one touch and pass back to the middle players with their second touch to continue the drill.

Variations

• Middle players fake to receive the ball with the front foot but let the ball run across their body to receive it with the back foot
• Middle players receive the ball and pass back to the same end player then turn to receive a pass from the opposite end player.
• As above but middle players use only one touch
• Everyone uses one touch whenever possible

Diagram 12

Follow Your Pass

In diagram 13, the players are split into two lines. The first player in line passes to the front player of the opposite line and then follows his pass to join the end of the opposite line. The player receiving the ball controls with one touch then passes with his second touch. He then follows his pass and joins the back of the opposite line. The drill continues with the next player in line making his pass.

Variation

Use one-touch passing.

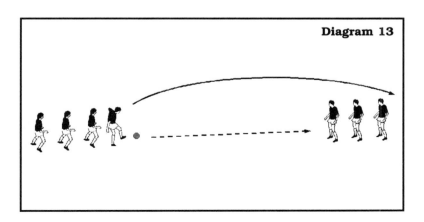

Diagram 13

Nottingham Forest

Earlier this year I had the opportunity to spend a day at Nottingham Forest. I watched both the first team and the youth team practice. Below are some drills from the first team.

Three Team Keep-Away

This drill was done as a warm-up for 12 - 15 minutes. In a field of 40 x 40 yards, three teams of five, each wearing different colors, one team starts as defenders the other two teams combine in possession of the ball. If the defending team wins possession of the ball then the five man team who lost possession becomes the defending team. Therefore it is always 10 v 5.

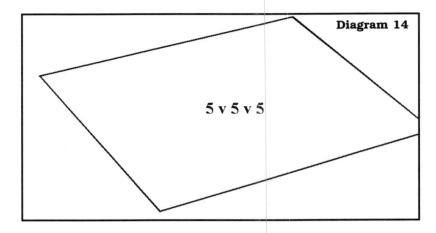

Diagram 14

5 v 5 v 5

2 v 2 Plus Servers

The grid is 40 x 20 yards. The middle 20 yards is occupied by four players in a 2 v 2 situation. Two servers are in each 10 yard end zone. A server starts by playing the ball into one of the players in the middle section. Once in possession, the player attempts to pass the ball to a server at the opposite end. He can do this directly or by using his teammate in a passing combination. If the defending team gains possession they pass it to a server and then become the attacking team.

When a server receives a ball he can either play it back to the attacking team with one touch or he can pass to the other server in his end zone to pass in.

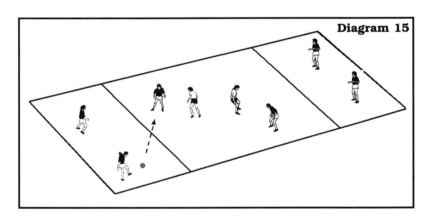

Diagram 15

Coaching Points

- Defend strongly, individually and as a pair
- Track your player defensively
- Look for give-and-go's offensively

Crossing and Finishing

A1 passes to A2.
A2 passes back to A3.
A3 passes to incoming A2 then a runs down the flank.
A2 controls with an open body position, turns and passes to A4 then runs to the edge of the 18 yard box.
A4 passes in front of running A3
A3 crosses to incoming A4, A5 and A6.
D1 defends the cross.
Continue the drill using both flanks.
Add defenders to make the drill progressively more game like.

Variation

A1 passes to A5.
A5 passes back to A1.
A1 passes in front of wide running A6.
A6 crosses.

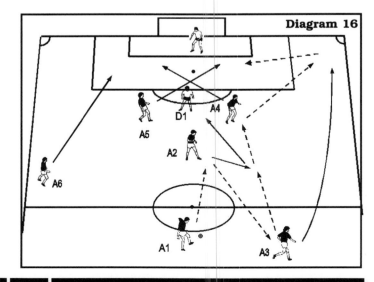

Diagram 16

Nottingham Forest

Crossing and Finishing

A1 passes to A4.

A4 passes to A7 then runs toward 18 yard goal-box.

A7 passes to incoming A6.

A6 passes in front of running A8 then runs toward the near post.

A8 crosses to incoming A3, A5, and A6.

A10 runs in on the opposite flank to cover over-hit crosses.

Continue the drill using both flanks.

Progressively add defenders to make the drill more game-like.

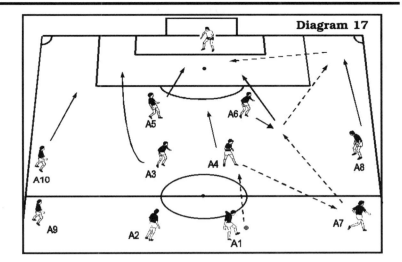

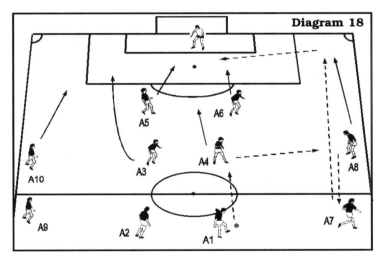

Variation of Diagram 17

As in the above drill but this time A4 passes to A8.

A8 lays off a pass to A7 then turns and runs down the flank.

A7 plays a first-touch pass into the path of running A8.

Variation of Diagram 17

As in diagram 17 but this time A8 plays a give-and-go with incoming A6.

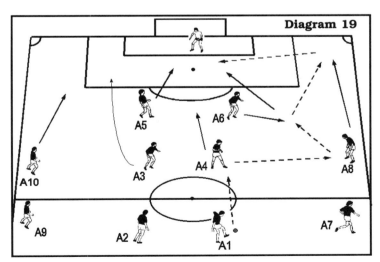

Editors Note... Both the youth team and the first team did many repetitions of these crossing and finishing drills. Many different combinations were done and defenders were always added to turn the drill into a more game-like situation. One noticeable point was that even without the defenders involved, the coach was constantly directing his players to play at game speed. The passes were quick and accurate and after each goal attempt the players jogged back to their starting positions which made the drill somewhat fitness orientated as well.

65

October 1998 Issue

Boca Juniors

In March, Dr. Jay Martin, Athletic Director and Men's Soccer Coach at Ohio Wesleyan University, led a delegation of soccer coaches with the Citizen Ambassador Program of People to People International to Brazil and Argentina. During their visit they held talks with various soccer clubs and coaches and observed games and practices. Below is a practice session of the Boca Juniors, Argentina U15 youth team.

Warm up
Speed work and agility work – 20 minutes.

Technique Work
The team began a series of juggling techniques. The trainer was very active and vocal. His talk was very positive and he constantly tried to challenge the players.

Sequence
Juggle and keep the ball below the knees.
Juggle foot-head-foot-head etc.
Juggle foot-chest-foot-chest.
Juggle foot-thigh-foot-thigh.
Juggle and move around the field on trainer's command.

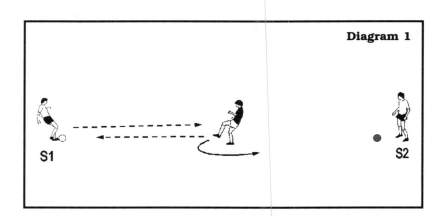

Diagram 1

The trainer kept the players juggling while he explained the next technique. He wanted the players to control the ball, knock it into the air, chase it, trap it and speed dribble to space. The whole team (about thirty players) did this in half field. He then added two passive defenders to force players to change direction with the speed dribble. The players worked extremely hard. The trainer stopped the activities often and had the players stretch.

The next technique was receiving the ball. Three men with two soccer balls lined up as seen in diagram 1. The player in the middle played the ball as quickly as possible. One server always played on the ground, the other server alternated balls in the air and on the ground on the coach's command.

In another drill, the whole team lined up facing the goal and the coach (diagram 2). One by one the players juggled from the first cone to the second cone and then:

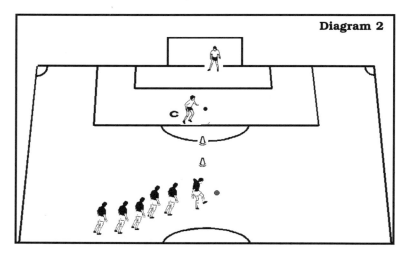

Diagram 2

"Beat the coach" for a shot.
Played a give-and-go with the coach for a shot.
Played a lofted ball to the coach for a shot.

The coach repeatedly urged the players to "…line up the body" and "improve the timing of the run and the shot".

Jay Martins note: This "drill" demonstrated poor teaching/coaching methods. It was very low intensity with only one player and goalkeeper involved at any time. The coach, however, did spend time and give attention to each player.

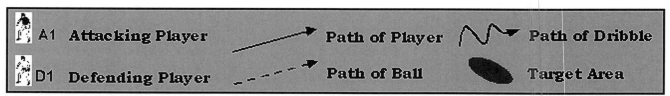

A1 Attacking Player	Path of Player	Path of Dribble
D1 Defending Player	Path of Ball	Target Area

Boca Juniors

The trainer/coach then placed a series of cones in front of the goal as shown in diagram 3. Each player in turn would dribble through the cones for a shot. The trainer emphasized sharp turns and change of pace. Demonstrating what he wanted a few times, he then asked the players to juggle to the cones, dribble and shoot.

End Game

The team played full field 11 x 11. The trainer asked for the following restrictions in turn:

- Low pressure defensive alignment and counter.
- Two-touch after a turnover (man with the ball plays two-touch) and looking forward.
- High pressure in attacking third after a turnover.
- Minimum three-touch, asking the players "to get into space".

The session ended with a warm-down and stretch.

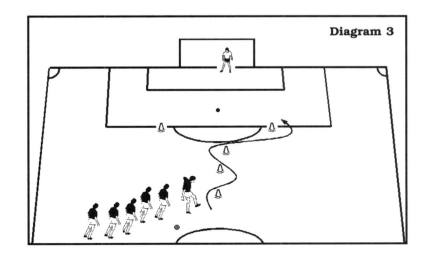

Diagram 3

Leeds United

A practice of the Leeds United Youth Team.

Shooting and Goalkeeping

The practice area is the 18 yard goalbox marked out as shown in diagram 4. The mid-area between the six yard boxes is the 'second six yard box' for both goals. Two servers with a supply of balls are positioned at the sides.

S1 serves to incoming A1.

A1 shoots one-touch toward the opposite post.

S2 serves to incoming A2.

A2 shoots one-touch toward the opposite post.

S1 then serves to incoming A3.

A3 shoots one-touch toward the opposite post.

S2 then serves to incoming A4.

A4 shoots one-touch toward the opposite post.

Once a player has taken a shot he joins the back of the other line behind his goal. For instance, A1 will join the back of the A3 line.

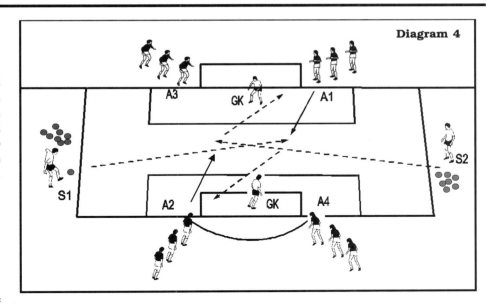

Diagram 4

- Wide focus of attention is needed to finish down the sides of the goalkeeper.
- Finish any rebounds.

Coaching Points - Forwards

- Make a straight run to the ball.
- Get to the ball early. Stretch to finish or slide if necessary.

Coaching Points - Goalkeepers

- Ensure goalkeepers have a correct starting position and are ready before serving.
- Goalkeepers to close down the space when ever possible.

Dutch National Team

A practice observed during preparations for the World Cup warm-up game against the U.S. earlier this year.

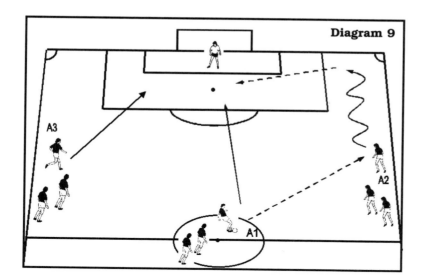

Diagram 9

Crossing And Finishing

Start with three lines of players as shown in diagram 9.

A1 passes to A2 with a lofted pass.

A1 then sprints to the edge of the 18 yard goalbox.

A2 controls the ball, dribbles to the end-line and crosses for incoming A1 and A3.

As A2 is dribbling to the end-line A3 makes a run to the far post.

Continue using both flanks.

Coaching Points

- A1 and A 3 must finish with one touch
- A2 varies his crosses

Columbus Crew

Contributed by Greg Andrulis, Assistant Coach of the Columbus Crew.

Warm-up

Players begin practice with an informal game of 5 v 2 as shown in diagram 10. Two or three games will be played until everyone is involved.

The next 20 - 25 minutes are spent on footwork and plyometrics using agility ladders and hurdles. The warm-up is progressive and includes active rest and static stretching.

The warm-up continues with the field players divided into six groups of three, one ball per group. Using one half of the field, the players inter-pass within their own group whilst moving around the field.

The goalkeepers spend this time in a specific goalkeeper warm-up that includes various catching and diving exercises

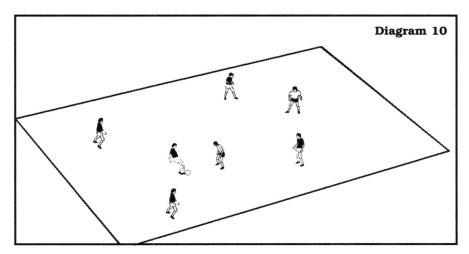

Diagram 10

Small-Sided Game

In diagram 11, the field is twice the size of the 18 yard goalbox (36 x 44 yards). Full size goals with goalkeepers and three teams of six are utilized. Two teams play and one team acts as 'active walls' on the perimeter. The perimeter players are encouraged to move along their lines. The perimeter players play for the team in possession of the ball and are limited to one touch. Inside it is 6 v 6. Two points are awarded for a goal scored from the defending half and one point is awarded for goals scored in the attacking half. The center line is used to enforce offside.

The games are five minutes long in duration with the winning team staying on to play again and the losing team swapping places with the perimeter players.

Progression

- Three-touch inside, one-touch perimeter.
- Two-touch inside, one-touch perimeter.
- One-touch in defensive half, unlimited in attacking half, one-touch perimeter.

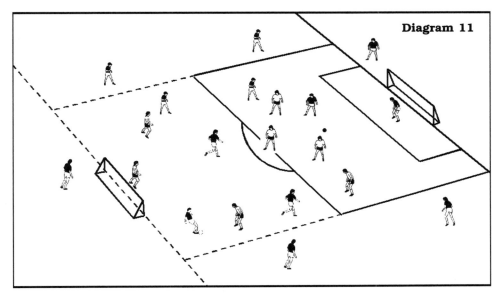

Diagram 11

Coaching Points

- Quick play
- Combinations
- Movement without the ball
- Take shooting opportunities
- Transition
- Everyone is active

After each team has played through all three progressions, the winning team is decided based on wins and goal differential. The winning team does some fun finishing and the losing teams do fitness. Practice concludes with a 15 minute cool down.

Martin Hunter

Martin Hunter was the FA's Regional Coach in the North East from 1990 to 1996. He has staffed both national and international courses for the FA and has coached England youth sides from Under 16's up to Under 20's. During 1993, Martin coached the Under 20's squad that won the Bronze Medal at the World Youth Championship in Australia. Martin is now the first team coach at Stoke City. This is Part One of 'Individual Play In The Middle Third Of The Field'. Part two will appear in the November issue of WORLD CLASS COACHING.
This article is reprinted with the kind consent of CATALYST, the official journal of AFCAT.

Individual Play In The Middle Third Of The Field

Stage 1 – Warm-up

Martin began with a warm up that enabled his players to practice one of the most important techniques of the overall practice.

In a grid 20 x 10 yards, A1 passes to A2 and A2 passes to A3. Repeat in the opposite direction and rotate the players occasionally.

Coaching Points For Middle Player

- Receive side on (look over shoulder before receiving).
- Judge the pace of the pass. If it's hard, take two touches, if it's soft, let it run or hook it on.

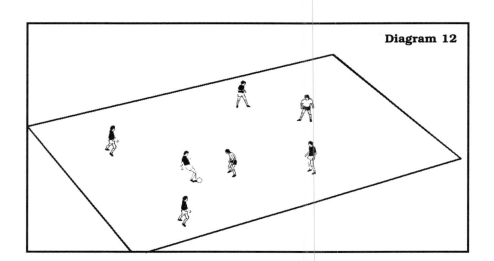

Diagram 12

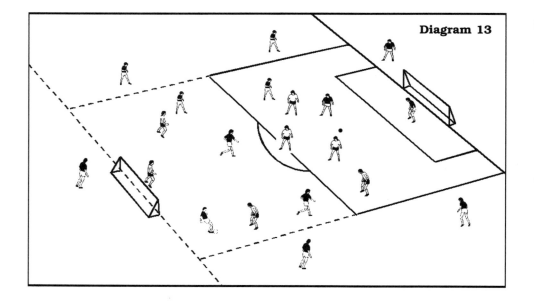

Diagram 13

Stage 2

In diagram 13, A1 passes to A2.
A2 should open up and look forward. As the ball travels to A2, A3 should move away and then check back to receive the ball from A2.
A3 passes up to either A5 or A6.
If A3 elects to pass to A6, they should pass down the side of the player.
If the pass is to A5, play around the corner.

Practice down both sides.

Stage 2 Continued

Next, A2 plays a diagonal pass to A4.

Coaching Points
- A1 and A2 should open up.
- Quality of pass to the mid-field.
- The mid-field and front players should make angled runs.
- Be positioned side on.
- Encourage players to be smart with their turns and angled passes.

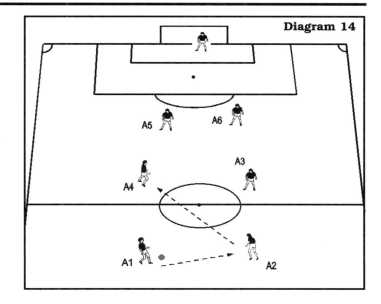

Diagram 14

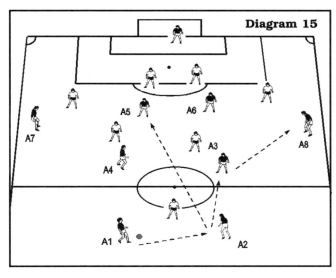

Diagram 15

Stage 3

Opposed practice. Coach the A's only. The organization should be as follows:

One player from the defending team versus A1 and A2, two versus two in mid-field, two versus two in attack and two wide players versus two full-backs.

Start with A1 and A2 passing into the mid-field. Progress by allowing the back players to pass up to the forwards too. Next, work on the mid-field getting the ball to the wide players. Finish with free play.

Coaching Points
- Support angles with open body.
- Quality and selection of pass angle and pace of pass (play the pass away from defenders, i.e. the safe-side).
- Smart play in the final third.

The "3-5-2 System of Play"

Stage 1

Unopposed practice. A1 passes to A2 or A3 to start the practice (work alternate sides). Condition the play to two-touch. Work on the movement of the two strikers and the "man in the hole", A4.

Firstly, A2 passes down the line for A5 as A4 and A6 make their runs.

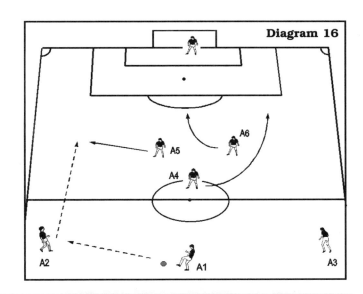

Diagram 16

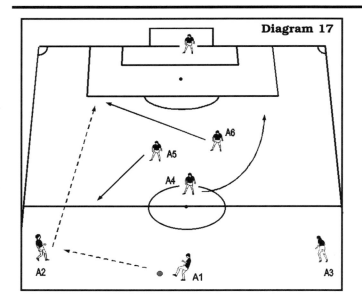

Diagram 17

Now, give A2 various options.
A5 moves towards the ball and A4 peels away, A2 passes down the line for A6 who has made a run behind A5.

Variations

- A2 plays a give-and-go with A5 before passing down the line
- After the give-and-go A2 sends a diagonal pass to A4.

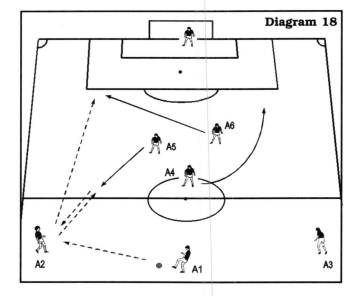

Diagram 18

Progression

Finally, as for the previous drills except that A6 pulls away as A2 and A5 play a give-and-go to enable A4 to make a diagonal run behind A5 for the pass up the line.
In the final drill, A4's run must be late.
Encourage A4 to work off the front two.

Coaching Points

- Weight and accuracy of passes
- Timing of runs
- Angle of runs
- Movement off the ball

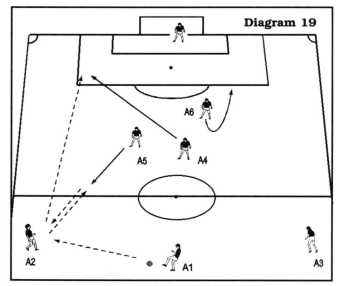

Diagram 19

Miami Fusion

Observed at a regular season practice.

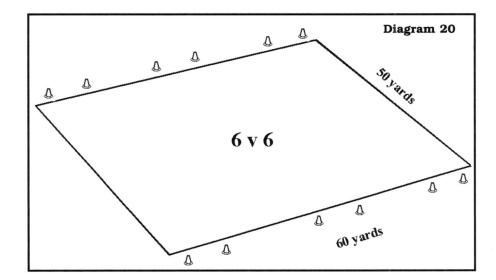

Diagram 20

50 yards

6 v 6

60 yards

Six Goal Game

In an area of 50 x 60 yards, place six small goals using cones as shown in diagram 20.

Play 6 v 6 with the conditions of two-touch and passing on the ground only.

Coaching Points

* Move the ball quickly
* Get the ball wide
* Look for quick combinations

Kansas City Wizards

A look at Ron Newman's corner kick philosophy. Adapted from an article in the Kansas City Star.

Wizards head coach Ron Newman said, typically, he likes to have a player move to the near post, try and get in front of a defender and flick the ball with his head to the far post for a waiting teammate. Or, the corner kicker can aim straight to the far post. He gives a hand signal before kicking as to which post he will be aiming for.

Newman likes to get two good headers of the ball like Paul Rideout and Mo Johnston and have one go to the near post and one far post. A player is placed near the goalkeeper to keep him from coming out. Two players are kept back to stop any quick breakaways and the rest of the players form what he calls an umbrella around the penalty area.

Another option Newman uses is to play a short corner. This is used to pull a few defenders out of the box and create some one-on-one opportunities inside the penalty area.

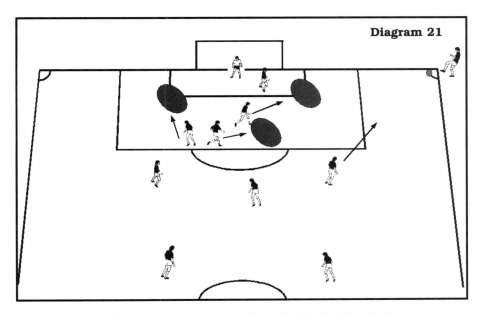

Diagram 21

November 1998 Issue

Nottingham Forest Youth Team

Contributed by Nottingham Forest youth team coach, Peter Cooper. Peter has experience coaching youth players of different ages at a number of Premier League clubs including Leeds United and now Nottingham Forest. Last season he worked with the U14 boys, this season he is the coach of the U11 boys.

Keeping Team Shape

Mark a field of 60 x 40 yards with four lanes as shown in diagram 1. The field size can be changed depending on the age of the players.

Four players in each team have to stay in the lanes they are positioned in. These players can only move up and down in these lanes. The other two players in each team are target players positioned either side of the goal.

The objective is for each team to play 4 v 4 but stay in their lanes and try to make a pass to one of their target players.

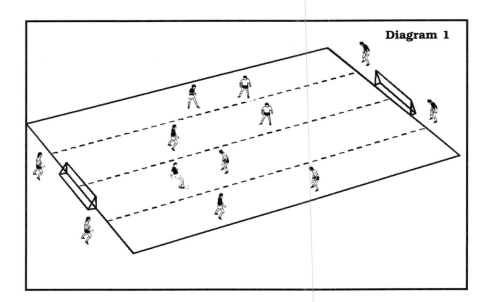
Diagram 1

Progression

Once a target player receives a pass he changes position with the player that passed the ball.

Game Two

The same 4 v 4 in the lanes but this time the two target players now move onto the field and play behind the four players as sweepers. These two players are allowed to move anywhere except in front the four teammates in front of him. The objective this time is to shoot on goal.

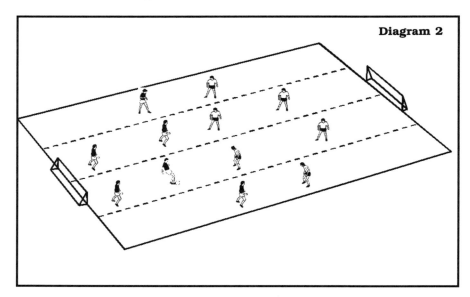
Diagram 2

Coaching Points

- Rotate the players
- Team and individuals to keep good team shape
- Normal defensive strategies can be used – pressure, cover, balance
- Covering defenders are to cover on the nearest side of their lane
- Good communication
- Encourage players to play forward or back – not square

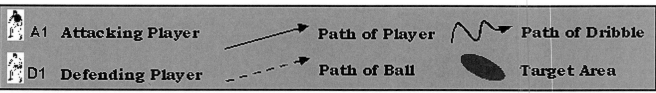

A1 **Attacking Player**	→ **Path of Player**	⌇ **Path of Dribble**
D1 **Defending Player**	⇢ **Path of Ball**	⬮ **Target Area**

Running With The Ball

Set up four lines of players in a 50 x 20 yard grid as shown in diagram 3.

Player A runs with the ball, passes to the front player in line D and joins the back of line C.
Player D runs with the ball, passes to the front player in line A and joins the back of line B.
When a player joins the back of line C and B the front player from these lines joins the back of lines D and A respectfully.

Coaching Points
- Keep your head up.
- Good first touch.
- Use the laces of the shoe.
- Have few touches when running with the ball.
- Quality passes.

Progressions
- Change the direction of play to use the other foot.
- On the player's first touch to receive the ball, the player behind chases as a passive defender.

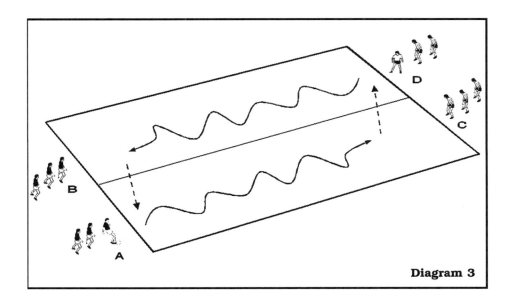

Diagram 3

Running With the Ball

All the players have a ball and position themselves on the perimeter of a 40 x 40-yard grid. All the players run with the ball at the same time using the coaching points described in the previous drill (diagram 3). There are three progressions for this drill.
1. Players run with the ball to the opposite side of the grid, execute a turn and stop the ball.
2. Players run with the ball to one side of the grid, execute a turn, then run with the ball to another side of the grid, execute a turn and stop the ball.
3. Players then run to all four sides executing turns on each side.

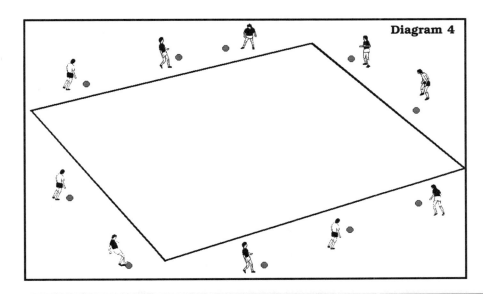

Diagram 4

Coaching Points
- Good turning techniques.
- Acceleration away from turns into space.
- Avoid collisions with other players by keeping your head up.
- Firm touches into space.
- Use more controlling touches in confined areas.

Running With the Ball – Small-Sided Game

Diagram 5 is set up with a 60 x 40-yard field with a five yard end zone at each end of the field. Two teams of 6 v 6 + 2 floaters can score a goal by running the ball into the end zone. When a team has scored they keep possession and play going in the other direction.

Coaching Points

- Run with the ball whenever possible.
- First touch to be forward.
- Keep the ball moving.
- If you can't run with the ball, look for a give-and-go and then run again.
- Have the attitude of 'run at them'.

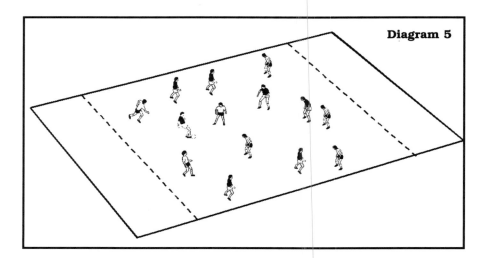

Diagram 5

Small-Sided Game for Awareness

The small-sided game in diagram 6 is designed to improve movement and positional sense both on and off the ball as well as improving awareness during transition from attacking to defending. Two teams of 6 v 6 play in a 40 x 40-yard grid. Each team plays 4 v 4 inside the grid with two target players on opposite sides of the grid as shown. One team plays in a north/south direction the other team plays simultaneously in an east/west direction. The objective is to pass to one of their target players. The target player then has three touches to play the ball back to a teammate.

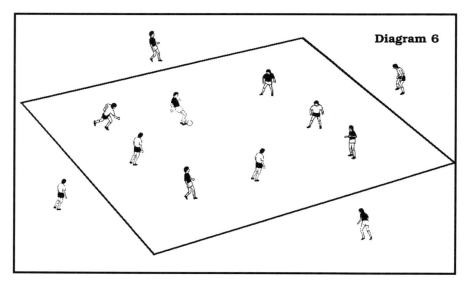

Diagram 6

Possession Coaching Points

- Open body position to receive the ball.
- Move towards the ball to play early.
- Move away from the ball for more time.
- Do not give the ball away.
- Look for give-and-go's.

Defensive Coaching Points

- Switch on quickly.
- Change body position.
- Pressure the player in possession quickly.
- Cover and balance.

Interview with Bob Warming

The architect of two of the biggest turn-arounds in NCAA soccer history, Bob Warming has taken the Saint Louis University program back to the Final Four for the second time since 1974. Previously, Warming built the Creighton University program from scratch into a national power in the early 90's.

What do you believe to be the key aspects in team success?

I believe the two main aspects are team chemistry and talented players.

What is your preferred playing style?

If I had a preferred playing system it would be the Dutch system of 3 – 4 – 3. However, I don't think it is something that is easy to accomplish with the typical American player because there are very few American players that have been taught to play as wing players. Therefore, I usually play a slight variation of a 4 – 4 – 2.

Do you prefer to man mark with a sweeper or use a zonal defending system?

I would prefer to play using a zonal defending system. However, the players I inherited are better suited to playing with markers and a sweeper.

Do you feel the typical American players are suited to playing with markers and a sweeper?

There is no question that the American players are much more comfortable playing with markers and a sweeper and I have my own theory as to why that is. The most important aspect is that the American players have just not seen enough zonal defending. They haven't learned to read the game well enough by watching enough of the top players and teams in the world play. For example, just over half of our players at St. Louis University have actually seen a live professional soccer game. So unless you've seen it, how can you do it? Unless you've seen it done well, how can you do it well? I think that as a result of our players not having a chance to see zonal defending done correctly at the top level it is much easier for players and coaches at this time to play with marking back systems.

Do you ever change your playing style or formation?

Unfortunately yes. Last season for example, we lost seven starters to injury during the first two weeks of the season and because we are allowed only 9.9 scholarships, you don't have that much depth in your team and you sometimes need to make changes depending on the players you have available. It is very rare that I would change how we would play because of another team. Do we make adjustments sometimes? Absolutely, but we go in prepared to play the way we want to play.

Do you utilize videotape sessions with your players?

Yes, very much so. I think when I was at Creighton we were the first school in the country to use the Avid Editing System. This allowed us to isolate certain parts of the game and individual players on tape. For example, if we wanted to talk with the wide defenders about the right time to attack out of the back, we could edit the tape to show just the times when the defenders had the ball and point out the opportunities they might have to move forward from the back. In fact, we could easily edit the tape to show just about anything we wanted such as the forwards playing with their back toward goal, crossing situations, runs into the goalbox, etc. Yes, I am very much into what you can do with videotape, particularly because of the fact that our players don't get to see enough quality soccer.

How often do you practice shooting and finishing?

Every practice, either with the 3 v 2 to 2 v 1 game described on the following pages or with some crossing and finishing drills.

How often do you work on restarts and set plays?

Probably not enough. We spend a lot of our time just learning to play the game.

What kind of practice do you do regularly with your team?

The first thing I try and do is to set an attitude at the start of practice. Almost always we try and do something that is fun. One of the things about coaching at the college level, for example, is that you might find yourself dealing with a play-

> **There is no question that the American players are much more comfortable playing with markers and a sweeper. They just haven't seen enough zonal defending.**

er that just came out of a physics test that he bombed. I think it is important that they look forward to practice, so we start off the first five to ten minutes with some sort of fun activity. We usually follow this with some sort of possession games. We almost always utilize small-sided games with neutral players that play for the team in possession. Then we move on to the tactical part which might be looking at what we did in our last game and how we can correct that or looking at our future opposition and deciding how we can best take advantage of any weakness they might have. We then move on to some finishing drills and sometimes we will end with a 15 – 20-minute scrimmage.

Bob Warming - A Favorite Practice

3 v 2 to 2 v 1

Two teams line up either side of the goal post of a goal that is placed 40 yards out as shown in diagram 7. The game starts with three players from team A, A1, A2 and A3 playing offense against two players from team D, D1 and D2. Once team A has taken a shot, the goalkeeper plays a ball to team D who now plays 2 v 1 going in the opposite direction against the player from team A that took the shot. The other two players from team A now stay where they are as they become the defending team next time around. After team D has taken a shot, both D players join the back of their line as does the player from team A that was defending the two players from team D. Then the next three players from team D play 3 v 2 against the two players from team A that stayed on the field and the game continues. Goalkeepers are used and a supply of balls is placed by each goal post.

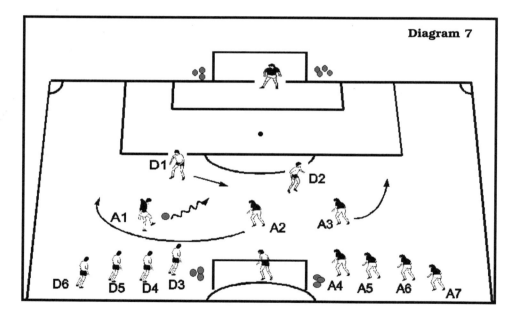

Diagram 7

In this example, A1 starts with the ball and runs inside in an attempt to move D1 closer to D2 creating room on the outside for the overlapping A2. A3 also runs wide in an effort to move D2 from the middle.

Bob Warming - A Favorite Practice

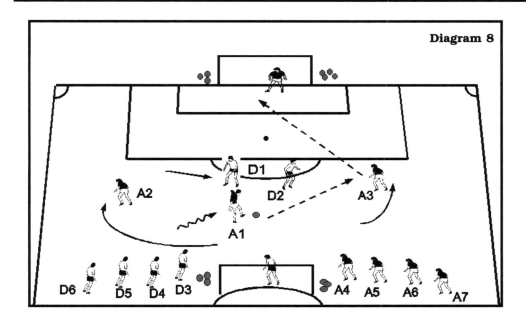

A1 has now moved toward the middle bringing D1 inside. A2 has made an overlapping run and A3 has moved out wide stretching the defense and giving A1 two options – to take a shot or to pass.

In diagram 8, A1 passes to A3 who shoots on goal.

As soon as A3 has taken the shot, the goalkeeper passes the ball to D1 or D2 to play 2 v 1 in the opposite direction. A3 then runs back to defend against D1 and D2. A1 and A2 stay where they are as they become the two defenders next time around.

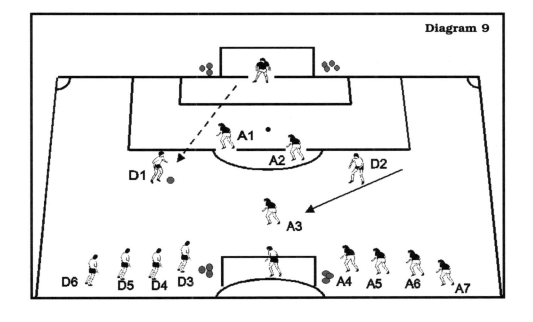

Bob Warming - A Favorite Practice

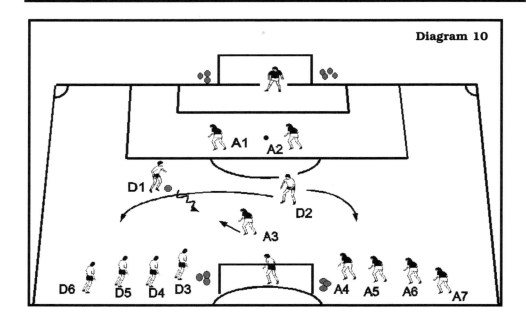

In diagram 10, D1 is encouraged to attack the middle of the field forcing A3 to engage him to deny a shooting opportunity. D2 has the option of making an overlapping run, supporting D1 for a give-and-go or staying wide for a pass.

Following a shot by D1 or D2, the game continues as shown in diagram 11.

Encourage overlaps, takeovers, dribble penetration and give-and-go's.

Following a shot by D1 or D2 in the previous diagram the game continues with D3, D4 and D5 playing 3 v 2 against A1 and A2. A3, D1 and D2 join the back of their respective lines.

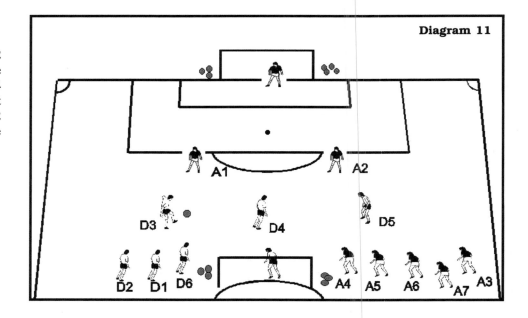

Coaching Points for 3 v 2 to 2 v 1

- Encourage attackers to dribble at the nearest defender at an angle and at speed.
- Encourage attackers without the ball to bend their runs so that they can run onto the path of the ball instead of away from goal.
- Encourage players to combine by giving an extra point for a successful overlap, takeover or fake. takeover.
- Make the exercise competitive – award three points for a goal, one point for a shot on goal and deduct five points for shooting over the crossbar.

Pia Sundhage

Pia Sundhage gained 146 caps playing for her native country, Sweden. Sweden brings it's coaches up through the ranks, and Pia has been coach of the U16, U18, and now the U20 national team as well as the assistant coach to Sweden's national team. Below Pia describes some drills used to practice isolated techniques.

This article is reprinted with the consent of Catalyst, the official journal of AFCAT.

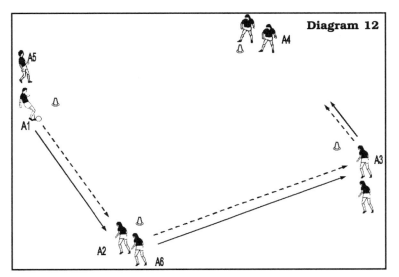

Diagram 12

Practice One

Mark a grid 10 x 10 yards (grid size depends on age and ability of players) with cones at each corner. Two players are placed at each corner.
A1 passes to A2 then follows the pass.
A2 receives and passes to A3 then follows the pass.
A3 receives and passes to A4 then follows the pass.
A4 receives and passes to A5 then follows the pass.
The drill continues with A5 passing to A6 and so on.

Practice Two

A1 dribbles the ball inside A2's cone then turns and screens the ball from the 'opponent'. A1 then quickly moves away with the ball, passes to A3 and follows the pass.

At the same time A4 dribbles the ball inside A1's cone and passes to A2.

The drill continues with A2 and A3 now dribbling the ball.

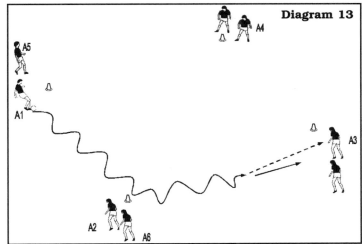

Diagram 13

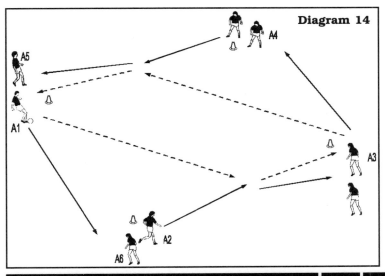

Diagram 14

Practice Three

A1 passes in front of A2.
A2 sprints to receive the ball from A1.
A2 receives the ball, passes to A3, then runs behind A3's line.
A3 prepares to make the next pass to sprinting A4 with one touch, then joins the back of A4's line.
The drill continues with A4 passing to A5 and so on.

Pia Sundhage

Practice Four

Development and realism of practice three is increased by introducing goals on a slightly larger field. The organization is the same but now the players attempt to score.

Use more balls and players to get increased activity – learn by doing! Adjust the passing distance according to the age group of the players.

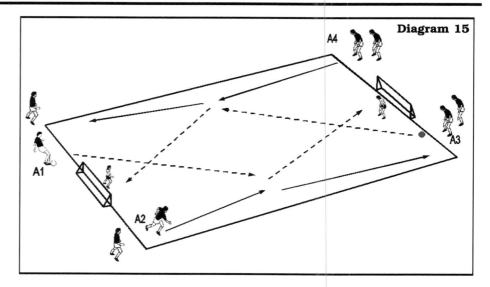

Diagram 15

Coaching Points – All Four Practices

- Quality of the pass.
- Preparing to receive the ball.
- Controlling the ball by increasing the concentration of the 'first-touch' to obtain more time and space to increase movement and to improve playing angles.

Michael Hennigan

Michael Hennigan has an extensive soccer pedigree, playing professionally in England, South Africa and Australia. Following his playing days he coached at just about every level of the game including eight years as assistant manager/first team coach with Leeds United F.C. highlighted with the English Premier League Championship in 1992. Hennigan is currently the first team coach at Blackpool F.C.

One-Touch Finishing

Set up two goals with goalkeepers 40 yards apart as shown in diagram 16. In the middle are two receivers and one shooter. S1 serves to R1 who lays off a one-touch pass for the shooter to shoot. Following the shot S2 quickly serves to R2 who also lays off the pass for the shooter to shoot. Then S3 serves to R1 followed by S4 serving to R2 for the shooter to shoot in the opposite goal. The drill is designed to be played at a quick pace – work the shooter hard for 2 – 3 minutes. Change positions.

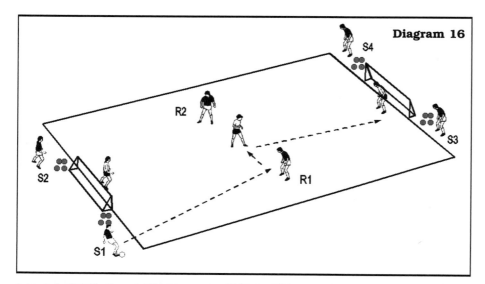

Coaching Points

- Servers to play balls in with pace.
- Shooter to keep close to receivers for quick shot.
- Quick feet with small step adjustments to get in position to shoot.
- Use both feet to shoot.
- Must hit the target.
- Worst place to shoot is over the crossbar.

Martin Hunter

This is the second in a two part series of 'Individual Play In The Middle Third Of The Field' from Martin Hunter. Martin has previously coached England youth sides from U16's to U20's including the U20 team that won the bronze medal at the 1993 World Youth Championship.

In the previous article Martin worked on midfielders and forwards making runs to receive the ball from defenders. The session continues with an opposed practice in a phase of play.

This article is reprinted with the kind consent of Catalyst, the official journal of AFCAT.

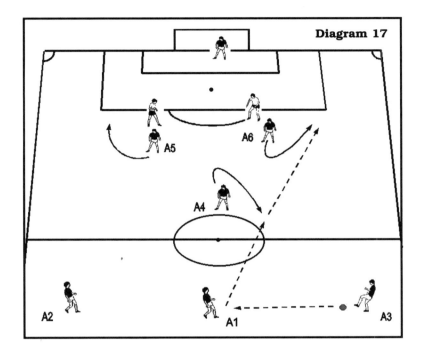

In the last issue we looked at the various options that A4, A5 and A6 had in making runs to receive the ball or to create space for another player to receive the ball. Defenders are now introduced to make it more game realistic.

Introduce two defenders to mark the two strikers A5 and A6. A2 or A3 begin by passing to A1. A4 checks away and comes off at an angle to receive with an open body from A1. A4 then turns to pass to either A5 or A6.

Progress by bringing on another defender to mark A4. If A4 is tightly marked, A1 should look to miss him out and pass up to the front two. A4 should then look to support.

Coaching Points
- Timing and angle of movement from A4.
- Accuracy and weight of pass.
- Correct selection by A1.
- Support.

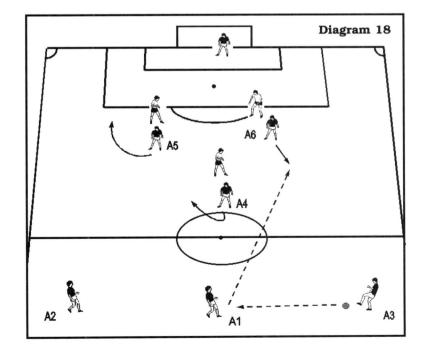

Conditioned Game

Play 7 v 11 on a 3/4-size field as shown in diagram 19. Add two wide players to the A's (A7 and A8) each with a marker with both the strikers and "the man in the hole" (A4) being marked. Place two in midfield versus one marker and add an opponent up against the back three. The ball should be played across the back with the coach calling the number of passes.

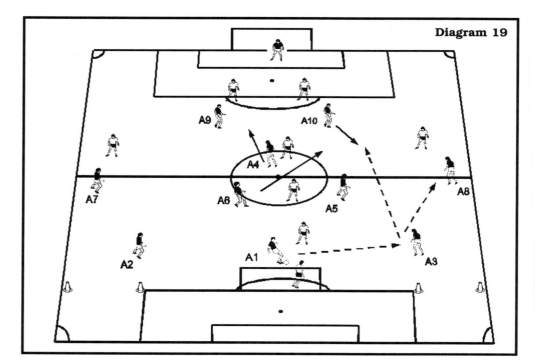

Diagram 19

Progressions

- Work on the back players playing up to the front players.
- Play the ball out to the two wide players.
- Finish with free play working on the understanding of the front three.

Coaching Points

- Quality of passes.
- Support.
- Late angled runs.

December 1998/January 1999 Issues

Bobby Houghton - Playing Against A Sweeper

Bobby Houghton has built championship clubs throughout the world including England, Sweden, Greece and Saudi Arabia. Following a short stint with the Colorado Rapids, Houghton was offered the job of National Team Coach of China where he now has the task of qualifying them for the 2002 World Cup.
Bobby's session looks at important aspect and one that is probably neglected at the lower levels of the game. How do you play against a sweeper?

Stage One

Using the full field (see diagram 1) organize as follows: three defenders on each side (two markers and a sweeper), a goal-keeper and two attackers in each team. Four midfield players play for both teams (A1, A2, A3 and A4). The midfield players always begin the practice from the halfway line and are limited to two touches.

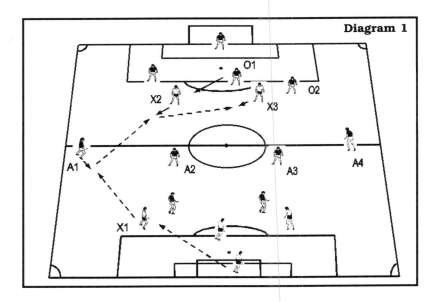

The goalkeeper throws the ball to X1. Midfielder A1 moves away from X1 before checking back and receiving a pass from him. A1 must receive the ball half turned, facing inside, and play a pass to X2, who has pulled off to drag the sweeper O1 across. X2 can then attempt to pass inside to X3, away from the sweeper O1. Finish with an attempt on goal. Repeat with O's goalkeeper throwing out to O2 and working back. Operate both flanks alternatively.

Coaching Points

* Timing of the runs.
* Angle of runs from midfielders and forwards.
* Move away from the passer before checking back quickly to receive.
* Use the direction of play to pull the sweeper out of position.
* Receive the pass side-on to give maximum viewing of options.

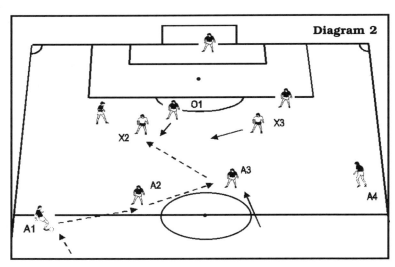

Coaching Points

* Encourage the midfield players to keep their heads up.
* Look for correct time to pass to the forwards.
* Play the ball when the sweeper is out of position.

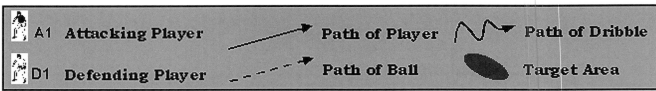

A1 **Attacking Player** → **Path of Player** ⌇ **Path of Dribble**

D1 **Defending Player** ⇢ **Path of Ball** ⬮ **Target Area**

Bobby Houghton - Playing Against A Sweeper

Stage Three

Encourage the midfield to play give-and-go's off the forwards to try to switch the direction of play. A1 passes to X2 who has pulled the sweeper (O1) out. X2 can pass back to any of the midfielders who must try to get the second forward, X3, in with a quick pass.

Coaching Points

- Draw defenders out of position and create space to play in.
- Play the ball in where there are no defenders.
- Encourage quick passing.

This article was reprinted with the kink permission of CATALYST the offical journal of AFCAT.

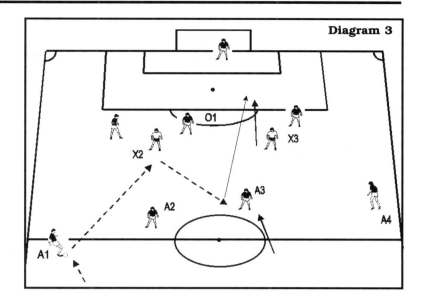

Diagram 3

MLS Practices

Various MLS team practices observed during pre-season training in Florida – February 1998.

NY/NJ MetroStars – Technique Practices

The players stand in pairs ten yards apart. The front player from each pair at one side juggles the ball toward the front player in the opposite line, passes him the ball and joins the back of the line. The player that receives the ball does the same in the opposite direction. Each different technique is practiced for one minute. The following techniques are used:
Juggle with foot, thigh or head.

Juggle with feet only.
Juggle with thighs only.
Juggle with head only.
Two-touch passing, keeping the ball in the air.
One-touch passing, keeping the ball in the air.

The pairs of players then move fifteen yards apart for the following techniques:
Dribble to opposite side leaving the ball for a takeover.
Dribble using many fast touches with instep only, leaving the ball for a takeover.
Pass, receive with one foot, pass back with opposite foot.
Pass, receive with outside of foot, pass back with same foot.

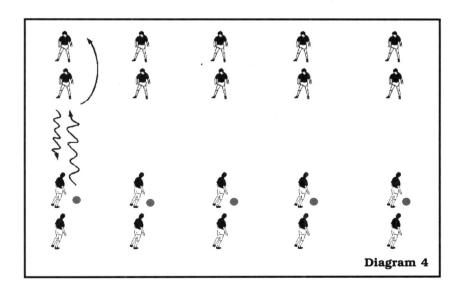

Diagram 4

MLS Practices

NY/NJ MetroStars – Technique Practice

Players group into lines of three. The outside players are 15 yards apart and have balls. An outside player passes to the middle player who passes back and quickly turns to receive a pass from the other outside player. He again passes back and turns to receive a pass from the opposite side again. The drill continues for 30 seconds then the players change positions. Once all three players have been in the middle a new technique is introduced. The following techniques were practiced.

Two-touch passing.
One-touch passing.
Short one-touch passes to make the middle player come to meet the ball.

Serve the ball in the air with the hands for:
Alternate feet for one touch passes.
To the chest for control and pass back.
To the thigh for control and pass back.
To the head (serve so the player needs to jump to make the header).

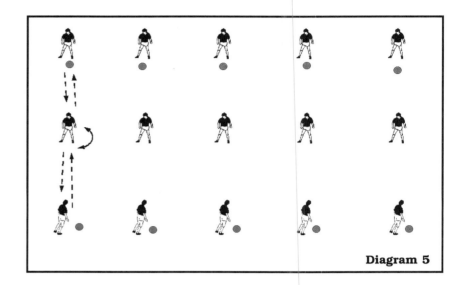

Diagram 5

San Jose Clash – Fast Break Game

Mark half a field into thirds as shown in diagram 6. Three teams of six position themselves, one team in each third. Goalkeepers and full size goals are used. The team in the middle third (team A), starts the game.

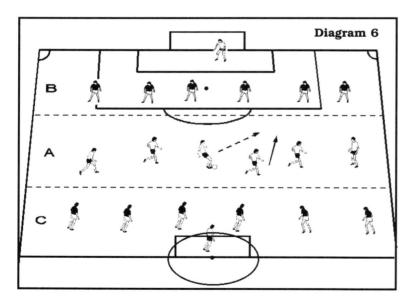

Diagram 6

Team A starts by attacking the goal defended by team B.

After a shot by team A, or a loss of possession, the goalkeeper throws a ball to a player in team B.

Team B then attacks the goal defended by team C.

Team A waits in the third of the field they have just attacked which was initially occupied by team B.

After team B takes a shot on the goal defended by team C, or loses possession, the goalkeeper throws the ball to a player in team C.

Team C now attacks the opposite goal which is now defended by team A.

Team B waits in the third of the field they have just attacked which was initially occupied by team C.

Continue end-to-end play for 15 minutes.

The coach constantly asked his players to attack with speed as in a counter attack.

Prior to playing the Fast Break Game the team warmed up with twenty minutes of 10 v 10 keep-away in two thirds of the field.

Fred Schmalz - University of Evansville

Fred Schmalz has coached at the University of Evansville for 20 years. His record prior to the 1998 season stands at 268 – 111 – 42. His teams have competed in the NCAA Division One tournament eleven times, most recently in 1996 when they had a record of 18 – 5 – 0, won the Missouri Valley Conference tournament and finished 20th in the final national poll. Fred Schmalz shares with WORLD CLASS COACHING a typical training session with an emphasis on possession play.

At Evansville we devote portions of every practice to speed training, possession, and finishing. The amount and complexity of these activities will naturally vary with the time of season and our daily emphasis. The following is a typical training session with an emphasis on possession play.

Stage One – Warm-up

Start off with passing in pairs for three minutes. The ball and the players must keep moving at all times.

Stretch, then repeat with gradually longer passes.

Stretch, then play 3 v 1 in 12 x 12 yard grids as shown in diagram 7. Limit to two-touch, when all three players have touched the ball, they can move to an adjacent empty grid. The player in the middle switches position on loss of possession.

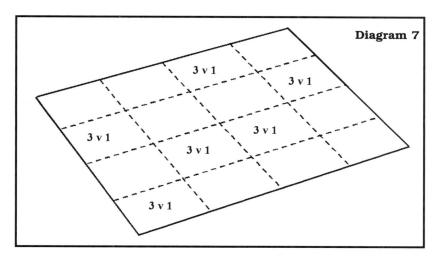

Diagram 7

Coaching Points

- Angle to support the ball.
- Keep maximum space between players.
- Quick ball movement.

Stage Two – Possession Activity

Play with three teams of four in a 35 x 45 yard area. One team is the perimeter team with two neutral players on the side and two target players on the end-lines. Two teams play directional 4 v 4. The objective is to pass the ball to your team's target player. Following a score, the target player gives the ball to the defending team. Teams rotate every three minutes. The teams score one point for a pass to their target player or two points if the pass is from their own half. The game should be played quickly and use wide release to consolidate possession.

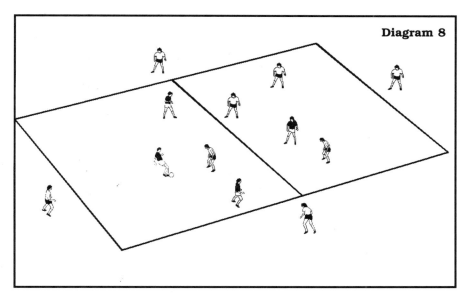

Diagram 8

Variations

- Play two-touch.
- Must make four passes before you can score (passes to neutral players do not count).
- Attacking team keeps possession after a score.

Coaching Points

- Consolidate possession by passing to support players early.
- Use wide or deep players to quickly relieve pressure.
- Immediate transition when you gain possession. Be sure to keep possession first – then build the attack.

Stage Three – Finishing

Activity

Three lines of players are set up 35 – 45 yards from goal as shown in diagram 9. Each line has two cones five yards apart. The defender (D) passes the ball from the rear cone to the forward (A) who is by the cone closest to goal.

On receiving the ball, the forward sprints towards goal and attempts to score.

As soon as the forward takes his first touch, the defender chases. If the defender gets goalside of the ball, he and the goalkeeper combine to defend.

One line goes at a time. Players change lines after each attempt and can alternate as forwards and defenders.

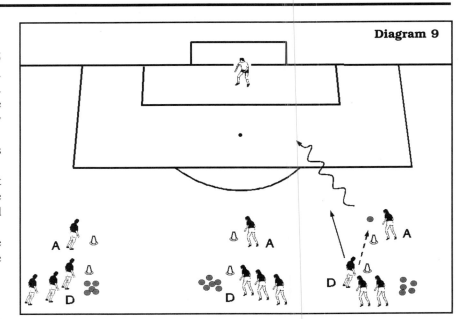

Diagram 9

Coaching Points

* Forwards take a big first touch so they can sprint toward goal.
* Run across the path of the defender – early.
* Forwards shouldn't run wide as this helps the goalkeeper narrow the shooting angle.
* Use fakes and feints.
* Forwards should keep the ball close to the feet once they have entered the 18 yard goalbox.
* Place your shot on goal – make sure you hit the target.

Stage Four – Buzz Game

Two teams of eight plus goalkeepers on a 3/4 size field. One team plays with just four players while the other four players act as ball retrievers behind their goal. The team of eight is limited to two-touch. The team of four has unlimited touches. Play for four minutes then alternate so the team of eight now plays with four and the team of four plays with eight players. Play for approximately 30 minutes.

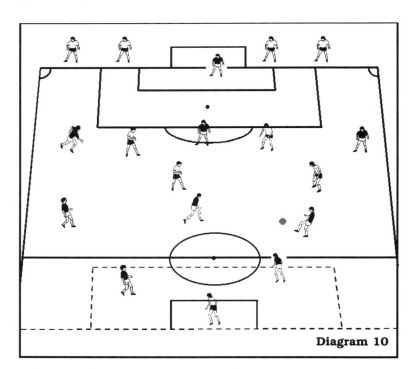

Diagram 10

Scoring System

Shot – one point.

Shot on goal – two points.

Goal – three points for the team of eight, five points for the team of four.

Team of four to have ball bounce in the attacking goalbox – one point.

Coaching Points

* Ball movement and quick shots for the team of eight.
* Constructive play under pressure for the team of four.
* Immediate pressure to win the ball and delay the long pass forward for the team of eight when they lose possession.
* Quick positive distribution by the goalkeepers.

Morning Session

Warm-up
Split into three groups of 5 v 2 and play one-touch keep-away for 7-8 minutes, then 7-8 minutes of light jogging interspersed with short sprints.

Technical
The players stand in pairs eight yards apart and pass the ball back and forth using one-touch. Then the receiving player checks away and turns 360 degrees to receive the ball and plays it back with one touch to his partner who does the same.

Attacking Combinations
A1 passes to A2 who passes back to A1 with one touch.

A1 then turns and passes to A3 who passes back to A1 with one touch, then makes a run toward the near post.

A1 then drives a pass to the far side for running A5 and then makes a run toward the far post.

A5 crosses the ball into the goal box for incoming A1 and A3.

A4 makes a run to the edge goalbox.

A1, A3 and A4 finish with one touch.

Repeat using opposite flank starting with A4.

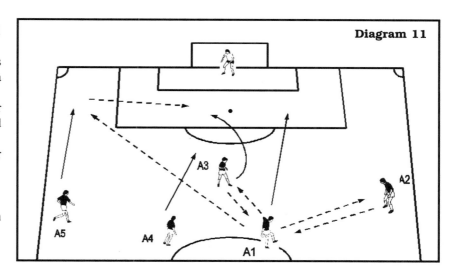

Diagram 11

Afternoon Session

Warm-up
Players divide into groups of three and stand 10 yards apart with one player on one side and two players on the other side. The drill starts on the side of the two players. Player A dribbles the ball to player B at the other end who does a takeover and dribbles to the opposite end toward player C who does a takeover. The drill continues with each of the following skills practiced for approximately 90 seconds each.

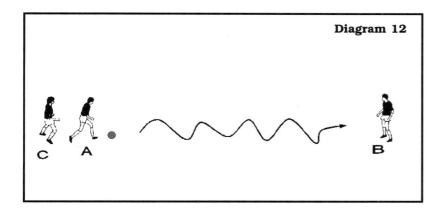

Diagram 12

- Increase speed of dribble.
- Dribble using only the instep.
- Dribble using alternate feet with each touch.
- Speed dribble.
- Dribble halfway, do an instep turn, sprint back to start, do an instep turn then dribble.
- Dribble halfway, turn using the outside of the foot, sprint back to start, turn using the outside of the foot then dribble.
- Dribble halfway, do a Cruyff turn, sprint back to start, do a Cruyff turn then dribble.
- Dribble halfway, do any turn, sprint back to start, do any turn then dribble.

U.S. U20 National Team

Small-Sided Game

The team splits into two groups of nine players. Each group of nine splits into teams of three and plays 3 v 3 v 3 keep-away. Each team of three has a different colored jersey (red, white and blue). Two teams of three combine to play keep-away from the other team of three. The team of three that is responsible for losing possession becomes the defending team.

Play for ten minutes, starting off with two-touch then progressing to one-touch.

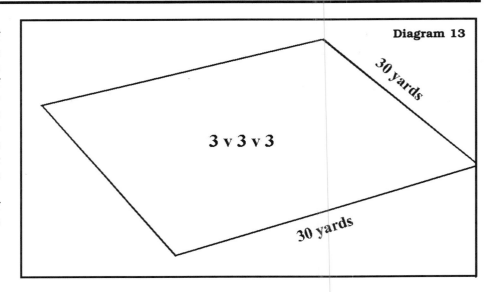

Diagram 13

3 v 3 v 3

30 yards

30 yards

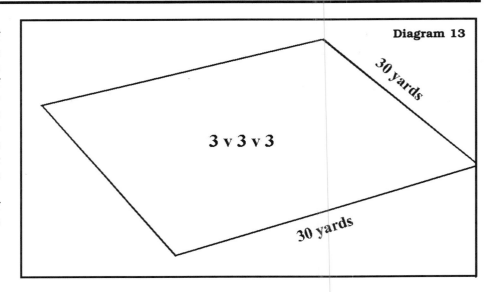

Diagram 14

Full-Sided Game

9 v 9 plus goalkeepers on a 3/4 size field as shown in diagram 14. Play for 30 minutes with unlimited touches and an emphasis on high pressure. Goals from crosses, combination play or from a one-touch finish score two points. Goals from anything else score one point.

Fitness

The practice ends with the players in four groups of five doing sprints over distances of 20, 30, 40, 60, and 75 yards. This is followed by a cool down of a light jog and stretches.

Kansas City Wizards

A complete practice observed September 1998.

Warm-up

The team splits into four groups of five. Two games of 5 v 5 one-touch keep-away are played in each goalbox. A point is scored for 10 consecutive passes.

Play for five minutes then stretch for two minutes. Repeat with another five minute game followed by two minutes of stretches.

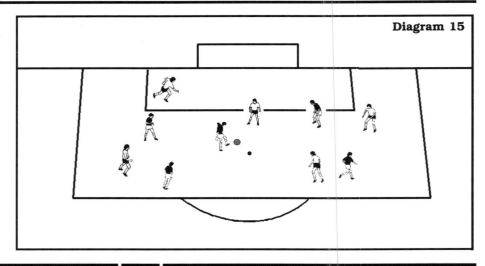

Diagram 15

Kansas City Wizards

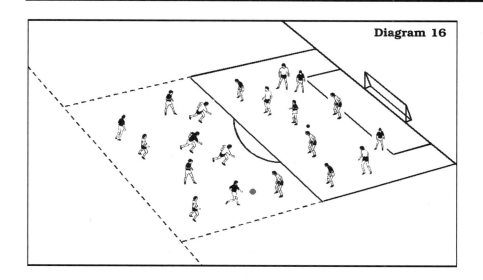

Diagram 16

Warm-Up Stage Two

The two groups combine and play 10 v 10 one-touch keep-away in an area the size of two goalboxes. Again, keep count of the passes, a point is scored for ten consecutive passes.

Play for eight minutes followed by four minutes of stretching.

One-Touch Passing

The players then split into two groups of ten, each group doing the passing drill shown in diagram 17. The cones are 12 yards apart. For ease of explanation, I will describe just the movement of one line. However, both lines play at the same time with A1 and A6 starting the drill by passing at the same time.

A1 passes to A2 who passes straight back then turns and runs toward A4.

A1 drives a pass to A4 who lays off a pass to incoming A2.

A2 passes straight back to A4 who then passes to the front player in A6's line.

A1 takes A2's position. A2 takes A4's position and A4 joins the back of A6's line.

All passes are one-touch whenever possible.

Play for four minutes, rest for one minute and repeat three further times. The players are challenged to increase the quality of passes and the speed of play after each rest period.

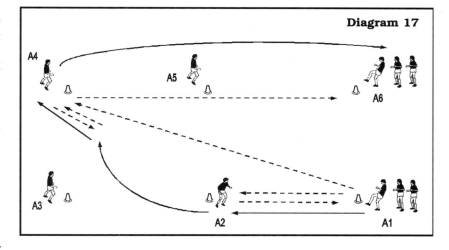

Diagram 17

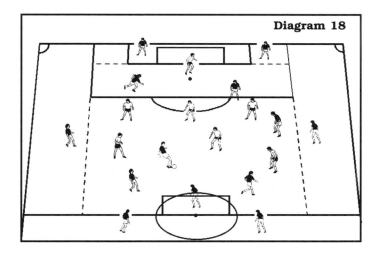

Diagram 18

Small-Sided Game

Mark out the field as shown in diagram 18. The players split into three teams of six. Two teams play 6 v 6 while the third team positions themselves on the perimeter with one player either side of the goal and one player on each side-line. The field players have unlimited touches but the perimeter players are limited to one-touch.

The games are played at a quick pace. Each game lasts for four minutes or when one team scores two goals. The winning team stays on the field, the losing team changes with the perimeter team.

F.C. Petrolul Ploiesti - Romania

F.C. Petrolul Ploiesti plays in Division One of the Romanian Football League. In this article, coach John Eparu shares some practices to aid the participation of the outside defenders in the attack.

Having outside defenders participate and contribute in the building and finishing of attacking moves creates two major benefits. Firstly, the element of surprise and secondly, the freedom of movement since they are not marked as closely as forwards or midfielders. There are two ways that the outside defender can participate and contribute in building up an attack: through participation starting in the defending third immediately after taking possession of the ball, and through direct participation in the finalization of the attack in the attacking third by crossing, passing, heading, or shooting.

In diagram 20, the goalkeeper passes to the outside defender, A1, who immediately passes to the defensive midfielder, A2. A2 passes to the outside midfielder, A3, who controls and leaves the ball for A1.
After each pass, the players move forward and the passing combination is repeated until they reach approximately 35 yards from goal.

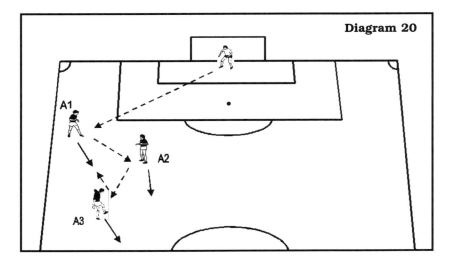

Diagram 20

F.C. Petrolul Ploiesti - Romania

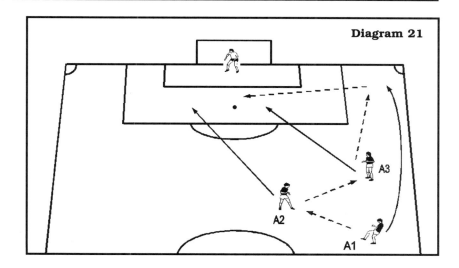

Diagram 21

Once the players have reached approximately 35 yards from goal, A3, instead of leaving the ball for A1, passes toward the end-line.

A2 and A3 then make runs into the goal-box.

A1 makes an overlapping run and crosses the ball into the goalbox for incoming A2 and A3.

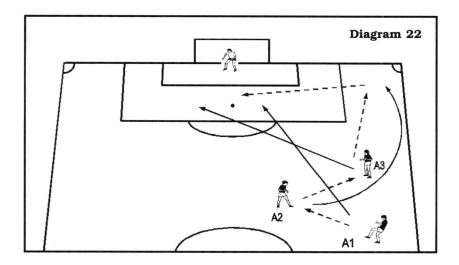

Diagram 22

Variation

Same exercise up until reaching 35 yards from goal.

This time A1 makes a run into the goalbox and A2 overlaps A3 and crosses to incoming A1 and A3.

Coaching Points

- Crisp one-touch passing whenever possible.
- When making runs into the goalbox, the players must sprint.
- Always have one player running toward the near post and the other toward the far post.
- Crosses should be varied and be hit with the first touch.

Practices observed July 1998.

6 v 6 To Goal

Mark a field by extending the lines of the goal-box to the half-line as shown in diagram 1. Use full size goals and goalkeepers. Split into three teams of six, two teams play 6 v 6, the other team is positioned on the perimeter as shown. The perimeter players are limited to two-touch, the field players have unlimited touches.

Play five-minute games with the losing team switching with the perimeter team.

Look for a quick, fast paced game with plenty of shooting opportunities.

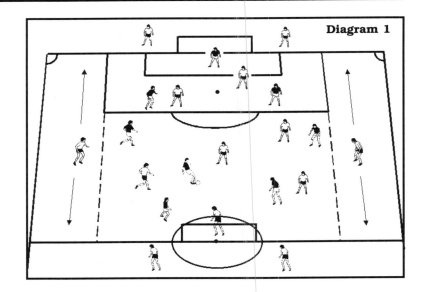

Diagram 1

Unopposed Finishing

The players line up as shown in diagram 2. The coach has a supply of balls and serves to the players for them to finish with one-touch. No goalkeeper is used. To start, the coach serves from just outside the post and the players finish into the opposite corner from six yards out. The following three finishing techniques are practiced:

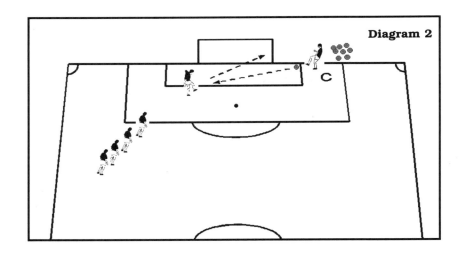

Diagram 2

1. From an easy paced service on the ground, finish by placing the ball with side foot.
2. From a service about knee high, finish with an inside foot volley.
3. Serve for the players to jump and head the ball.

As the practice progresses, the coach will serve from further away, eventually serving from outside the 18-yard goalbox.

The players also finish from further out, moving in stages to 12, 18, 25, and 35 yards out.

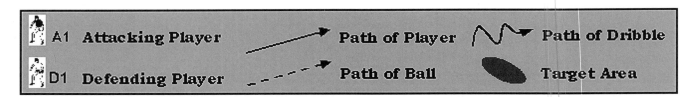

A1 **Attacking Player**	⟶ **Path of Player**	⟿ **Path of Dribble**
D1 **Defending Player**	- - -> **Path of Ball**	⬬ **Target Area**

Midfield Runs

Start with 2 v 2, A's attacking the goal and D's defending. The ball is passed in by the server, S, from the center circle. Once the ball is played in, the A's attack the goal. The coach constantly stresses that the players should be patient when looking to create opportunities.

Example One

A2 checks to the server to receive the ball. If the server doesn't pass him the ball, A2 continues his run away from his original starting position.
A1 moves into the space left by A2 leaving and receives the pass from the server.

The defenders start by playing passively until the players become familiar with the drill.

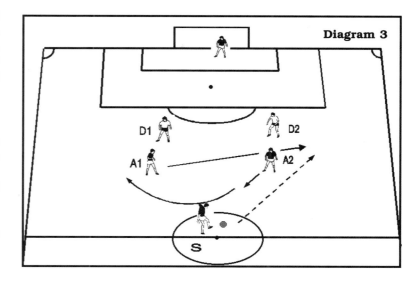

Diagram 3

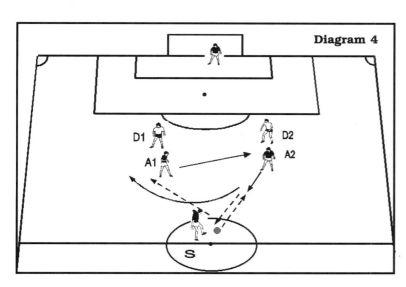

Diagram 4

Midfield Runs

Example Two

A2 checks to the server to receive the ball, passes it back immediately with one touch and continues his run away from his original starting position.
A1 moves into the space created by A2's run.
The server now passes into the path of A2 who can now run at D1 and attack facing the goal.

A1 and A2 explored different options of runs to receive the ball and create space for themselves and each other. The practice progresses to 4 v 4 and finally 6 v 6.

Keep-Away

Used as a warm-up, the players play 4 v 4 with two neutral players in a 30 x 25 yard grid.

Variations

- Unlimited touches.
- Two-touch.
- One-touch.

Coaching Points

- Someone needs to check into the middle to receive the ball.
- Keep the ball moving.
- Keep the hips and body open to the field.

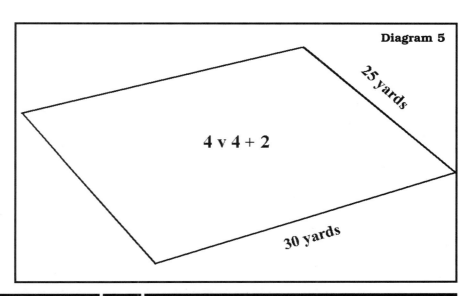

Diagram 5

4 v 4 + 2

25 yards

30 yards

U.S. U20 National Team

Runs To Goal

A1 passes to A2 then makes an overlapping run outside A2.

A2 touches the ball inside then plays the ball toward the corner for overlapping A1.

A1 crosses with his first touch, if possible, to incoming A3, A4, and A5.

A3 makes a straight run to the edge of the goalbox.

A4 makes a curved run toward the near post.

A5 makes a curved run toward the far post.

Continue the practice from the other flank with A6 passing to A7.

A3, A4, and A5 vary their runs. However, they must communicate with each other when doing so.

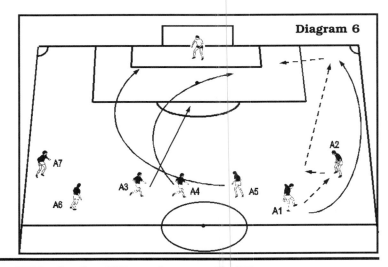

Diagram 6

Game Analysis - Welsh National Team

The use of sports science has become an integral part of the coaching process. Richard Donnelly is a former Sports Science lecturer with experience in analyzing English Premiership and international games.

Soccer, regardless of ability, experience and skill level is played with varying degrees of technical and tactical awareness. As coaches, we are always searching for ways of helping individual players or teams to maintain or improve performance, whether this is technical, tactical or even fitness based.

The capacity to accurately observe and analyze performance, or factors which effect performance, are essential and it is here the coaching process ultimately begins.

Individual or team tactics can best be decided upon if the coach has identified the strengths and weaknesses of the teams involved. So what can help us identify these strengths & weaknesses? For many years the general format has relied on the coach simply watching and evaluating the opposition as well as their own players. There are serious flaws in using this method as the human brain has a limited capacity for observation and recall. The coach may also allow personal opinion to distort the facts therefore causing the whole coaching process to collapse.

ENTER SPORTS NOTATION!

The term 'Notational Analysis' describes any system that gathers accurate & objective performance information that can be used by the coach to structure game tactics or team practices. The players themselves should use the gathered information to monitor their own strengths, weaknesses, adherence to tactical requirements and fitness levels at varying points of the season. Many coaches already use notation in one form or another, some without realizing it. Some use a Dictaphone to note events in real time while others may

use video so as to review the game in lapsed time. Coaches without the resources of computers or videotapes could make use of pen and paper with symbols similar to shorthand. As an example, a complex play such as a successful lofted 30 meter pass by player #10 to player #8 could be notated as 110 P30m - 8✓. This shorthand allows information to be gathered without the note taker taking their eyes off the game.

It is extremely important to gather accurate data on performance during games so that practices can be structured to help improve the team's weakness or expose a weak area of an upcoming opponent. Basic information may be supplied at half time or at key points in the game, e.g. positive or negative passes, tackles, fouls, off-sides, shots on target/off target, etc. This basic information may alter the tactics or structure of play.

For example, within soccer, the following is typical of the kind of data necessary to collect during a game.

BALL POSSESSION
Gained/Lost
Location
Specify position
Player/s involved
How gained / lost
Specify action

During the games I analyzed for the Welsh National Team and in many of the English Premier games, player performance was analyzed with all aspects of the game being diagnosed. For example, passes were broken down into those that were lofted, driven and played on the ground, whether they were successful (accurate) or unsuccessful (inaccurate), distance played, between which players, time played and field location. This analysis was followed for heading, shooting, tackling, interceptions, corners, throw-ins, free kicks, fouls, goals, etc. This in-depth analysis would hopefully identify patterns of play. The table below shows the main points of the data gathered for the Welsh National Team in a World Cup qualifying game between Wales and Belgium.

Based on the information, especially the poor percentages of unsuccessful passes between defenders and forwards, lost goalkicks/punts and unsuccessful lofted passes over 20 meters, practice was structured with an emphasis on ball retention, patience in build up and positional structure. Drills such as 'keep-ball' and 15 consecutive passes to score were utilized to emphasize speed and movement on and off the ball. This would hopefully shake off the old fashioned long ball game that can be easy to defend when playing international teams.

Future game plans were changed tactically. The rotation of midfielders to support defense and attack would hopefully reduce overall ground coverage and therefore cause less fatigue and errors. The long ball game was restricted and a build up requiring the keeper to roll the ball out to wide defenders who in turn covered behind each other before the ball was passed to switching midfield/forward players was utilized. The aim was to hit a player on the move instead of passing to static players.

Computerized and videotape game analysis is used frequently by many U.S. college programs as well as MLS teams. Two of our most well known college coaches Anson Dorrance – University of North Carolina and Bob Warming - St. Louis University are strong proponents of game analysis

Advantages of game analysis:
Builds a database of information, motivates players, reinforces the coaches subjective assessment, provides the coach with a greater understanding of the game.

Disadvantages of game analysis:
Time consuming, used wrongly - de-motivates players, endangers coach credibility.

As a coach, I see this method of analysis as an essential part of the coaching process. Only in the last few years have top international and club teams identified it's importance in maintaining or improving individual or team performance. No aspects of play and indeed levels of players are exempt – Notation is here to stay!

Positives	Negatives
• Shots on target = 8	• **Shots conceded on goal = 9** (defense/midfield slow closing down)
• Goals = 1	• **1 midfield player attempting and failing all 12 interception attempts** (arousal level too high or poor situation assessment)
• Clearance headers won by defense = 29	• **73% of balls from defense to offence = unsuccessful** (lack of midfield movement/support to act as a pivot between defense and offence)
• Opponents headers at goal = 0	• **92% of all goalkicks/punts lost directly to opposition** (lack of passing options?)
• Penetrating runs by midfield through opponents defense = 7	• **63% of all lofted passes over 20m were lost** (technique or decision making problems?)
	• **Only 3 sequences of 12 passes or more** (patience while under pressure?)
• Two midfield players making 12 or more tackles in each half.	• **Shots off target = 6**
	• **Defenders lost ball 8 times when dribbling out of defense** (lack of passing options?)
	• **14 crosses made - only 1 successful** (problems with offensive angles of run/positioning or quality of crosses)
	• **38% of errors occurred in final 12 minutes of each half** (possible fitness problems)

F.C. Petrolul Ploiesti - Romania

F.C. Petrolul Ploiesti plays in Division One of the Romanian Football League. In the last issue, we focused on the outside defenders in attack. In this article, coach Nicu Lazar focuses on defending in the defending third of the field, concentrating on double-teaming.

Defending Using The 'Double-Team'

The coaching staff at F.C. Petrolul Ploiesti believe that equal participation of all the players in both the attacking and the defending phases of the game is mandatory. In the attacking phase, not just the forwards, but the entire team needs to be inventive and creative. The same applies to defending. The defense has to be strengthened through the participation of every player, regardless of the positions and functions they have to fulfill on the team.

The forwards apply the pressure directly on the opponent's defenders. The midfielders and the defenders using "zone" defense make sure that the midfield third and the defensive third is all covered. It is also very important to have adaptable players who can play more than one position and be efficient doing so.

Here at F.C. Petrolul Ploiesti, our defensive system of play is based on collective play in which double-teaming and re-doubling are very important. Double-team (doubling) engages at least a couple of players within an optimal distance of each other. One will attack the forward, trying to repossess the ball, delay the attack or channel the forward away from the goal, and the second defender will back him up (will double him) being ready for attacking the forward again in order to repossess the ball if the forward passes the first defender. The distance between the two defenders decreases the closer the forward gets to the goal.

Below are some of our practices for learning double-team defense.

Double-Team Defending

In the following examples we focus on double-teaming in the defending third of the field. Although these examples highlight the role of the sweeper, double-teaming is not limited to the sweeper. In the defending and middle thirds of the field the nearest player should pressure the ball and the closest player in a supporting position should double-team.

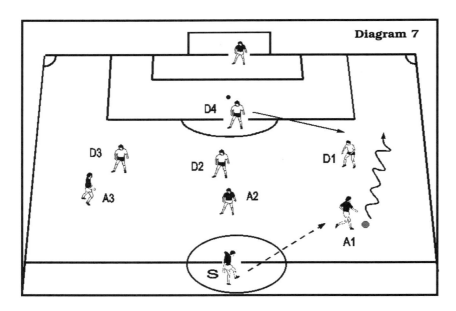

Diagram 7

In diagram 7, the practice is set up with a server playing balls in to any of the three forwards. The forwards are all marked by defenders. D4 plays the sweeper position. In this example, the server passes to A1 who dribbles past his defender, D1.
As D1 engages A1, the sweeper, D4, slides over to double team A1.
If D4 can get over early enough to double-team, it should force A1 to look for other options instead of dribbling past D1 only to encounter another defender, D4.

Progression

Now that D4 has moved over to double-team A1, the closest players to the ball need to react and adjust their positions accordingly.

As D4 slides over to double-team A1, D2 slides into the sweeper position to take the place of D4 and gets ready to double-team with D4 if A1 is successful in getting past D1.

If D1 gets beat by A1 he should slide over to take D2's position and guard A2.

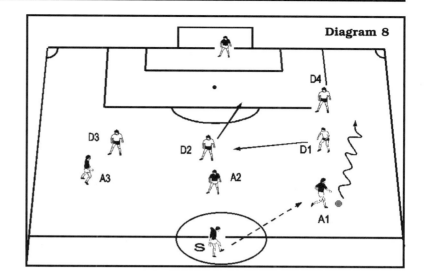

Diagram 8

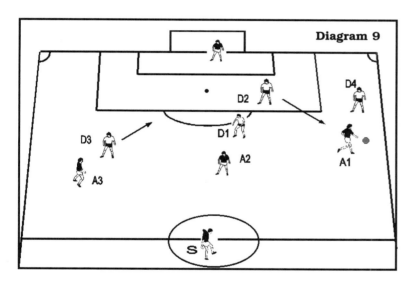

Diagram 9

Progression

In diagram 9, if A1 has beaten D1, D4 now pressures the ball and is forcing A1 inside to take him off his stronger foot and force him into D2 and the double-team.

In this example, D4 forces A1 to go inside. The decision of whether to force players outside or inside depends on a number of variables including how good the forward is at crossing, can he cross or shoot well with his weaker foot, etc.

It is not only the players that are close to the ball that need to make adjustments. Every player should adjust their position depending on where the ball is. For instance, in this example, D3 should drop back in a covering position, as that is more important than guarding A3 who is outside the box.

Progression – Variation

The practice continues with the server playing balls in to any of the three forwards who combine in an attempt at a scoring opportunity. The defenders now play at game pace.

In Diagram 10, the ball is played in to A2, who quickly passes to A1 who has run by his defender, D1.

All the same things should happen that took place in the earlier example.

D4 should slide to pressure A1.

D2 should drop back to take D4's place and then slide over to double-team A1.

D1 should slide inside to take D2's place and cover A2.

D3 should start dropping back in a covering position.

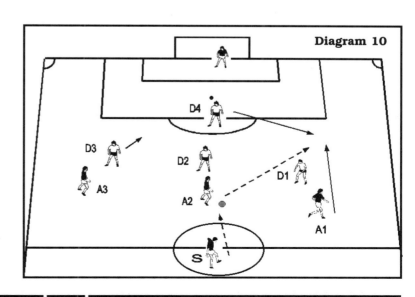

Diagram 10

Kansas City Wizards - Fitness

Misha Bacic played professional soccer in Germany, France, and his native country, Yugoslavia. Now the Kansas City Wizards conditioning coach, Bacic has previously worked with the Houston Hotshots of the CISL and individually with MLS players such as Frank Klopas, Preki and Goran Hunjak. In this article, he shares some of the Wizard's ball related fitness drills.

The following drills are based on jogging and sprinting and incorporate technical aspects such as shooting, dribbling and passing. They can be used as part of pre-season conditioning, as a warm-up or to top up fitness levels during the regular season. For instance, we would use these kind of drills early in the week if we had no mid-week game scheduled. On all of the drills, the players, when running, should sprint at 90% of their maximum. Typically each player would do two sets of 8-10 repetitions of each line. Between sets the players would stretch for five minutes.

In diagram 11, two players stand in the center circle and two lines of players position themselves at each end of the field. Both lines go at the same time. The front player in the line dribbles the ball quickly for 10 yards then drives a firm pass to the player in the center circle. The player in the center circle passes with one touch in front of the running player who shoots with one touch if possible. Once the player has passed to the center circle player, he must sprint at 90% pace to receive the return pass. After shooting, the players join the opposite line. The next player in line starts when the player in front has passed to the center circle player.

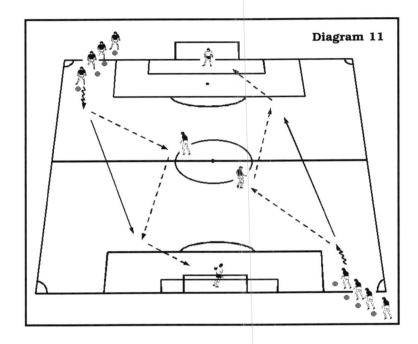

Diagram 11

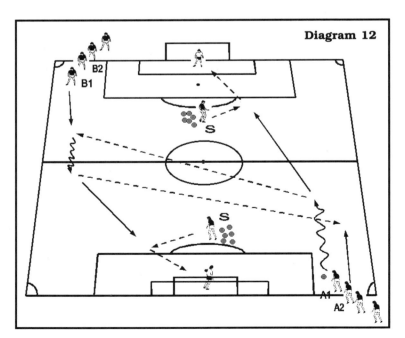

Diagram 12

In diagram 12, two servers with a supply of balls are positioned outside each goalbox. The players are lined up on each end of the field. To start the drill, A1 dribbles the ball approximately 25-30 yards and passes across the field to running B1. B1 dribbles the ball until he crosses the half-line and passes back across the field to the second person in line, A2, who continues the drill.

As soon as A1 and B1 have made their cross-field passes they sprint at 90% pace to the edge of the goalbox where the servers pass them a ball for a one-touch shot.

The players then join the opposite line.

In diagram 13, the players line up in three lines at one end of the field. The players in line A each have a ball. The drill starts with player A passing in front of running player B.

Player B passes across the field to running player C.

After making their passes, A and B sprint at 90% pace toward the opposite goalbox.

Player C runs with the ball into the opposite corner and crosses for incoming A and B to shoot with one touch.

All three players then jog back and join a different line. As soon as player C receives the ball the next players in line start.

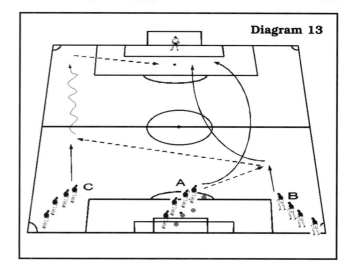

Diagram 13

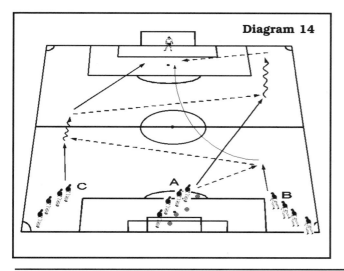

Diagram 14

Diagram 14 is a variation of diagram 13.

This time when C receives the ball, he passes it across the field for running A, then makes an angled run into the goalbox.

A receives the ball and runs into the corner and crosses for incoming B and C to shoot with one touch.

Attacking From Midfield

Ray Lewington, the former Chelsea player and Crystal Palace coach who is now the coach at Brentford F.C., shares his practices to improve 'Attacking From Midfield'.

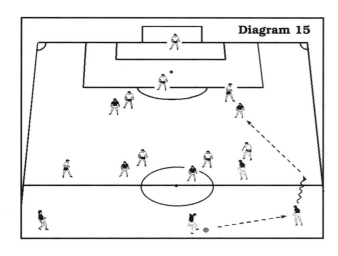

Diagram 15

Play 8 v 8 using 3/4 of a field. The defending team has three defenders and four midfielders plus the keeper. The attacking team has two forwards, three midfield players, two wingbacks and a sweeper. To begin, the sweeper passes to the right back, who plays the ball in to the forwards. When the ball has been played to the forward and they have held the ball up, the wing back and midfield players should look to get forward and support.

Coaching Points
• The forward must take up a closed body position to hold off his marker.
• The pass to the forward should be to the safe side and not the defender's side.

Attacking From Midfield

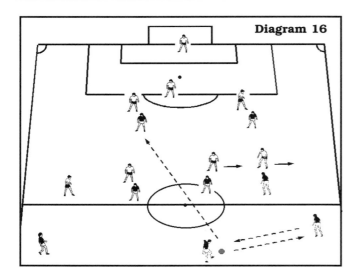

Diagram 16

If the wing back cannot play the ball up to the forward, they may pass back to the sweeper who can play the ball to the other forward.

Coaching Points
- Only play the ball forward when one of the forwards looks set and ready to receive
- Midfielders should only push on when the forwards have good possession

Encourage the midfield players to arrive into space between them and the forwards. The space will only be there if players hold their run until late and then move quickly.

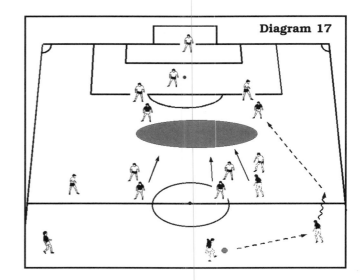

Diagram 17

Develop the practice: Take away three of the opposition midfielders and put the other one into defense. The defending team will now play with a back four but no midfield. This allows the attacking midfield side to build the play with no pressure from opposition.

Progress by bringing back two opposition midfield players to mark the central midfielders from the attacking team.

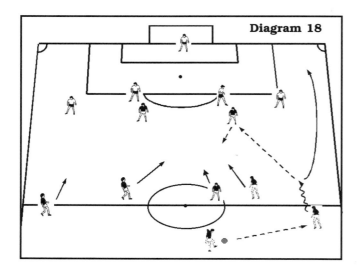

Diagram 18

Attacking From Midfield

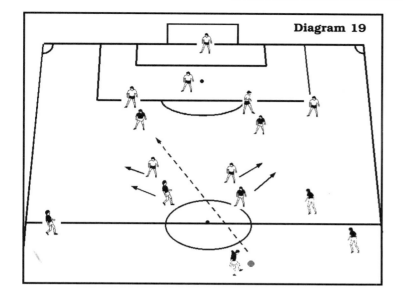

Diagram 19

The two central midfield players must create space for the sweeper to pass to the forwards by making diagonal runs away from the center of the pitch.

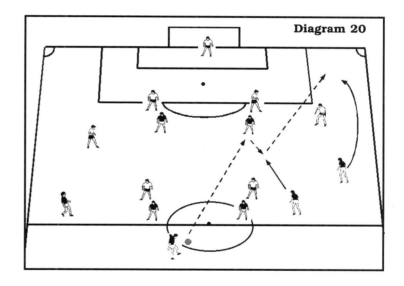

Diagram 20

The forward can now play the ball into the space for the spare midfield player who may play the ball into the space behind the defending full back for the wing back to run on to.

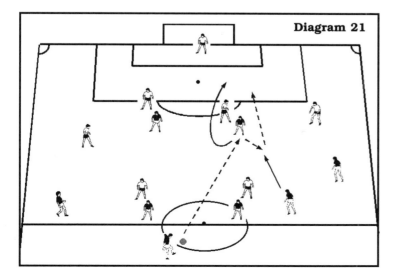

Diagram 21

Alternatively, if the midfield player that has received the ball back from the forward has time on the ball, he may be able to play the ball in behind the central defender with the forward "rolling off" their marker.

Coaching Point
- The forward must be aware of offsides and look along the line of the defenders

Progression
Free play with full opposition

Columbus Crew - Goalkeeping

Ideas and a practice session on integrating the goalkeeper in team training sessions, contributed by Greg Andrulis, assistant coach of the Columbus Crew.

One of the most important facets of training the goalkeeper is the integration of the goalkeeper in team training sessions. Although specialized training is an important component that affords the goalkeeper the opportunity to maintain a decent physical and technical level, the tactical and psychological dimensions are often neglected. In order to assist the goalkeeper to improve in the areas of reading the game, decision making, communication and leadership, it is necessary for the goalkeeper to be put in a training environment that will explore these components. For many coaches, "integration of the goalkeeper" involves having them involved in small-sided games, full-sided games and finishing exercises. To truly foster the development of the goalkeeper beyond the physical and technical dimensions, this integration in tactical situations has to be treated as an important training environment for the goalkeeper.

Listed below are some suggestions on ways to integrate the goalkeeper in the team's training environment.

1. Include the goalkeeper in team warm-up exercises that involve physical and technical components such as footwork, running, dribbling, passing, etc. The modern goalkeeper needs to be more than competent with the field player skills. With the advent of the pass back rule, the demands for technical competence is greater than ever. In most training situations, the goalkeeper receives more training as the last line of defense than as the first line of attack. The ramifications of having a goalkeeper that can correctly distribute the ball, as compared to the goalkeeper who is involved in emergency clearances, is quite profound. In addition, the more time that the goalkeeper and field players play together, the greater understanding they will have for each other.

2. When designing tactical training sessions for the team, utilize this opportunity for coachable moments with the goalkeeper. These include reading the game, positioning and decision making. For example, if the team is working on changing the point of attack, check the position of the goalkeeper in relation to the ball and play. As the ball moves, so should the goalkeeper. Has the goalkeeper made the proper adjustment relative to the movement and distance of the ball from the goal? And, is the goalkeeper making the correct positional changes based on the players in front of him/her?

Practice does not make perfect. Practice makes permanent.

3. Reading the game situations create the opportunity for the coach to insure that the goalkeeper is giving the correct information to the field players. The elimination of goal scoring opportunities begins with communication, proper positioning and understanding of the tactical responsibilities of the rest of the team. It is important that the field players and the goalkeepers all have an understanding of team tactics. Off field video review, match analysis and "chalk board" talk are great supplements to on field match related games.

There are many variables that influence the decision making process of a goalkeeper. One such variable is the assessment of the strengths and weaknesses in each dimension of their game. Part of our responsibility as coach is to properly assess our goalkeeper's strengths and weaknesses and develop team tactics that compliment them. If, for example, we have a goalkeeper that is very good at dealing with crosses, but lacks competence in breakaway situations, would it be logical to rely on the offside trap as a defensive tool? Probably not. It would be prudent in this situation to design tactics that limit breakaway situations and forces the attacking team wide, into crossing situations. The development of the goalkeeper's decision-making ability occurs in every exercise that they are involved in. Whether its finishing exercises, small-sided or match related games, the goalkeeper and the decision making process need to be analyzed and critiqued. It is important that proper decisions are recognized and reinforced. Practice does not make perfect. Practice makes permanent.

What you see in practice, you will certainly see in a match. Take the initiative when dealing with your goalkeeper to assist them in increasing their reading of the game and decision making ability.

The training session that follows is an example of the integration of the goalkeeper from the beginning of the training session to the conclusion. It provides the goalkeeper and the coach with numerous opportunities to explore the tactical and psychological dimensions.

Columbus Crew - Goalkeeping

Warm-Up

The warm-up consists of numerous touches and demands on the players and goalkeepers. The field players are encouraged to think of placement with their passes to the goalkeepers. Each exercise is done for three to five minutes with stretching in between exercises. The demands on the players should be progressive.

Mark a field as shown in diagram 22. GK1 rolls the ball into space for A1. A1 passes the ball forward with one touch to C1 and follows his pass with a change of pace to

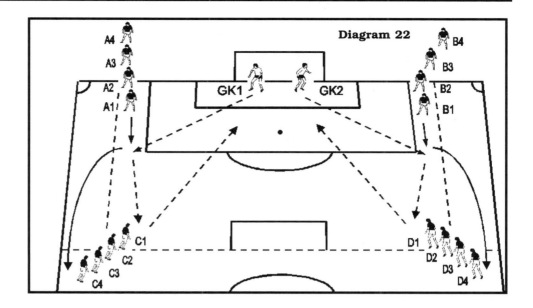

the end of line C. C1 uses one touch to play the ball back to GK1. While this is going on, GK2 repeats the same sequence with B1 and D1. The demands on the players can be changed quite frequently. Passes with the inside of the foot, outside of the foot, right foot, left foot, chipping, etc.

Progression One

The set up is the same as in diagram 22. This time the goalkeepers will start each sequence with a pass in the air for the field players who use a controlling touch prior to playing the ball forward.

Progression Two

Diagram 23 is the same set up as in diagram 22, with the exception that the goalkeepers serve the ball forward to C1 and D1 who then collect the ball and take on A1 and B1 respectively to create one-on-one situations.

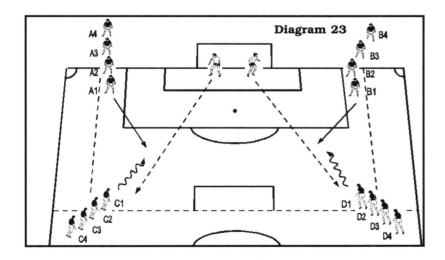

Coaching Points

- As the warm-up, it's important to take time between exercises to stretch.
- Make the exercises progressive and use your imagination to challenge the players.
- Have the goalkeepers take time between each serve so that both sides are not playing balls back to the goalkeepers at the same time.
- The field players and goalkeepers are expected to execute the exercises cleanly.

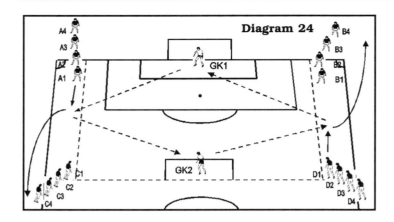

Diagram 24

Practice

Use the same marked field from the warm-up. This time the field players play in the channels that are 10 yards wide from the touch-line.

GK1 plays the ball into space for A1 who collects the ball with a forward touch and crosses with a second touch. GK2 collects the cross and plays the ball forward to D1 who, with two touches, crosses the ball back to GK1. The exercise is repeated, GK1 to A2, etc. The goalkeepers can switch the play, i.e. GK1 serving the ball to B1 to change the direction. With a little coordination, the exercise can have two balls in play at the same time.

Progression One

The set up is the same with this addition. After the goalkeeper serves the ball wide, the player on the other side joins in to become an attacker. For example, GK1 serves the ball to A1, B1 joins the play and A1 and B1 attempt to score. This also creates an opportunity to institute demands on the server, in this case A1. GK2 then collects the ball and starts the sequence in the other direction.

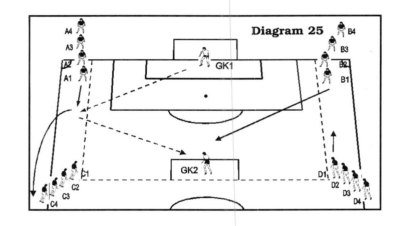

Diagram 25

Progression Two

The set up is the same with the addition of a defender who will join the play from the side that is being attacked. GK1 serves the ball wide to A1, B1 joins A1 as a second attacker. C1 will step into the field and defend the two attackers A1 and B1. Once the attack is concluded, the two versus one situation continues in the other direction with two new offensive players and a new defender. GK2 serves the ball to D1 who is joined by C1 to attack the goal of GK1 and defender B2.

Diagram 26

Other Progressions

- The same set-up with the addition of a second defender to create two versus two situations to goal.
- The same set-up with the addition of designated wide players who are responsible for serving the ball into the box where two attacking players are met by two defenders.

Coaching points

- Time and patterns of attacking runs to goal
- Service choices from wide players
- Combinations to goal

- Defensive positioning and goalkeeper communication
- Goalkeepers dealing with crosses.
- Goalkeepers dealing with distribution choices.
- Transition play.

Columbus Crew - Goalkeeping

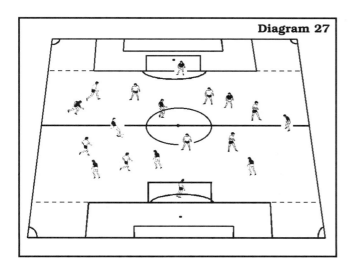

Diagram 27

Game Situation

The field is now extended to the top of the penalty boxes. The game is 8 v 8 with goalkeepers

Coaching points

The situations that are created by the demands placed on the players will become your coaching points. From this exercise you have numerous opportunities to manufacture a game to fit your specific needs for that particular training session (such as scoring from crosses only).

West Ham United - Youth Team

West Ham United youth team manager Tony Carr shares his practices of how to create goalscoring opportunities with a session of working in and around the penalty area.
This article is reprinted with the consent of CATALYST, the official journal of AFCAT.

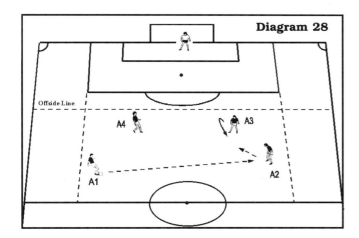

Diagram 28

Mark a field as shown in diagram 28, with lines extending from the penalty area and an offside line 25 yards from goal.

Start the practice with shadow play using four players playing in an area only as wide as the penalty area.

A1 passes to A2 who receives with an open body. A3 checks and shows for a ball off A2. A2 plays the ball into the space in front of A3.

A2 then moves wider at an angle to receive a return pass from A3.

A2 then moves wider at an angle to receive a return pass from A3.
A2 then passes into the space behind A3 for A4 who has made a diagonal run. A3 then peels off to the far post area.

Coaching Points
- Receive the ball with an open body.
- Angled runs.
- A4 must push up with A3 before making a diagonal run to prevent offside.
- Pass into space.
- Timing of runs.
- Weight of pass.

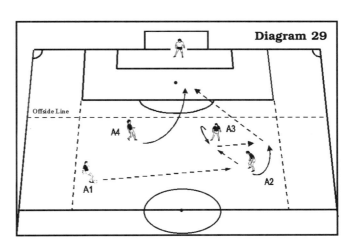

Diagram 29

Progress by adding three defenders. Two must mark the forwards. One must fill the area between the forwards and the midfield. Encourage players to make their own decisions and to be creative. See if they can use the points they have practiced in the shadow play. Develop the play by removing the offside line and play offside from the last defender.

A2 makes a diagonal run to receive from A3. A1 pulls out and spins off to receive from A2.

Coaching Points
- Receive with an open body
- Get away from marker
- Good movement
- Individual skill (dribbling and turning)

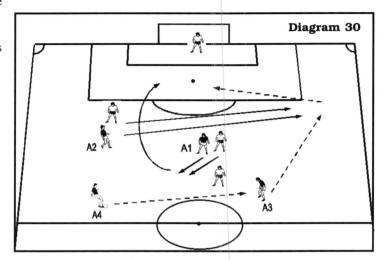

Diagram 30

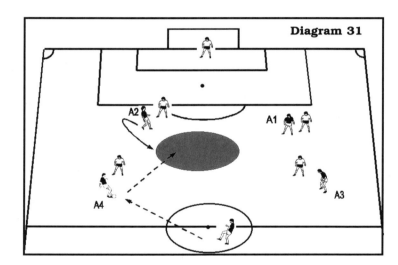

Diagram 31

Add one more defender and a server. The server feeds one of the midfield players.

Coaching Points
- Timing of passes and runs
- Weight of pass
- Forwards should push defenders back as far as possible to create space in front (shaded area) to drop in short.

Use the areas wide of the penalty box and position two attacking players in these areas. Forwards may now take the option of passing to these wide players as per the diagram.

A1 receives the ball and passes to A2. A2 may either pass in to the forward or pass on to A3 who has made an overlap.

Final Coaching Points
Teach the players to know what type of passes to make by looking at the positioning and movements of the forwards. Try to encourage them to see situations and to make good decisions.

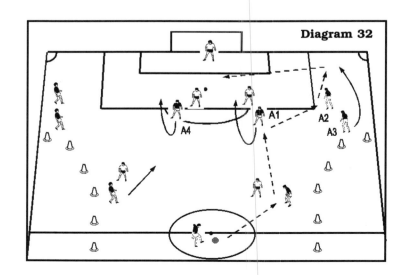

Diagram 32

Snickers National Champions

The West Coast Shamrocks won the U19 Girls Snickers National Championship in July 1998. They have previously been California South State Champions six times, Far West Regional Champions four times and Snickers National Championship runners-up once. As well as coaching the Shamrocks, Bobby Bruch also serves as head coach of the entire West Coast F.C. Bobby also enjoyed success as a player winning two NCAA National Championships and playing professionally for eight years. In this issue, Bobby shares his favorite practices for improving midfield play.

Midfield Runs and Crossing

A1 passes to A2.

A2 passes the ball toward the end line.

A1 overlaps A2 and crosses with her first touch.

The three lines of players all make angled runs into the goalbox as shown and finish with one touch if possible.

The crosses should be varied, i.e. near and far post, high and low, etc.

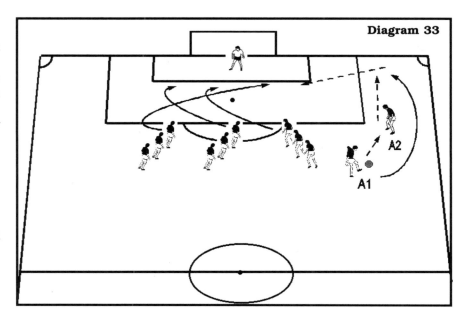

Coaching Points

- Great first touch
- Angle and speed of overlapping run
- Time the runs into the goalbox
- Quality crosses, bend them away from the goalkeeper and drive them near and far post.

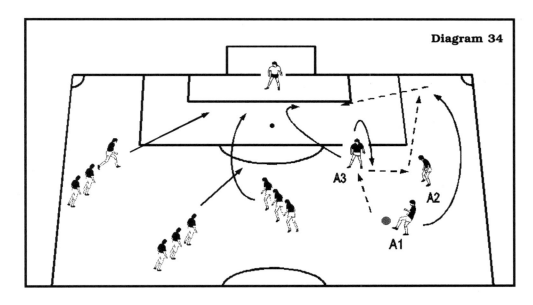

Variation

This time A1 combines with the 'striker', A3.

A3 moves away then checks back to receive a pass from A1.

A3 passes to A2 then turns and runs into the penalty area.

A2 passes toward the end line.

A1 overlaps A2 and crosses with her first touch.

The three lines of players all make angled runs into the goalbox.

Coaching Points

- As per the previous drill
- Pace of pass
- Quality of first touch
- Checking run of A3

Other Variations

The drill can be started with a throw-in or a re-start.

Brazilian Olympic Team

Practice observed in Florida, March 1998.

Used as a warm-up or cool-down, this drill is excellent for fine tuning technique. The players assemble in groups of three and pass the ball as shown in diagram 35. A1 and A3 are approximately four yards apart.
A1 passes to A2.

A2 returns the pass with one touch to A1 then runs around A3 to his other side to receive another pass from A1.

The drill continues with A2 running around A3 with A1 making passes to each side of A3 to keep A2 moving.

The players attempt to work into a rhythm. Work for one minute then change positions.

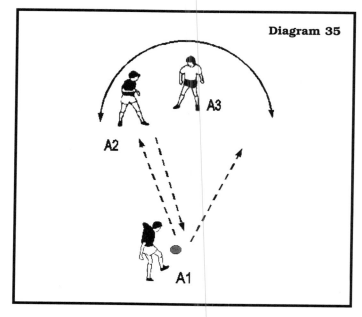

Coaching Points

- It is important that A2 receives the ball in front of A3.
- Change positions
- Can toss the ball with hands for volleys, etc.

Variations

There are many variations including:
- Instep
- Outside of foot
- Volley
- Chest then pass back
- Thigh then pass back
- Headers

Progression

The players start on one side of the field and A3 walks backwards during the passing until the players reach the other side of the field. Then change positions.

Jamaican U20 National Team

A practice observed in Florida, July 1998.

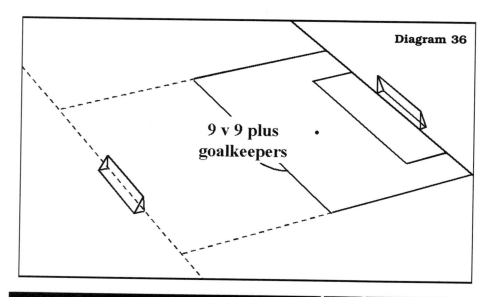

In a field the size of two goalboxes, two teams play 9 v 9. The small field size puts the players in tight space situations.

Coaching Points

- Two-touch
- Look for combinations
- Keep the ball moving
- Look for quick shots

March/April 1999 Issue

Goalkeeping - U.S. National Teams

In August 1998 I attended a CEU weekend with featured clinicians Peter Mellor, U.S. Soccer National Goalkeeping Coaching Coordinator and Steve Aldard, Marquette University men's soccer coach and Region Two Boys ODP Goalkeeper Coach. Both coaches proved extremely knowledgeable and the weekend proved just how important specialist goalkeeping coaches are. Below are some of the drills demonstrated during the course and used by the U.S. National Teams goalkeepers.

Warm-Up

Arrange two goals 15 yards apart as shown in diagram 9. There are four goalkeepers, two in each goal. A1 and A3 start with a ball. Rolling the ball underhand, A1 and A3 pass the ball at the same time to A2 and A4 respectively and then follow their pass. When they receive the ball, A2 and A4 slide over to A3 and A1's positions and continue the drill. Therefore the goalkeepers should continue in a rotating pattern.

Coaching Points

- Keep a good shape with body weight forward
- Shoulders should be square to the ball
- Shuffle feet when moving sideways – don't cross feet
- Move towards the ball to meet it – don't wait for it to reach you

Progression

Same as diagram 9 but throw balls to the goalkeepers midsection area.

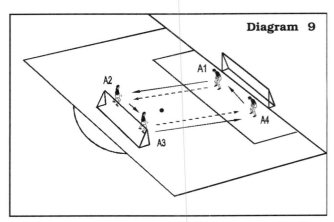

Diagram 9

Coaching Points

- Step/jump backwards to cushion the catch.
- Keep elbows in.

Other Progressions

- Same as diagram 9 but throw balls head-height
- Same as diagram 9 but throw balls high for the goalkeeper to come out and take the ball at its highest point.

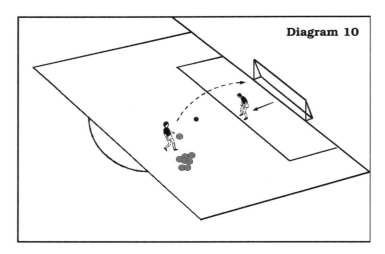

Diagram 10

Chip Shots

The coach positions himself about 15 yards from goal with a supply of balls. The goalkeeper starts on his line then quickly moves to the six yard line and sets his feet. The coach then throws a ball over the goalkeeper's head to either upper corner of the goal and the goalkeeper backs up to make the save. The ball should be thrown just as if a player was attempting to chip the goalkeeper.

Coaching Points

- Footwork – the first step backwards should be with an open step which will turn the upper body a little sideways.
- The second step should cross the first then back pedal.

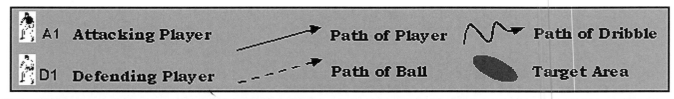

Diving

The goalkeeper steps off his line – sets his feet, then the server throws or kicks the ball on the ground to the side of the goalkeeper. The goalkeeper dives to save the shot.

Coaching Points

- Step forward to dive – narrow the angle
- The first step is a collapse
- Use the ground as a 'third hand' - with one hand behind the ball and one hand on top of the ball to trap it to the ground.

Progression One

Serve balls waist high. The goalkeeper should dive, trap the ball to the ground and pull it into his body.

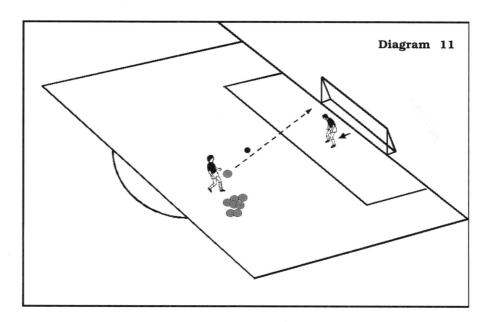

Diagram 11

Progression Two

Serve balls to upper corners. For this the goalkeeper should be in a 'ready stance' looking at the ground psyching himself for the save. When he his ready he looks up and the server then plays the ball to the upper corner.

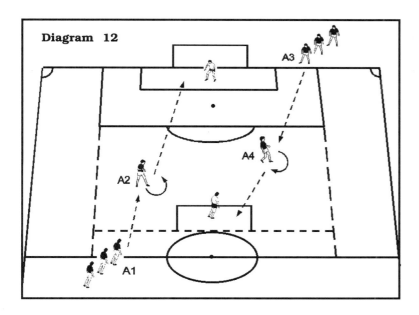

Diagram 12

Shot Stopping

Set the field with two full size goals as shown in diagram 12. Work both goals at the same time. Spare goalkeepers can stand behind the goals and alternate every few shots.

A1 passes to A2. A2 turns and shoots on goal. A3 and A4 go at the same time.

After a shot, A1 takes A2's position. A2 goes to the back of A3's line. A3 takes A4's position and A4 goes to the back of A1's line.

As the ball is passed to the shooter, the goalkeeper should be approximately 4 – 6 yards off his goal line. The shooters should vary their attack with chips, close range shots, long range shots, power shots, curved shots, etc.

As the shooter turns, the goalkeeper should drop back a little in case the shooter decides to attempt a chip shot. If the shooter decides to move closer to goal, the goalkeeper should come back out and close the gap between him and the shooter. For every touch of the ball the shooter takes when advancing on goal, the goalkeeper should close the gap on the shooter.

This drill is excellent for teaching the goalkeeper the correct distance needed to be off his line and between him and the shooter.

Progression

A2 and A4 serve crosses from outside of the extended lines of the 18 yard box.

Positioning and Distances

A 50-yard rope is staked to the center of the goal-line with the coach at the other end representing an attacking player with the ball. The coach moves with the rope from side to side and north and south. The goalkeeper should straddle the rope at all times.

The objective is to teach the goalkeeper the correct lateral positioning and how far off his line he needs to be depending on where the ball is.

A second person can be introduced. He can be positioned as a defender at varying distances from the coach to simulate different kinds of defensive pressure on the ball.

Once the coach passes into the shaded area straddling the line doesn't apply because of the danger of crosses.

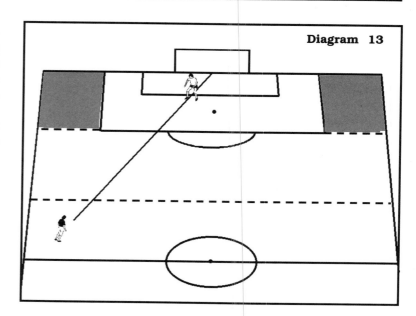

Diagram 13

Coaching Point

• Make small adjustments often – not fewer big adjustments

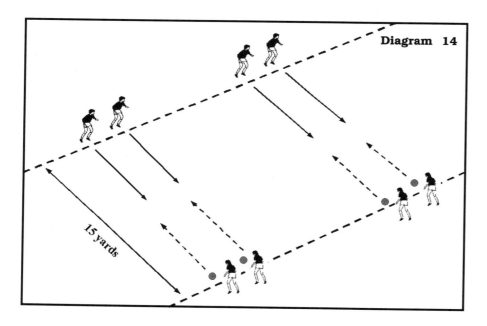

Diagram 14

15 yards

Goalkeeper Fitness

The players are lined up in pairs 15 yards apart as shown in diagram 14. The two players at one end roll the balls underhand toward the two players at the other end who come to collect the ball by scooping it into their body. The first person to collect the ball wins, therefore the players rolling the balls need to roll at the same time and at the same speed. After 10 repetitions, change ends.

Progression

Roll only one ball and have the two players at the other end compete to see who collects the ball.

Coaching Point

• Must stay on your feet when collecting the ball

Goalkeeping - U.S. National Teams

The number of repetitions and amount of rest in the following drills in diagrams 15, 16, 17, 18 and 19 should be related to the fitness level, age, ability, etc. of the goalkeeper.

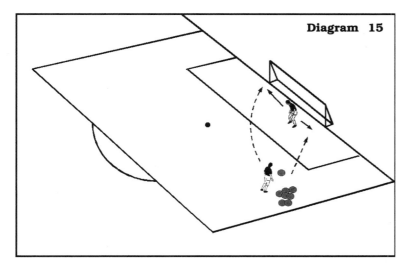

Diagram 15

Goalkeeper Fitness

The goalkeeper starts in the correct position related to the server, as if he was positioning to save a shot. The server rolls the ball to the near post and the goalkeeper makes the save and back pedals. Once the goalkeeper has collected the near post ball, the server throws a ball to the opposite upper corner for the goalkeeper to back pedal and save. After the save, the server rolls a ball to the near post again and the drill continues.

Goalkeeper Fitness

The goalkeeper starts in the middle of the goal. The server throws the ball to the upper left hand corner of the goal. The goalkeeper collects the ball, throws it back to the server and returns to the middle of the goal. The server then continues the drill by throwing to the same corner. For the next set of repetitions, work the other corner.

Coaching Points

- Be aware of the goal post
- Concentrate on foot work – side-step, don't cross-step

Progression

Alternate corners every throw

Diagram 16

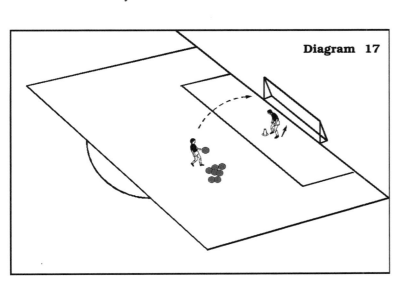

Diagram 17

Goalkeeper Fitness

The goalkeeper starts at the cone, which is 3 yards from the goal-line. The server throws the ball high over the goalkeepers head as if he were attempting to chip over the goalkeeper.

The goalkeeper's footwork should take him back quickly so he is able to catch the ball in front of his body.

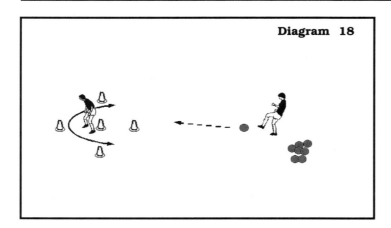

Diagram 18

Goalkeeper Fitness

Mark five cones as shown in diagram 18. The goalkeeper starts with his back to the server, straddling the center cone. The server shouts 'turn' and then half-volley's a shot at the goalkeeper. The goalkeeper turns, stops the shot, throws the ball back to the server and returns to his starting position to continue the drill.

Work on footwork and turning technique by avoiding knocking over the cones.

Goalkeeper Fitness

Place two servers with a supply of balls as shown in diagram 19. One server is at an angle approximately eight yards from goal. He serves high shots. The other server is straight on, 15 – 20 yards from goal. He serves half volleys waist high or below.

As soon as the goalkeeper makes the save from one server, the next server should shoot to goal. The servers should time their shots to make the goalkeeper work on his recovery speed.

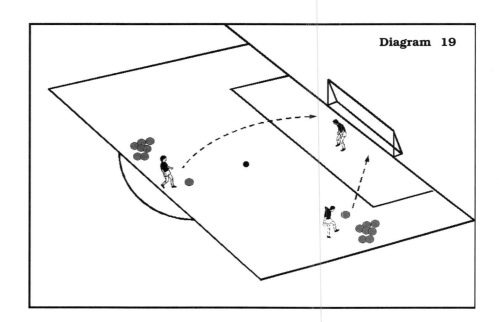

Diagram 19

Diagram 20

Diving

Line six balls two yards away from a marked line as shown in diagram 20. The server passes firmly towards the goalkeeper who dives forward to save the ball in the upper body area. As soon as he has made the save, he returns to the line ready for the second ball to be passed. After completing all six balls, return in the other direction.

Do one part drill to three to five parts rest.

Goalkeeping - U.S. National Teams

Peter Mellor demonstrated three plyometric exercises that added up to three inches to the vertical leaps of some of the U.S. National Team's goalkeepers.

- The coach and goalkeeper stand side-by-side. The coach extends his hand above his head and the goalkeeper 'frog jumps' to try and get his head above the height of the coaches hand
- The coach crouches over and the goalkeeper leapfrogs back and forth over the coach
- The coach crouches low on the ground and the goalkeeper side-jumps back and forth over the coach

The goalkeepers for the U20 and U23 National Teams did the following repetitions of the above exercises twice a week.

- One minute each exercise – continuous. (Three minutes total) followed by five times rest = 15 minutes
- Thirty seconds each exercise – continuous. (90 seconds total) followed by five times rest = 7 1/2 minutes
- Fifteen seconds each exercise – continuous. (45 seconds total)

England U15 National Team

Steve Avory describes a training session from when he was the coach of the England Schoolboys U15 Squad. This article is reprinted with the kind permission CATALYST, the official journal of AFCAT.

The session delivered was typical of how I got the England Schoolboys started once the final squad had been selected. Preparation time for matches was always precious (two hours the day before, one hour or so set play practice on match day). I always felt the most valuable practices were the functionals, presenting the picture that players could hopefully make happen. Such team understanding practice was always uppermost in my mind, considering the time available. However, there had to be other dynamic, enjoyable and productive practices which was nearly always devoted to receiving, passing and movement before getting onto the "meat" of the session. So here it is, Attacking Play.

Practice One
All players work in a 40 x 40-yard area, i.e. 14 players, four to five balls. Make ground pass to player supporting/calling, then move off to demand/receive another ball.

Coaching Points
- Body position "open" to receive ball. Have a look before ball arrives.
- Create space on controlling touch – set up for pass or run with ball – various conditions can be brought in here, i.e. must take with outside foot, let ball run across and take away with furthest foot.
- Quality pass – accuracy and pace.

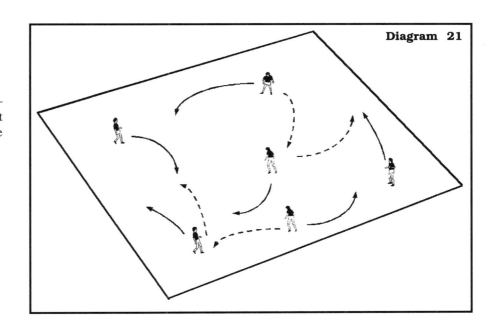

Diagram 21

Practice Two

Play 3 v 3 inside a fairly large circle formed by the other eight players, positioned alternately. Dark team can play to team mates inside circle or use dark players on outside. If pass is made to outside player, then replace. The receiver then becomes one of the 3 v 3 inside the circle. Outside players are not fixed in position. They can move sideways in the space between opposition. Easy option of pass to outside player will probably be used too much initially. This is acceptable and the point of switching play can be brought out. Gradually challenge inside players to look for passes through opponents to team mates. Also, progress to outside players having one touch.

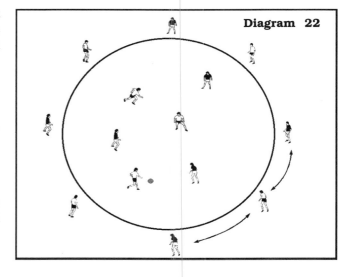

Diagram 22

Coaching Points

- Create space as a team, i.e. spread.
- Create space individually, i.e. check away and then receive.
- Body position correct in approach to ball, i.e. "open up"
- Receiving touch to create space – effected by getting body position correct and then making the appropriate decision, i.e. touch away from defender or shield the ball.
- Support early – angle/distance – can be brought out clearly when a pass is made to outside player. Other players must move to support as ball is travelling to outside player, particularly if he only has one touch.
- Passing – short when necessary, encourage combination play, i.e. long pass to get out of tight areas.
- Open up the play when required, i.e. switching play, create space for fresh runs.
- Quick play, dependent on other factors being right, i.e. early support, preparation by receiver with body position correct to see early passing opportunity.

Functional Practice – Creating Space As A Team – Exploiting Space Created

Play 10 v 8 on a field as shown. Coach the 'A' team. Practice starts with the 'D' team delivering a comfortable cross for the GK to intercept, who then looks for a quick delivery to 'A' players. To make it realistic the 'A' players must take up realistic defensive positions in relation to the cross. 'A' players must look to move toward the goal on delivery of the ball.

Diagram 23

Target Line

Coaching Points

- Reaction on a team to regained possession – spread wide/long. Note all A players movement away from ball, keeping body position open to see developments and prepare for movement to receive ball
- A3, obvious target for GK to switch play quickly. Angle of run/body position to receive important, i.e. see the whole picture. Receive/touch if necessary to go forward and then pass decision
- Option to A7 (feet or space). A7 should get wide early and look to receive feet or space, determined by D's defending.

Space opened for early pass to A9. A5 run important here (away from A3) to open space for pass to A9 (A8/A9 movement possibilities, see next practice). A4/A5 movement also considered, but at this point A5 needs to be aware of checking back to receive from A3 if necessary, but also appreciate his role in creating initial team space. Obviously creating space as a team doesn't just happen when the GK regains possession but I have found this a sound starting point for understanding the value of spreading wide/long. It puts great emphasis for the support/passing decision making to achieve quality possession.

Creating Space/Exploiting Space – Movement of Midfield and Strikers

Starting point with center back pass to A3. Team space already created. Now working towards goal (so 9 v 9). From previous practice, players should be aware of passing possibilities but more attention given to midfield/strikers movement and attacking space created.

Target Line for D Team   Diagram 24

Coaching Points to Emphasize

- If A5/A4 prove understanding and make fast movement away, pass to A9 is on.
- A9 movement should also be away (keeping body open to observe build up from back players). Timing of run important – A9 makes movement as A3 lifts head making a shallow diagonal run to receive to feet or a diagonal run for ball to space and ahead of defender. A8/A9 could of course cross-over but not essential.
- A8 continue movement away to opposite direction.
- Other players have movement decision to make on pass to A9.
- Example: Pass to A9's feet, A5 supports behind. A4 anticipates with forward run into space created ahead of ball by A8/A9 movement. A6 could also make an out-to-in run if A8 continues movement wide. A7 works the line for ball to feet or space.

Again, I emphasize this is a good starting point for understanding the movement possibilities from the middle 1/3 to attacking 1/3, showing how space can be created and exploited. The points above and indeed other possibilities can be brought out clearly with the above organization, but obviously the "acid" test is during the play to see whether players really do understand. The pictures created in the controlled practice situation do not automatically happen and occur in exactly the same way in a game and players need to appreciate this, but understand that if team space is created and the defending team stretched, there is a basis for such passing and movement ideas. I always found myself in future sessions stressing the need to pass and keep possession as well as pass to get behind the opposition when good attacking space is created. It is a fine balance between the two, but good players and good teams make the right decisions.

Mike Smith - Defending

Mike Smith is one of the world's most experienced international coaches. To date he has coached teams in 212 international games. From 1974 to 1980 he was the manager of the Welsh National Team. From 1985 to 1988 he was manager of the Egypt National team where he won the African Nations Cup and the African Olympics. Currently Mike is at Wolverhampton Wanderers of the English First Division where he works with the youth team players.

As FIFA came down heavily on tackles from behind, defending has become a much greater skill. The techniques of defending now require:

- Quick feet – to adjust quickly
- Reading the game to intercept
- Close enough to be able to finger touch your opponent
- Keep your eyes moving from your opponent to the ball – always 'man and ball' not just man or ball

You can coach defending from the principles, delay – slowing down your opponents attacks, balance – numerically coping with your opponents attack and depth/cover – being able to defend spaces behind colleagues.

But in the ebb and flow of the game and dealing with counter-attacks, speed and communication are vital. As one side loses possession, all of their players have to work to defend. The front players have to pressure the opposing defenders slowing the delivery. All other players have to get behind the ball and hold their position.

What happens next?

Wherever the ball is played, a defender engages and tries to intercept. If not, he must jockey then tackle. All other defenders must do their job and half of the surrounding defenders job.

In diagram 25, D2 does his job of engaging the player with the ball.
D1 does his job and half of D2's job.
D3 does his job and half of D2's job.
D4 does his job and half of D3's job.

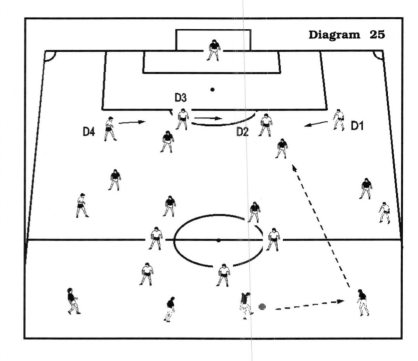

Diagram 25

The concept of doing half of the other players' jobs alerts them to the possibility of their colleague being beaten. Therefore, cover and depth is part of that decision. Now the art of defending comes in actually winning the ball. So when a ball is played to your opponent with his back to you, don't get boxed in right behind him because there is little chance that you can get a touch on the ball without fouling. What you must do is give yourself room by positioning yourself at the side so you are able to 'get a foot in' and 'nick' the ball away. When the ball is played to a player facing you, you need to attack his first touch, but only if you are absolutely sure you can win the ball. So you need to be close enough to play the ball away from your opponent. If your opponent's first touch is excellent, you have to work hard enough to get close, stay on your feet and run with your opponent until you have the opportunity to tackle and steal the ball.

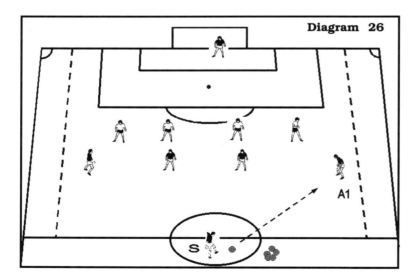

Diagram 26

Mark two lines approximately 8-10 yards inside the touch-line as shown in diagram 26. The coach has a supply of balls and serves passes in to the forwards who attempt to score, or if they are defended well, can pass back to the coach. After a scoring attempt or a pass back, the coach passes in again to any of the forwards.

The coach uses his judgement and passes balls in to create different situations for the defenders.

For example, he can pass to forwards who have their back to goal or to forwards that are running at the defenders. He should also play some bad passes so the defenders have the chance of intercepting.

Mike Smith - Defending

Each time the ball is played in, the defenders have to make decisions (do their job and half of their colleague's job). Each defender has to retain his distance from his colleague – like being tied together with a rope both forwards, back and sideways.

In diagram 26, the ball is played in to A1. Diagram 27 shows how the defenders need to react and adjust their positions.

The Challenge

Can you challenge the first touch of your opponent when the ball arrives at his feet?

Is your approach correct? Do you know the line from the near post to your opponent?

Can you get a foot in to knock the ball away?

Can you work your body against him and 'jockey' him where you want him to go?

Do you know his strongest foot, and can you keep him off that?

But as the pass was on its way, do you think you could intercept the ball?

This is reading the game!

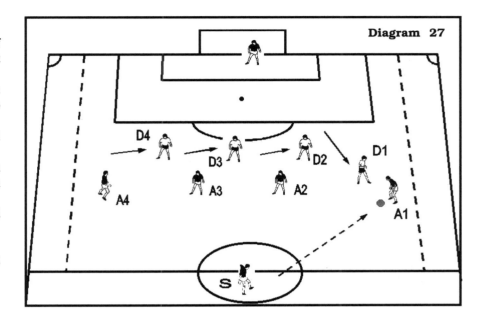

Diagram 27

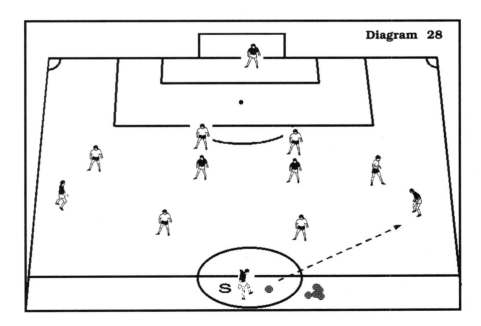

Diagram 28

Progression

Once the defenders have become more familiar with the concept of doing their job and half of a colleagues job as well as understanding the need to retain the correct distance from each other (like being tied together), we add two central midfielders to defend in front of the back four.

Take away the marked lines and play using the half-field. The coach stays as a server, plays into midfield or wide or off the front players allowing the defenders to make the right decision and to keep pulling the defenders out until they reach the half-line.

Mike Smith - Defending

Progression

The final progression to create realistic game situations is for the six players to defend against 8-10 players in a game situation on 3/4 of a field. The attacking team starts with their defenders passing the ball to each other until they get an opportunity to pass to one of the forwards/midfielders. Once the forwards/midfielders have the ball, they attempt to combine for a scoring opportunity. If they are defended well, they pass the ball back to their defenders and the practice continues.

The objective of the defending team of six is obviously to deny scoring opportunities and if they win possession of the ball to get it over the half-line.

The defending team should be able to go for long periods of time without conceding a goal and the coach will have plenty of opportunities to work on the coaching points described throughout this session.

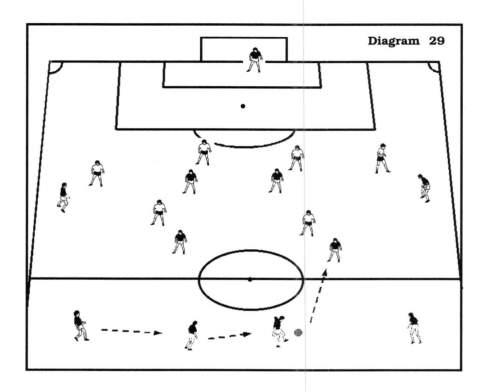

Diagram 29

Coaching Points

- Quick feet – adjust quickly against your opponent if he gets good possession.
- Read the intended next pass – in order to intercept.
- Get close to your opponent as the ball is moved around – arms length.
- Keep your eyes moving – defend MAN & BALL.
- Do your job and half of a colleague's job.
- Retain the correct distance from your colleagues – like being tied together.
- Emphasize the challenge.

In the previous diagrams there is not a spare defender. Every defender picks up an opponent, i.e. 1 v 1, but the two full-backs close in on the opposite side to the ball and shift defenders across to create a spare defender, much like diagram 18. Some teams adjust their defense and play a 'sweeper' or 'libero'. This allows the central defenders to mark and keep their distances tight with opponents.

Some teams readjust tactically and play three center-backs with two marking backs and one spare to cover and maybe move through and play in midfield. These are all progressions and are usually determined by opponents and the tactics employed by opponents.

So when you coach defenders, make them understand distances; marking between each other; like being tied together; recovery; the necessity for quick feet against an opponent. Read the intended next pass in order to intercept. Do your job and half of a colleague's job. Defend **MAN AND BALL.**

Finally, beware as you work through your practices of two factors:

1. Repetition work of attack v defense often results in the defense defending too deep. So after each wave of attack, make sure the defenders push out towards the half-line.
2. Repetition work also produces the fact that defenders are always facing the ball. So, on occasions when the defenders push out, really make them get to the half-line and then play a ball past them to make them turn and recover.

Coaching Set Plays

'Coaching Set Plays' is a book recently published by Tony Waiters which is the product of 30 years of joyful -- and painful! -- Experiences, both as a player and a coach. The truth is, Waiters' experiences as a coach were much happier with regard to Set Plays because of lessons learned as a player and then quickly learned as a rookie coach. It helped win a European championship (England Youth team, 1973), and two North American championships (Vancouver Whitecaps, 1979 and Canadian National Team, 1991). And, the two goals that finally qualified Canada for its only appearance in the men's World Cup (Mexico '86) both came from set-plays (Canada 2: Honduras 1).

The book covers every type of set play imaginable, both defending and attacking with research from literally hundreds of games including previous World Cups. In this article we look at chapter Two – Attacking Corners.

Why are set plays so important? In a 20 game season, what if you could guarantee scoring five more goals and conceding five less? -- A 10 goal spread; the difference between a championship and mediocrity; or a good, fun season rather than a miserable one.

Chapter Two – Attacking Corners

In recent years, Corner Kicks have superseded Free Kicks in goals scored at Set-Plays. Overall, Penalty Kicks are #1 in goals from re-starts in most levels of competition and we will come to them in Chapter Seven.

The fact is your team will attack and defend many, many more corners than penalties.

There are a number of different types of Corner Kicks. I'm going to deal with the four most successful ones -- both from an attacking and a defending perspective.

They are:
1. The Near Post Corner
2. The Far Post Corner
3. The Short Corner
4. The Pull Back

Before going into the detail let me introduce you to the "Black Hole." (Diagram 30).

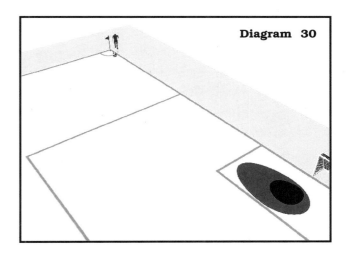

Diagram 30

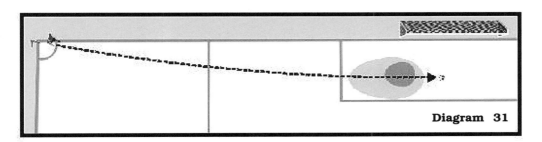

Diagram 31

Any well-hit, well-flighted, usually inswinging ball, arriving head-height in the black area gives great potential for a goal to be scored.

Coaching Set Plays

As you can see from diagram 32, most times the Corner Kick is merely helped on its way by a little "bump" of the head, wrong-footing defenders and the goalkeeper, but easily read by the rehearsed attacking team players coming in center goal and at the far post.

I find it difficult to believe the number of teams that still ignore the great opportunity of scoring created by balls into the "Black Hole" area. How often do you see them ballooning the ball to the Far Post areas only to see the central defenders time and time again rise to make the head clearance?

I'm not saying Far Post balls are a waste of time. Of course they are not. What I am saying is that in most competitions more goals are scored from balls played initially to the Near Post "black hole" area than hit to the Far Post area. Facts don't lie.

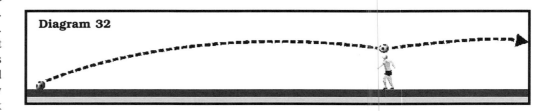

Diagram 32

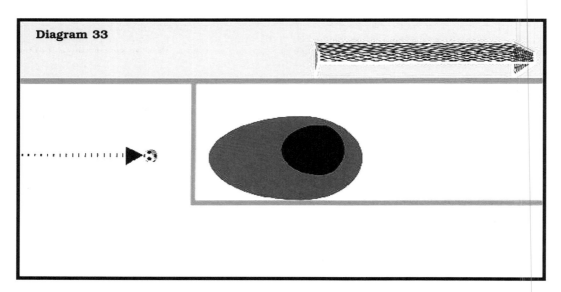

Diagram 33

The "perfect" ball is a well-flighted inswinger arriving head-height into the mini "hole" -- the "Bull's Eye" -- just too far forward and out for the keeper to take comfortably.

The Near Post (Inswinging or Inswinger) Corner

Most "Near Post" corners are inswingers -- with the left foot from the right side and the right foot from the left side. However, there are some very skillful kickers of the ball who can swerve an inswinging ball with the right foot from the right side (or the left foot from the left side). Teams containing only "normal mortals" will have to settle for right from left and vice-versa and make the necessary organizational arrangements.

Defending teams sometimes put a defender 10 yds. from the corner kick to make the kicking job more difficult, but the 10 yd. rule means it is not that much of a deterrent to the kicker (that defender may be more useful in another critical defending area.) Nevertheless, in practice, it will be worthwhile practicing the kick with and without a 10-yard marker.

It really doesn't matter what the opposition does with regard to its defensive organization if the "execution" of the planned corner kick is good. So let's look at the set up and the positions and actions that are required.

The initial ball in will greatly increase the chances of success and we'll go into more detail about that kick later in the chapter.

To cause greater confusion to the defending team, it is worth considering putting two players out at the corner kick to give the alternative of a short corner, and the option of an inswinger or an outswinger. However, a team has only so many players. We will see with the "runs" required to maximize the opportunity at the Inswinging Corner, we may run out of available players if we want to retain a safety "balance" -- to avoid too many players being caught "wrong side of the ball" if there is a clearance and counter attack. Two attackers at the corner will be a judgment call by the coach.

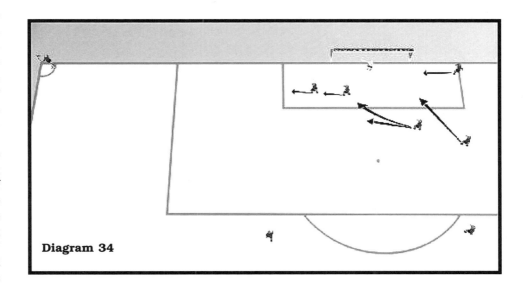

Diagram 34

First of all, let's take the situation we see in the diagram 34 and look at the roles and expectations of each player.

(In the manual, Waiters then goes into detailed "Job Descriptions" of each of the attacking players -- that means the whole team -- in terms of their roles, duties and expectations at the corner).

May/June 1999 Issue

Indiana University

Indiana University Men's Soccer program has been college soccer's most successful program since its inception in 1973. Since then, Indiana has won more NCAA tournament games than any other school including four NCAA titles. The program also has 11 Final Four appearances which is more than any other school. Head Coach Jerry Yeagley has been the architect of college soccer's premier program since 1973. Along with Assistant Coach, John Trask, Yeagley shares a training session used by Indiana University Men's Soccer team to improve ball movement and transition (both offensively and defensively).

Diagram 1

Warm-Up
1. Static stretching
2. 5 v 2 keep-away in a 10 yard circle as shown in diagram 1. The outside players are limited to one touch. The player responsible for losing possession changes places with the defender who caused the loss of possession.

Coaching Points
- Quality of Pass
- Support positions
- When to penetrate

Tactical Training Progression

8 v 4 Keep-Away

Play 8 v 4 keep-away in a 25 x 35 yard area as shown in diagram 2. The coach begins the activity by kicking the ball into play and the eight attacking players attempt to keep possession for as long as possible. The four defenders attempt to clear the ball out of bounds. We usually play a total of five balls before changing the defenders but have used up to ten balls if fitness is part of the training session. To keep things competitive in our training session the coach usually times how long it takes for the defenders to clear all five balls.

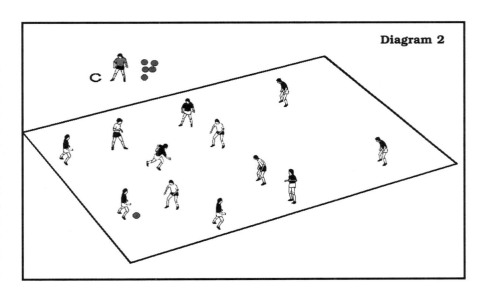

Diagram 2

Key: If we can increase the pressure applied to the offensive unit, they will learn how to cope with less time and space.

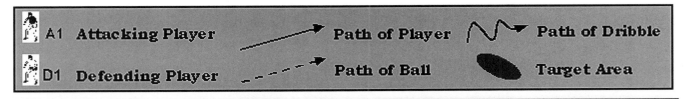

A1 **Attacking Player**   **Path of Player**   **Path of Dribble**

D1 **Defending Player**   **Path of Ball**   **Target Area**

Indiana University

8 v 4 Breakout

As in the previous game, the eight offensive players attempt to keep possession from the four defenders. When one of the four defenders wins possession he attempts to play the ball outside of the grid to another defensive player who is breaking outside the grid. If we are playing a total of five balls and the defensive unit can complete the breakout, we have them defend one less ball.

Key: Which players always seem to be on the end of the breakout or create the opportunity by winning the ball.

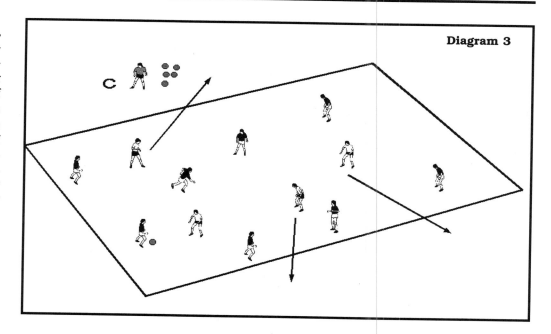

Diagram 3

Diagram 4

4 v 4 v 4

In the same 25 x 35-yard area, separate 12 players into three teams of four in different colors. Two of the teams attempt to keep the ball away from the third team. When one of the attacking players loses possession of the ball, his team must now transition and become the defending team. The ball can be put back into play by a throw-in or a kick-in depending on what you would like to stress.

Place a supply of balls around the perimeter to help keep the game flowing.

Variation

After the ball has gone out of play, restart from the opposite side of where the ball went out of bounds – Rational: If the throw-in or kick-in is coming from the opposite side, can the defensive group organize during this transition time?

8 v 4 Plus 4 to Goal

Using the same area, position two goals with goalkeepers approximately 20 yards from the sides of the grid and four cones approximately 10 yards from the ends of the grid as shown in diagram 5. The goalkeeper begins by distributing the ball to the eight attackers. The goalkeeper keeps count of the number of passes (usually 10). When the attacking team of eight completes 10 passes, they attack the goalkeeper who was counting and the defenders attempt to clear the danger. If the four defenders steal the ball before the target number of consecutive passes is achieved, they can attack either goal after passing to one of the four extra players positioned outside the grid by the cones. The four original defenders then transition to offense and attempt to score on the original offensive unit. Make the activity competitive by allowing each group of eight two or three sets of five balls and keep the total score.

Coaching Points

- Which players react quickly to loss of possession and understand their role to get behind the ball and clear the danger?
- Which players have the ability to spring the counterattack to one of the four options outside the grid?
- Transition from offense to defense and defense to offense.
- Decision making from wide players.
- Speed of play – attempt to get behind them quickly.

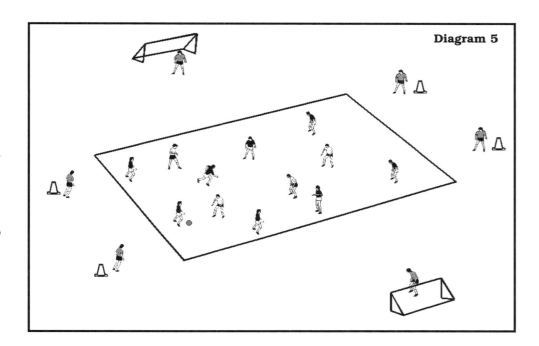

Diagram 5

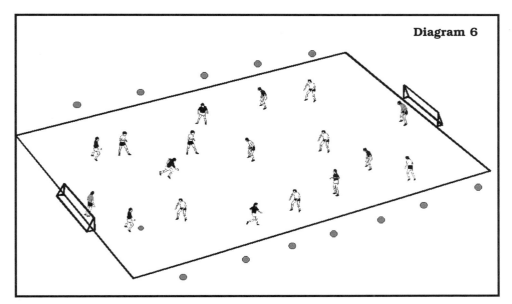

Diagram 6

Game Environment

Play 8 v 8 plus goalkeepers in a 75 x 50-yard area.

Coaching Points

- Place additional balls around the field to encourage quick restarts and transition.
- Be creative, there are many subtle changes in terms of scoring and modification of rules which will stress various components of possession and transition.

Sheffield United U16 Youth Team

Contributed by Sam Saif, coach of the U16 youth team at Sheffield United F.C., England. Sam first took part in the F.A. coaching schools at the age of 21. After attaining the F.A. Preliminary Award, Sam went on to coach teams at the youth and semi-pro level. Always looking to improve, Sam continued his soccer education with the F.A. coaching schools and received his F.A. Full Badge a few years later. In 1989, Sam became part of the coaching staff at the Center of Excellence for Sheffield United F.C. In 1995, Sam joined the coaching staff at the Leeds United F.C. Center of Excellence coaching the U14 team. He returned to Sheffield United F.C. in 1997 to coach the U16 youth team. In this article Sam shares a practice he learned from Frank Barlow who is currently the First Team Coach at Sheffield Wednesday which is used to improve 'Running With the Ball'.

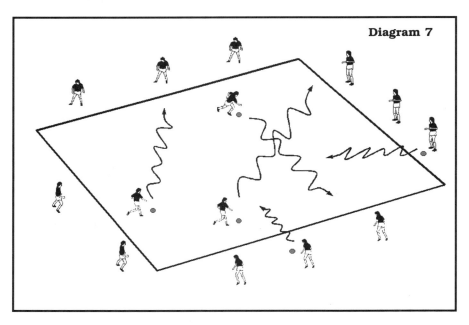

Diagram 7

Warm-Up

In a 30 x 30-yard area, organize 14 players with five balls. The players run with the ball across the square and pass it on to another player on the perimeter who does the same. Make sure the runs are not just directly across the square. Players need to scan to look and find where the space is and make their runs there.

Coaching Points

- When accepting the ball – make your first touch into space ahead of you.
- After receiving the ball – reappraise the situation, settle and make your run.
- Run the ball in then settle and turn into a different area.
- Run the ball with little changes of pace and direction.

Note: Players run with the ball differently and in individual ways. Don't make them conform. Instead allow them to experiment and try various ideas. They could try straight runs with pace or weaving-twisting runs with changes of pace and direction.

Possession Game

Split the players into two teams of seven and play in the same 30 x 30 yard area. Four players from each team are on the perimeter and the others play 3 v 3 possession inside the grid. The inside players have unlimited touches and can use their teammates on the perimeter. If a pass is made to a perimeter player, that perimeter player has to run the ball back into the square and change places with the passer.

Coaching Points

- As in diagram 7
- The perimeter players coming in with the ball cannot use just one touch – they must run in with the ball
- Start to look for takeovers

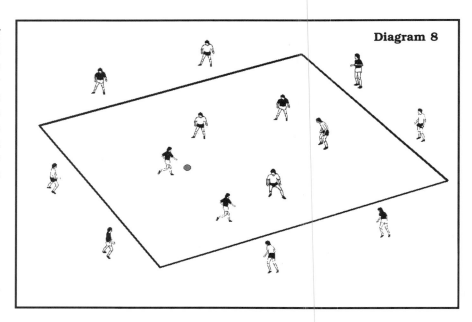

Diagram 8

May/June 1999   137   © WORLD CLASS COACHING

Sheffield United U16 Youth Team

Playing to a Line

In a 70 x 30 yard area, two teams of seven play a possession game attacking their opponent's 30 yard end-line. The shaded areas are 'safe areas'. These shaded areas must be left clear. Players are encouraged to run with the ball whenever possible. If they get into trouble they can run in the shaded areas with the ball and once in, cannot be challenged. This gives players the confidence to run with the ball without the fear of losing possession.

Once in the shaded areas, players should look to get back into play at the earliest opportunity by using diagonal runs.

Coaching Points

• Players that run with the ball always attract players from the opposition. Therefore, we must have support behind them.
• Once in the shaded areas, players must keep moving with the ball

Variation

The shaded areas can be positioned wherever you wish – even inside the playing area.

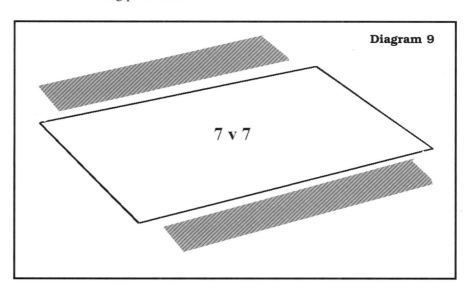

Diagram 9

7 v 7

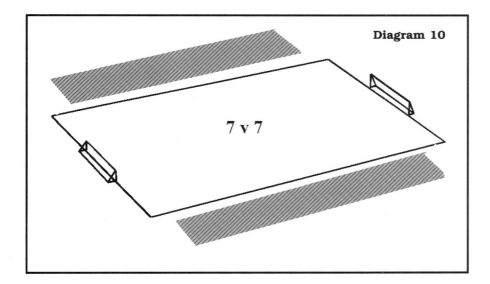

Diagram 10

7 v 7

Small-Sided Game With Goals

As in the previous game except add goals and goalkeepers.

Coaching Point

Don't expect total success – ENCOURAGE the players to run with the ball.

U.S. U20 National Team

A practice observed in Florida, March 1999.

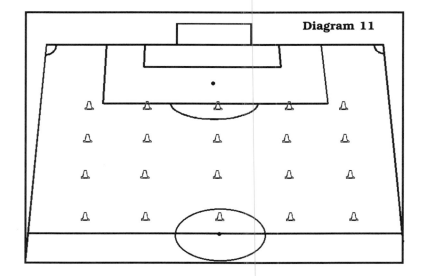

Diagram 11

Warm-Up

Cones are placed in rows covering half a field as shown in diagram 11. All 22 players jogged around the cones in different directions and different patterns for ten minutes.

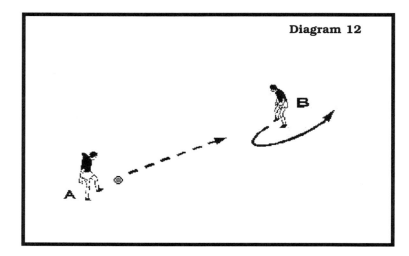

Diagram 12

Technical Practice

Players work in pairs 10 yards apart. Player A passes to player B who receives and turns, quickly sprints away for 5 yards and then turns to face player A again. Player B continues the drill by passing to player A.

Work on various turning techniques such as receiving the ball with different parts of the foot, turning different ways and disguising with fakes, etc.

Pass-and-Move

Players are in groups of three. Player A passes to player B and follows his pass to apply pressure. As player A gets close, player B passes to player C then makes a run to receive the one-touch return pass from player C. Player B then continues the drill by passing to player C.

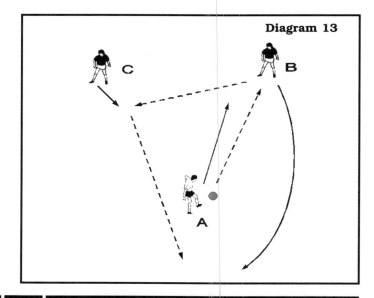

Diagram 13

The players were then split into two groups, one group played the half-field game, the other group worked in the coned area used for the warm-up. After 20 minutes the groups switched practices.

Half-Field Game

Play 4 v 4 + 1 on half a field with lines extending from the penalty area as shown in diagram 14.

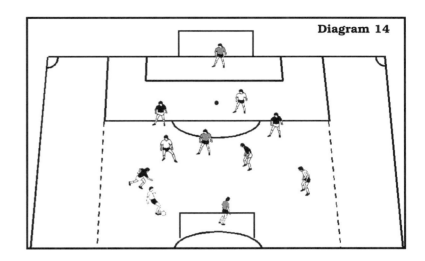

Diagram 14

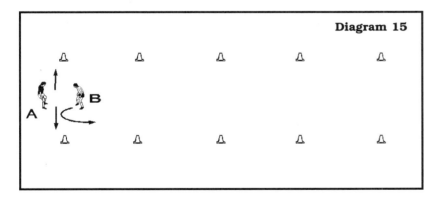

Diagram 15

Shadow Defending

Using the same cones set up from the warm-up, two players line up in between each row of cones. The drill starts with the player with his back to the cones, B, moving from side-to-side and the player facing the cones, A, shadowing him. On the coaches whistle, player B turns and sprints and player A follows and attempts to beat him to the end of the cones.

Variation

Both players lay down. On the coaches whistle the players get up and race to the end of the cones.

Ball Shuttles

On the coaches whistle, player B turns and runs to the first set of cones then turns to run back to the starting line. As he turns back to the starting line, player A passes him a ball and player B passes it back one-touch. Player B then turns and sprints to the second set of cones, turns and sprints back to the starting line. Player A passes the ball to player B as he approaches the first set of cones on his way back. The drill continues until all sets of cones have been done.

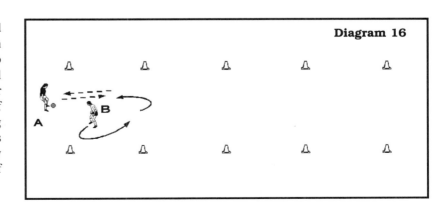

Diagram 16

Variation

Player A serves the ball with his hands for player B to volley.

The Liverpool F.C. Academy

One of the many highlights of my recent visit to England was the day I spent at the Liverpool F.C. Academy. The Academy is a facility solely for use by the players in the youth system of Liverpool F.C. This includes the full-time youth players age 16 – 19 and the younger players age 8 – 15 that practice two or three times a week in the evenings. Frank McParland, Director of Recruitment was my host for the day where I had the pleasure of observing Academy Director, Steve Heighway and U17 and U19 coaches Hugh McCauley and Dave Shannon take the youth players through their paces.

The Liverpool Academy

The Academy at Liverpool is part of a mini-revolution that English soccer is currently experiencing that is designed to improve the quality of soccer education and development of their gifted youth players. The major English clubs are now required to have a 'Football Academy' for their youth players. These Football Academies have to have certain requirements such as a minimum of six full-time staff including coaches, physiotherapists and a doctor available on call 24 hours a day. Part-time coaches are normally used for the U9 – U15 players that attend in the evenings. The Academy facilities are also required to have a certain number of fields per number of players registered. Other necessary facilities include a medical treatment room, classroom area and an artificial playing area. Most of the academies also include full-time living facilities for the U17 – U19 players.

The artificial field with lighted grass fields in the background.

English clubs now sign players starting at the U9 age group. Up until the end of the U16 season, players practice usually three times a week in the evenings during the season and play one game a weekend. Players are limited to a minimum of 24 games and a maximum of 30 games. Academy players usually play only with the Academy team as any games played with their school or elsewhere are counted toward the maximum of the 30 games allowed. Starting with the U17 season, players are full-time and receive a minimum of 12 hours coaching a week excluding games.

The Academy at Liverpool Football Club is a recently completed state-of-the-art facility containing a gymnasium, two weight rooms, offices for coaches and administrative staff, whirlpool, medical treatment room, locker rooms, restaurant, study/homework room and a parent's lounge. Outside there are eleven finely manicured playing fields of varying sizes to accommodate the different age groups, including a stadium field, a large artificial playing field and an indoor field that is currently under construction. Construction costs were over $17 million dollars with estimated annual operating expenses of over $1.5 million dollars.

During my visit I observed the U17's and U19's in an afternoon session, and in the evening I observed the U9, U10, U11 and U12 teams. I was struck by the intensity and business-like manner the U9 – U12 kids showed during practice. They obviously enjoyed playing at a competitive level and were eager to learn anything the coaches could show them. The evening sessions consisted of a 10 minute warm-up of Coerver type skills followed by 45 minutes of technique work that was designed to improve the quality of the pass, quality of the first touch and movement off the ball. The practice ended with a 30 minute scrimmage where the coaches let them play with very little coaching, just plenty of encouragement.

The Liverpool F.C. Academy

The following session was with players from both the U17 and U19 teams. Both coaches Hugh McCauley and Dave Shannon conducted the session. Academy Director Steve Heighway was on hand to observe and offer specific coaching points. He talked to the players about working smart, taking the challenge of the session and making sure they got something out of the session. The session focused on 'finishing' and was fairly light as the players were due to train with weights later that evening.

After a light warm-up of jogging and stretching, the field was set up with three goals as shown in diagram 17. To start the drill, each goalkeeper threw the ball out to the first player in their line. After receiving the ball, the player would then attack the goalkeeper creating a one-on-one situation.

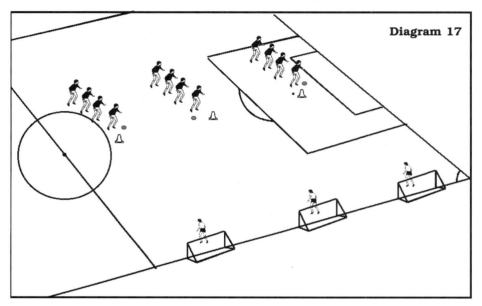

Diagram 17

Coaching Points
- Make sure your first touch puts the ball out in front of you
- Use the first 10 yards as sheer pace
- Experiment with different attacking options – be inventive
- Use fakes and disguise your intentions
- Use different body positions
- If you are close to the goalkeeper, try to slide it under his body
- Goalkeeper distribution should reach the player without bouncing

Editors note: The coaches also encouraged the players to try to emulate the moves that Arsenal's Dennis Berkamp used in scoring a one-on-one goal which appeared on national television the day before.

Progression
The players now line up at a cone placed five yards behind the original cone. The first player in line steps up to the front cone and receives the pass from the goalkeeper. On his first touch the next player in line, who is at the second cone, chases and attempts to disrupt the player's run at the goalkeeper.

Coaching Points
- First touch is critical
- Use the first 10 yards as sheer speed to get away from the chasing defender
- Run across the path of the chasing defender
- Finish in four touches or less

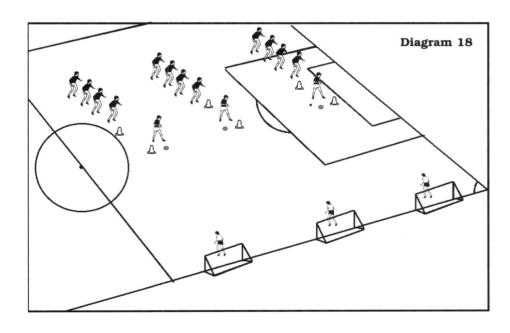

Diagram 18

The Liverpool F.C. Academy

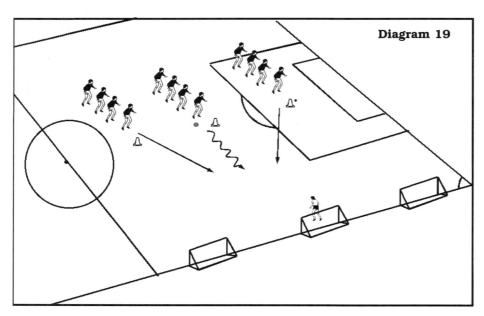

Diagram 19

Progression

The two outside lines of players are moved five yards closer to the center cone. Use just one goalkeeper in the middle goal. The goalkeeper throws the ball to the front player in the middle line. On that player's first touch, the front players in the outside lines chase the player with the ball and attempt to disrupt his run to goal. After each attempt, the players join the back of different lines.

Coaching Points

• Again, the first touch is critically important
• Composure
• Look to finish quickly before the chasing defenders reach you

Progression

Organize the players as shown in diagram 20 with a defender in front of each goal and defenders behind each goal ready to rotate in. The goalkeepers take turns throwing the ball to the front player in their line. Once the player has received the ball, the front players from the other two lines join in to play 3 v 3 against the three defenders. The attacking players can score in any of the three goals.

Coaching Points

• Look to get into 2 v 1 situations
• Switch the play
• Combinations – overlaps

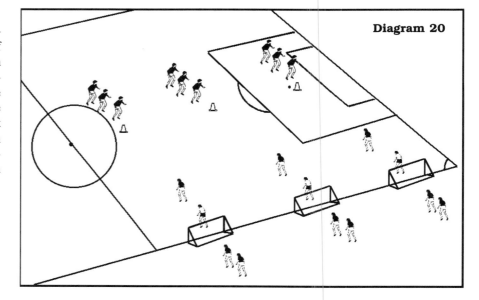

Diagram 20

The Liverpool F.C. Academy

The following session was observed in the evening with the U9 and U10 teams. Each team had their own coach who also coached the games at the weekend as well as the evening training sessions. However, the U17 and U19 coaches Dave Shannon and Hugh McCauley alternate staying behind each evening to observe and have some input into the sessions of the U9 – U15 teams. It struck me that having the full-time youth coaches stay behind and be involved in the development of the younger part-time players is critical in developing the players in the 'Liverpool way'. Steve Heighway, the Academy Director, also stays behind quite often to lend a hand. In fact, he stayed behind this evening to do sprint and agility tests for both teams. These tests, as well as others done during the season, are recorded and computerized to help monitor the development of the players. The session below is a combination of both the U9 and U10 teams that were practicing on different halves of the field.

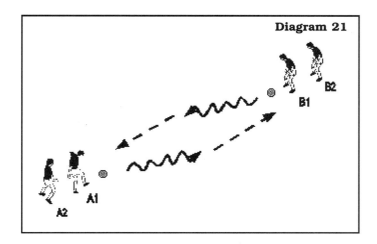

Diagram 21

Following a warm-up of seven to ten minutes of various Coerver type moves, the players went into groups of four as shown in diagram 21. The front players, A1 and B1 are 10 – 12 yards apart and dribble toward each other, do two Coerver type moves and pass to the player at the opposite end, i.e. A1 to B2 and B1 to A2 who continue the drill.

Coaching Points

- The coaches asked for various moves to be used then encouraged the players to experiment
- The quality of pass and first touch was also constantly emphasized even though the focus was on the Coerver type moves.

Progression

As in diagram 21, except after passing the ball, A1 and B1 move wide. The receiving players, A2 and B2 then play give-and-go's to start their turn.

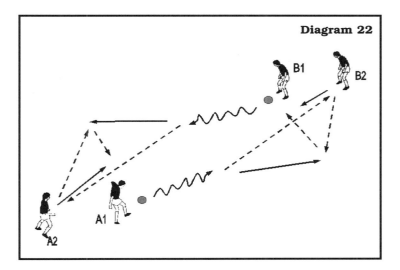

Diagram 22

In the same groups of four, the players form a square about 10 – 12 yards apart. The ball is simply passed around the square using two touches whenever possible. Then, move the ball in the opposite direction to practice with the other foot.

Coaching Points

- Quality of passes
- The first touch should be with an open body to allow for the next pass

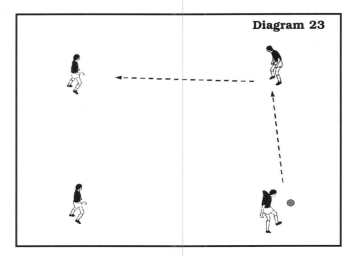

Diagram 23

The players then split into two groups with a coach in each group to work on the drill in diagram 24. The coach was constantly asking the players to focus on the quality and weighting of their passes.

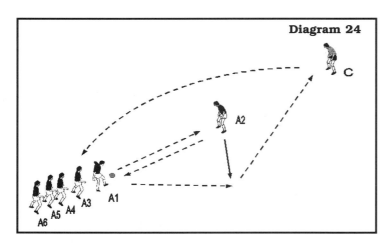

Diagram 24

A2 is 10 – 12 yards from A1.

A1 passes firmly to A2.

A2 passes back with one touch and moves into a wide position.

A1 passes wide to A2.

A2 controls the ball with an open body position and passes to the coach.

The coach then passes to the next player in line, A3, and the drill continues.

A1 takes A2's position and A2 joins the back of the line.

Coaching Points

- Firm passes on the ground
- Good first touch
- A2 backpedals to wide position so that he is in a sideways position to receive the next pass
- Use both feet

Variation

As the players become more familiar with the drill, a player can be used instead of the coach.

Set the cones up in a 40-yard area as shown with two players per set of cones. The players pass the ball back and forth through the cones using one touch if possible, whilst bouncing on their feet.

When the coach shouts 'turn', the inside player turns, dribbles to the opposite side of the grid with his head up and moves to a different set of cones. As the players are dribbling, the outside players move to the inside position so the players are always alternating positions.

If the coach shouts 'face', the outside players dribble with the ball.

Variations – Progressions

Practice different techniques of turns and passes.

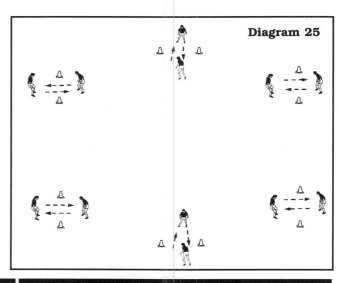

Diagram 25

Progression

As in the previous drill (diagram 25) except this time the waiting player (his partner) shouts 'turn' and the dribbling player turns and passes back to his partner. Again, the players should alternate inside and outside positions every time.

Progression

Diagram 26 shows a close up of two players from diagram 25. This time after dribbling, the player passes the ball back to his partner, shouts 'hold it' and runs around the back of his partner who passes into his path. Do three repetitions and change.

Coaching Point

The coaches stressed communication. The waiting player shouted 'turn'; after passing, the dribbling player shouted 'hold it'; then after running around his partner, he asks for the pass to be returned to him.

Variation

To start the drill, the ball can be passed through the middle of the legs or to either side.

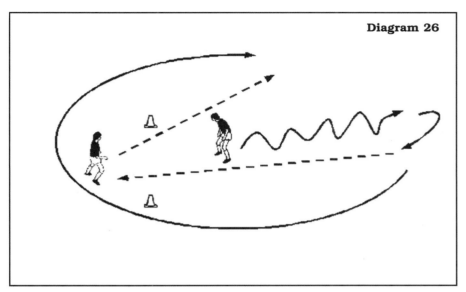

Diagram 26

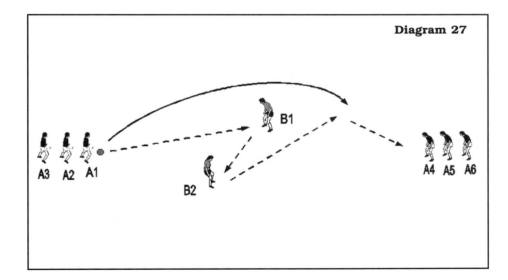

Diagram 27

The players again split into two groups.

A1 passes firmly to B1 then makes an overlap run around B1.

B1 'stuns' the pass with one touch to B2.

B2 passes with his first touch into the path of running A1.

A1 passes with one touch if possible to A4.

A4 takes a controlling touch and continues the drill by passing to B2.

Everyone takes turns at B1 and B2's position.

Editors note: I noticed that, with the exception of some Coerver type skills done as a warm-up, the practice focused mainly on three different areas; quality of the pass including the weight of the pass, a good first touch especially the ability to control the ball with an open body position, and, movement off the ball. The coaches also confirmed that they regularly spent time on 'finishing in the final third of the field' during practices.

Practice ended with a 25-minute scrimmage of 8 v 8 in a 50 x 35 yard area.

D.C. United

A pre-season practice observed at Myrtle Beach, February 1999.

Warm-Up
A five-minute light jog followed by 10 minutes of stretching.

Sprints
Cones are set up 15 yards apart as shown in diagram 28. The players line up in pairs at the starting position, A, and complete the circuit five times.

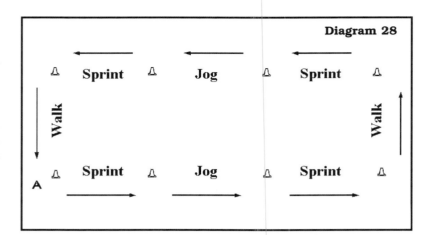

Diagram 28

Diagram 29

Keep-Away
The players then split into groups of five or six and played one-touch keep-away in a relatively small circle about six yards in diameter. Defender changes position with the player responsible for losing possession.

Progression
Keep-away by juggling the ball in the air. Players are limited to a maximum of three touches before they have to pass. The defender must steal the ball in the air.

5 v 5 + 1 Keep-Away
Split into three teams of five and mark the field as shown in diagram 30. One team positions themselves on the perimeter, the other two teams of five play keep-away. The team in possession uses the neutral player and the perimeter players. Both goalkeepers also play for the team in possession.

Games last for three minutes then the teams rotate, therefore each team plays the other two teams and takes a turn as the perimeter team.

First series of games
The field players have unlimited touches, the goalkeepers and neutral player are limited to two touches and the perimeter players are limited to one touch.

Second series of games
The field players are limited to two touches. Goalkeepers, neutral player and perimeter players are limited to one touch.

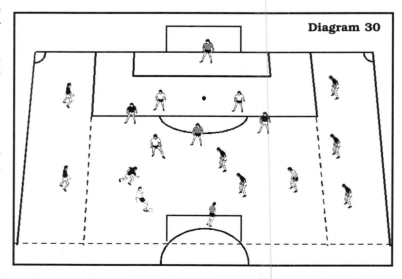

Diagram 30

5 v 5 + 1 To Goal

The same organization as the previous game except the objective is now to play directional and score goals. Also, there are now six perimeter players who are positioned as shown in diagram 31. The perimeter players behind the goal-line are limited to one touch, the neutral players and the perimeter players on the side-lines are limited to two touches. The field players have unlimited touches.

Play to a maximum of three minutes or until one team scores. The winning team stays on.

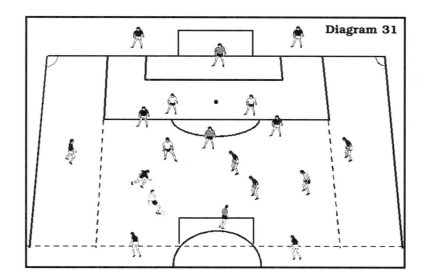

Diagram 31

As the field players were doing their fitness and technique work, the three goalkeepers worked with the goalkeeper coach doing their own goalkeeper related conditioning drills.

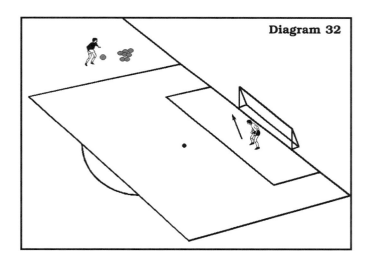

Diagram 32

Goalkeeper Conditioning

The coach positioned himself outside the penalty box with a supply of balls as shown in diagram 32. The goalkeeper starts off in the middle of his goal. He then moves to touch the post nearest the coach. As he touches the post, the coach throws the ball over the goalkeeper's head to the far post. The goalkeeper backpedals to make the save, throws the ball back to the coach then moves to the front post again to continue the drill.

Drill is for 40 seconds then rotate in the other two goalkeepers. Therefore, one part work – two parts rest. Do two sets for each goalkeeper.

Goalkeeper Conditioning

The coach positions himself with a supply of balls as shown in diagram 33. The goalkeeper starts on his goal-line, sprints out and dives at the feet of the coach who plays a short pass to the diving goalkeeper. The goalkeeper gets up and sprints to touch the goalpost then turns and sprints to the coach to continue the drill.

Do three times then rotate the other two goalkeepers in. Therefore, one part work – two parts rest. Do two sets for each goalkeeper.

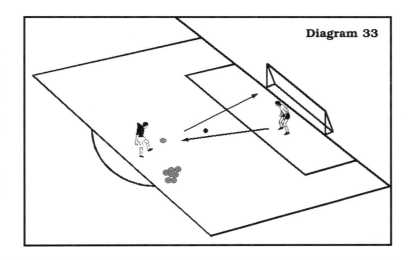

Diagram 33

Snickers National Champions

David 'Chaddy' Chadwick is the technical director of the AFC Lightning Club as well as the coach of the U18 boys Atlanta Lightning, the 1998 Snickers USYSA National Champions. Chaddy had played professionally in England for 15 years before arriving in America to play in the NASL. After three years with the Dallas Tornado and one year as player/coach with Ft. Lauderdale, Chaddy then moved full time into coaching with the Atlanta Chiefs and the Minnesota Strikers until the league folded in 1984. He then returned to Atlanta and has been involved with the GSSA for 14 years as a Staff Coach and USSF National Staff Coach. He has a USSF 'A' license and English F.A. Full Badge. Chaddy shares with us one of his favorite practices, taking into consideration the limitations usually imposed on the youth team coach.

Dog Owns the Yard

This practice is one we use a lot at AFC Lightning. It was handed down to me by our former Director of Coaching, Phil Neddo. I like it because it is a good 'economical training session'. Limited field space under lights means that we can only practice two nights per week and only for about an hour on the actual soccer field. This means I have to get the most out of each hour. Therefore I am a big believer in 'Economical Training' where I include technique training, tactical training and fitness training in a game related situation which is rewarding and fun for young players.

Seventeen players is the ideal number for 'Dog Owns The Yard' (15 field players and two goalkeepers). The goalkeepers stay in goal at all times, although I encourage them to take shooting opportunities if they arise and become an extra attacker. (With the new rules for goalkeepers I think it is good for them to use their feet as much as possible.) The 15 players are then divided into three teams of five. I try to pick the teams so that the players are playing in the positions that they play in games, i.e. sweeper, marking back, etc.

The field is 40 x 20 yards with full size goals. Two teams play each other. The team that is not playing is under the direction of an assistant coach and does some type of fitness training which is discussed before practice begins. This could be progressive laps around the field, some type of local muscle endurance exercises with the ball, speed training, etc. The two teams playing play either for a predetermined amount of time, between two to six minutes, or the first goal wins the game. I usually prefer a time limit. At the end of the game, the winning team stays on – hence the name of the game, 'Dog Owns The Yard'. The teams

keep score and at the end of practice the winning team is awarded Snicker Bars or Powerade drinks for being the 'dog who owned the yard'.

I try not to do too much coaching within the framework of the practice but I want the game to be intense and as game realistic as possible. I have found that this practice builds many qualities for the players.

If played at the right pace, the game can and will include a lot of decision making, passing, shooting, tackling, defending, movement off the ball, closing down attackers, getting back or forward to help their team mates, etc. These are all aspects that are found in every game of soccer and the players learn how to figure things out for themselves.

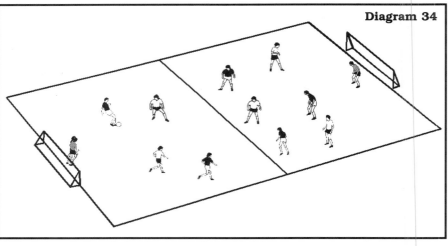

Diagram 34

Sometimes I will stop the game and bring in all three teams to get across a coaching point. However, the idea is the 'game is the teacher' and the success of the practice will rely on the players making the right decisions most of the time.

I occasionally condition the game. For example, if I want them to make quicker decisions under pressure, I have them play two-touch. When looking for movement, I condition the game so if they don't move after passing the ball, they have to do six push-ups on the spot.

I remember seeing the great German coach, Helmut Schoen at a coaches clinic for NASL coaches in 1978. He said the game was always about 2 v 1. When your team has the ball always try to get a 2 v 1 situation against the defender. When you lose the ball try to get a 2 v 1 situation against your attacker. Simple but very true.

F.C. Petrolul Ploiesti - Romania

F.C. Petrolul Ploiesti plays in Division One of the Romanian Football League. In previous issues, they have shared with WORLD CLASS COACHING practices for involving the outside defenders in attack and 'double team' defending. In this article, coaches Constantin Moldoveanu and John Eparu share some of their attacking combinations for midfielders and forwards.

Attacking Combination – One

A dribbles then passes firmly to B. B returns the pass then makes an angled run into the goalbox. A receives the pass from B, dribbles and passes to incoming C. C returns the pass and makes a run toward the corner. A receives the pass and plays it back one-touch to the corner for running C then runs into the goalbox. C dribbles to the end line and crosses for incoming A or B to finish.

Progression

Add 2 or 3 defenders who try to intercept the passes.

Coaching Points

- Player A should make angled runs to receive the return passes from B and C.
- The triangle passing combinations should be explosive like a give-and-go.

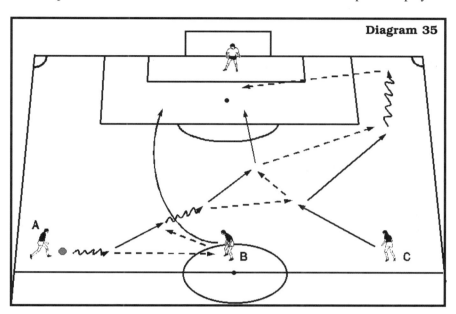

Attacking Combination – Two

A passes to incoming B then makes an angled run into the goalbox. B plays a one-touch pass to C then makes a run toward the corner. C plays the ball one-touch to incoming D then turns and runs into the goalbox. D turns with the ball giving time for B to make his run, then passes in the corner for running B.

B has the option of cutting the ball back for incoming C or crossing to the far post for A.

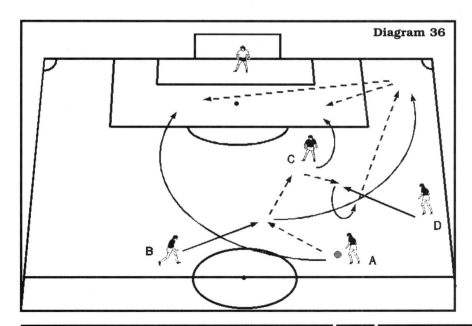

Coaching Points

- Players B, C and D always step away before checking back to receive the ball.
- Players should be moving all the time while maintaining proper distances between themselves.

F.C. Petrolul Ploiesti - Romania

Attacking Combination – Three

The ball is passed to the outside midfielder, A. A steps away then checks back to receive the ball, controls with an open body position and sends a firm pass to an inside midfielder, B. B controls with an open body position and passes into the path of running C, then runs into the goalbox. After making his pass, A makes a timed run into the goalbox. He should time his run so that he is close to C when C receives the ball in case C is under pressure and needs an outlet of a trail pass. C dribbles the ball toward the end-line and crosses into the goalbox. There are many different options when crossing into the goalbox. In this example, B knocks the ball down with one touch for incoming A to shoot.

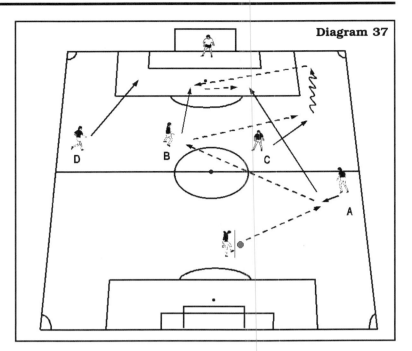

Diagram 37

Chicago Fire - Goalkeeping

The following conditioning drills were observed in February 1999 at Myrtle Beach during pre-season training. The goalkeeper coach worked with two goalkeepers therefore the conditioning element was one part work, one part rest.

The goalkeeper starts on his goal-line. The server plays in a high cross for the goalkeeper to collect. After he collects the cross, the goalkeeper throws the ball back to the server and then sprints to the goalpost nearest the coach and dives to his left as if he was saving a shot at the post. The goalkeeper then gets up right away and the coach half-volley's a shot to make the goalkeeper dive to his right to make the save. After the save, the goalkeeper dives to his left again, gets up and dives to his right to save another half volley shot from the coach. The goalkeeper saves five shots from the coach then continues the drill by starting on his goal-line and collecting a cross again.

After collecting this cross, the goalkeeper again sprints to the post near the coach but this time dives to his right first then the coach half volley's a shot to his left side. As before, do five shots.

The same was done for the second goalkeeper then the drill was repeated with the server at the opposite side of the field and the coach at the opposite goalpost.

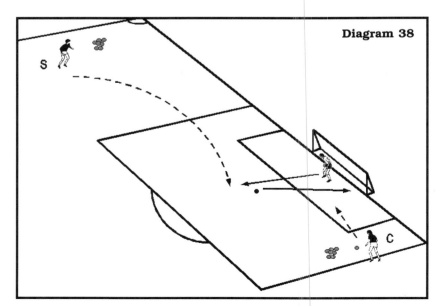

Diagram 38

The goalkeeper starts on his goal-line. The server plays in a high cross for the goalkeeper to collect. After he collects the cross the goalkeeper throws the ball back to the server and the coach throws a high ball for the goalkeeper to jump and save, then a low ball left, then right and then a waist-high ball left, then right. The goalkeeper goes back to his goal-line and repeats the drill.

Rotate the second goalkeeper in and then repeat with crosses from the other side of the field.

Coaching Point

The coach must serve the balls high and wide to make the goalkeeper stretch and dive to make the saves.

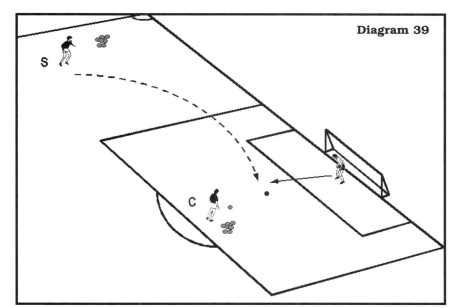

Diagram 39

July/August 1999 Issue

153

University of Florida

Contributed by Becky Burleigh, University of Florida women's soccer coach.

In just four seasons at the helm of the University of Florida women's soccer team, Becky Burleigh has taken UF from a start-up program in 1995 to the NCAA National Champions in 1998. Prior to taking the reigns at UF, Burleigh coached the Berry (Ga.) College Lady Fury for five seasons (1989 – 93) where she compiled a 82-23-6 record and won two NAIA National Championships in 1990 and 1993

Warm-Up – Gaelic Football

Play 6 v 6 on a half field with two goals as shown in diagram 1. Field size can vary with number of players. The object of the game is to score a goal by punting or drop-kicking the soccer ball from your hands into the goal.

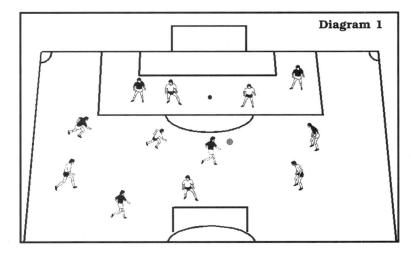

Diagram 1

Rules

1. With ball in hands, can only take three steps in any direction
2. Can pass the ball with a kick from the hands or a 'bump' with the hands (like volleyball)
3. Ball can bounce only once on any pass. If it bounces more than once, it is considered on the ground and it must be played with feet like regular soccer
4. To get the ball back into the hands to score – chip, scoop the ball, etc. to a teammate or to yourself (you cannot use hands to pick the ball off the ground)
5. Anything goes in defending – except full body tackling
6. No positions or goalkeepers – anyone can save a shot on goal
7. Play to a time limit or number of goals

Coaching Points

- Move the ball quickly
- Mix up short/long passes
- Work off the ball

3 v 3 v 3 Keep-Away

Three teams of three in different colored vests. In diagram 2, the dark and the gray team combine to play keep-away from the white team. The team that loses possession to the white team then plays defense against the other two teams. The playing area depends on the number of players and ability level.

Coaching Points

- Good shape by players in possession – how to receive the ball
- Try to split the defenders with passes if possible
- When to pass one-touch or use multiple touches
- Take advantage of disorganized defense

To utilize more players, have teams alternate in or play 4 v 4 v 4, etc.

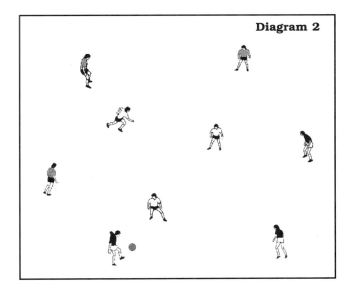

Diagram 2

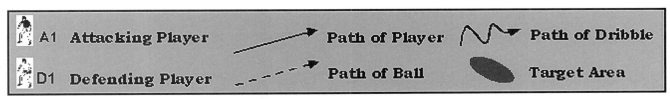

Small-Sided Game

Play 4 v 4 inside the penalty box with small goals or cones set up at each end as shown in diagram 3. One player for the defending team (A), kneels down and stays out of the play. Therefore, it is always 4 v 3 in favor of the team in possession.

Coaching Points

- Short support
- Open body position to receive passes
- Movement off the ball
- Depth of target player
- Target player must move to the ball to receive the pass
- Once the ball is played to the target player, others must support short and quickly
- Three man combinations
- Transition to offense

If utilizing more players, the other teams alternate in.

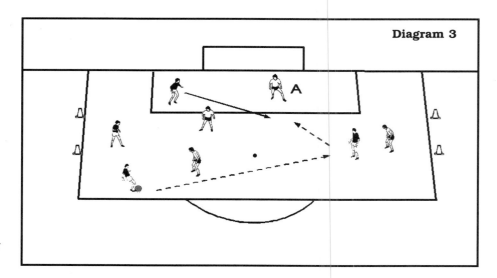

Diagram 3

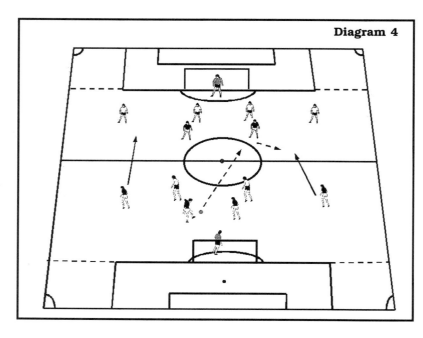

Diagram 4

Full-Field Game

Initially, position the goals on the top of each penalty box as shown in diagram 4. Play 6 v 6 with goalkeepers. The teams are organized with four defenders and two forwards. As in the previous game (diagram 3), the defenders in possession look to pass to a forward's feet. As the forward receives the ball, the defenders then support for a trail pass and they attempt to combine for a shooting opportunity.

Coaching Points

- Commit one defender forward on each attacking opportunity
- The forward must check back to the ball to receive the pass
- Passing combinations with defenders
- Use width and depth

Progression

Use the full field and add 4 v 4 in midfield.

Manchester United

Contributed by WORLD CLASS COACHING subscriber, Harry Oei. Harry previously coached with the girls program at Hoover High School and is now associated with various club teams in the LA area. In March Harry traveled with a group of the Manchester United Supporters Club to watch them play in Italy against Inter Milan in the quarterfinals of the European Champions League. Following that game the group returned to Manchester to watch them play against Everton in a Premier League game. In the days leading up to the Everton game, Harry and the group were fortunate enough to watch the team train at the famous Cliff Road Training Ground. Below is a session observed with just the defenders. The forwards were working on finishing drills in the other half of the field.

Warm-Up

After 10-15 minutes of jogging and stretching, the ten defenders are organized in pairs in the corner of the field as shown in diagram 5. The five white players dribble the ball at the same time about 25 yards across the field. The dark players retreat in a 'jockeying' position as the white players advance. After dribbling 25 yards, the white players then turn and dribble back to the starting position with the dark players following them, this time concentrating on shielding the ball from the dark player. The players then switch positions and the dark players dribble against the whites.

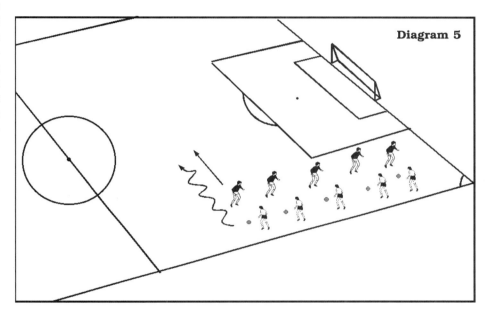

Diagram 5

Coaching Points

- Dribble at 75% pace
- Tight control when dribbling
- Defenders concentrate on technique

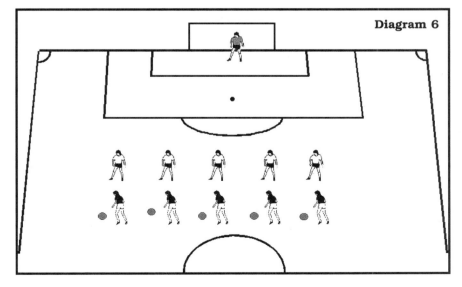

Diagram 6

One v One to Goal

The pairs line up 35 yards from goal with the dark players attacking the goal and the white players defending. This time only one pair goes at a time and a goalkeeper is used. When all five pairs have taken a turn the players switch roles and the white players attack against the dark players. Three rounds were done and the score was kept to keep the drill competitive.

Coaching Points

- When attacking, go at full speed
- Encourage defenders to feel comfortable taking on the forwards.

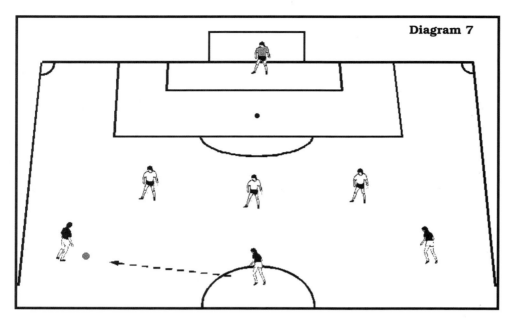

Diagram 7

Zonal Defending

The drill in diagram 7 is three forwards against three defenders. The forwards start with the ball on the half-line and attack the three defenders down the flanks or through the middle looking to create scoring opportunities. The teams switch after several minutes.

Three defenders are used instead of four as this makes it easier for the defenders to coordinate with each other during the initial stages of the practice.

Zonal Defending – Progression

In diagram 8, all ten defenders are utilized in a 5 v 5 drill. An extra defender is added to create a flat back four and a defensive midfielder is added to put pressure on the attacking team. For the attacking team, two forwards are added to put pressure on the center defenders.

The drill is played the same as in diagram 7 with the attacking team looking to combine to create scoring opportunities and the defending team working as a unit to stop them. Each time the defenders win

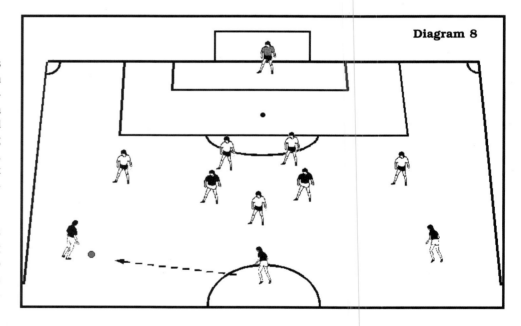

Diagram 8

the ball, the forwards start again from the half-line. The players switch positions after 10 minutes.

Coaching Points

- The drills in diagram 7 and 8 help the defenders become comfortable with each other and practices timing when to push out for offside and when and where to provide balance and cover, etc. The drill also provides the coach with the opportunity to work with the defenders in a game-realistic situation.

- For the final 15 minutes of the training session the forwards who were practicing shooting and finishing in the other half of the field, joined the defenders and played one v one as in diagram 6. The forwards played at full speed.

F.C. Onesti - Romania

F.C. Onesti plays in Division One in the Romanian Football League. Coach Teodor Stet shares a training session used to improve the passing game and finishing of midfielders in even numbers and numerical superiority.

3 v 3 v 3

In a 70 x 50-yard area, organize two goalkeepers and three teams of three. To start the drill, the goalkeeper passes to the dark team who passes to any of the gray midfielders. Once in possession the gray team attacks the goal defended by the white team. If they score, they keep the ball and attack in the other direction against the dark team. If the gray team doesn't score, then they change places with the white team and the white team then attacks the dark team. The drill then continues in the other direction.

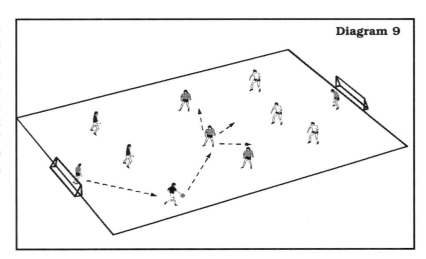

Diagram 9

Coaching Points

* Emphasize the quality of passing
* Two touches only
* Finish with one or two touch

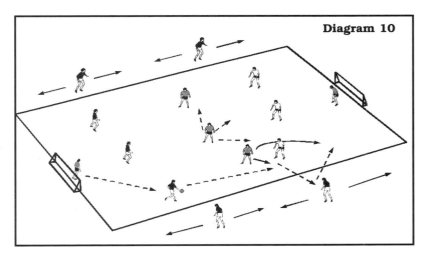

Diagram 10

Progression

Add two perimeter players on each flank. These players are limited to one or two touch. If possible, the attacking players should look to use the perimeter players for give-and-go's as shown in diagram 10.

Numerical Superiority

On a full field, organize two defenders in each half and four midfielders that attack in both directions. The drill starts with the goalkeeper distributing to a defender who passes to a midfielder. The midfielder then combines with the other three midfielders to create a scoring opportunity against the two defenders at the other end of the field. The drill then continues in the other direction.

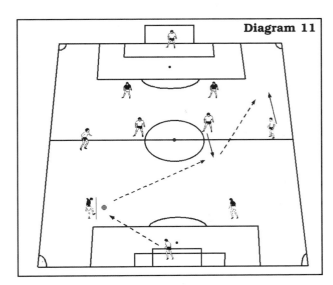

Diagram 11

Coaching Points

* Check in to receive the pass
* Use fakes and feints before shooting
* Place the shot on goal
* Use conditions such as two-touch, scoring from outside the penalty area, scoring from crosses, etc. to stress the parts of the game you would like to work on.

F.C. Onesti - Romania

Progression

This time in each half there are three defenders and two forwards. There are three midfielders instead of four. This creates a 5 v 3 situation for each attack.

Coaching Points

- Firm passes to the feet of the two forwards.
- Forwards should keep the ball close to their feet once they enter the box
- Look for through passes to the target players
- Keep heads up constantly
- Look to execute fake runs
- Fake in different direction before shooting
- Crosses to near and far post

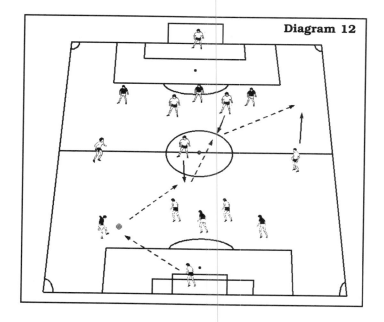

Diagram 12

ProZone Body Management System

In January while I was in England I caught a news feature on 'Sky Sports', the main satellite TV channel for watching the English Premier League and other soccer action. The topic of the feature was a new 'Training Preparation and Injury Prevention Room' that was recently installed at Premier League club, Derby County. It got my attention because of its high-tech nature and the remarkable claims of Derby County's coaching staff of fewer injuries, increased fitness and better communication during team meetings. Judge for yourself. Is this the way of the future for soccer and other sports?

The ProZone Body Management Center is a purpose built building that is basically a 'preparation chamber' for the team's players. It resembles a space-age cinema with individual seats resembling dentist chairs facing a large screen.

When operated, the chairs use sound waves that stimulate the responses/resonance frequency of the muscular and skeletal cells. This enables increased interstitial fluid flow, thus increasing muscular flexibility and relaxing tight and tense muscles. During warm-downs, after extensive exercise or activity, the ProZone chair enables the replacement of lost nutrients, removal of lactic acids and facilitates the removal of unwanted cells whilst increasing interstitial fluid flow; thus assuring consistent muscle tone and removing any risk of post training injuries through tired and unresponsive muscles.

While watching the big video screen, the players listen through individual sets of headphones that are linked to the sound system. Here team meetings are held prior to training while the players are relaxing and their bodies are being prepared for a vigorous training session.
The ProZone Body Management System has been designed and developed with the following in mind:

- Injury Prevention
- Accelerated Recovery from Training/Games
- Enhanced Rehabilitation & Recovery from Injuries

The system also provides state of the art facilities that enable the management and coaching staff to communicate effectively with the players in a formal and conducive training environment. The main purpose of the ProZone Body Management System is to allow the club to select their best players more often by reducing injuries and speeding up the time of rehabilitation from injuries.

Following fifteen years of development in both Europe and the United States, the ProZone Body Management System has been specially designed for professional soccer. The development has also been supplemented by clinical trials at Leeds University. The system thus developed:

- Increases flexibility in order to minimize the risk of strains and minor injuries
- Relaxes muscles and accelerates recovery following training/games in order to prepare for next day activity, resulting in fresher limbs and more alert players
- Accelerates the body's natural healing process by

increasing circulation enabling players to recover quicker from most skeletal injuries
- Targets specific injuries for healing

The aim of the ProZone Body Management System is to assist the body's natural healing mechanism enabling the team to have the players returning to full fitness quicker whilst providing effective preventative care for those non-injured players. The ProZone Body Management System should minimize the need for short term additions to a team due to injury and therefore reduce the club's spending in this area, in addition to the coach/manager being able to select preferred players more often.

The Derby County System

The system comprises of :
1. 22 ProZone Body Management units with a comprehensive array of programs enabling the players to be fully prepared for training and games.
2. The complete system is computer controlled for ease of operation and enables each of the 22 units to be independently programmed to suit the need of the team - collectively or individually.
3. Database to record and keep abreast of all medical treatments and usage of the ProZone BMS and printed reports.
4. The Audio/Video/Computer facility has been designed to enable:
- Reception of terrestrial and satellite TV
- Video recording, play-back (and a professional editing suite if required.)
- Multi-disc CD player piped to each unit with remote headphones
- High quality sound system with radio microphones
- Remote control of the full Audio/Video equipment by the presenter from a lectern at the front of the room
- Projection of all images (data, TV & video) on a large wall mounted screen
- Customized computer-based presentations to cover coaching, training, tactics, team issues, motivational presentations, etc.
- Scanning facility for presentations
5. White board and flip charts
6. Ergonomic work station
7. Full operator training and on-line 24-hour help and inter active maintenance support
8. The ProZone Body Management Center is housed in a supplied purpose-built building

All aspects of the above may be customized to meet the club's exact needs based on squad size. This includes the number of ProZone units needed and the building (which can be installed in 3 days).

Benefits from the ProZone Body Management System can be maximized by following a routine such as:

- Start and finish every training day in the ProZone Center
- Utilize the 12 minutes pre-training program and the 23 minute post-training program to ensure correct body and muscle tonality, a vital cog to sustain fitness and performance on the field
- Customized (by the medical staff) injured-players routines and regimes that target a specific injury allowing the medical staff to concentrate on their special skills
- Optimize time to conduct team meetings in a conducive environment using game analysis and Coaching Library Systems

For further information contact:
Ram Mylvaganam at Ramcms@netcomuk.co.uk

E.C. Vitoria - Brazil

Contributed by Vinicius Dos Santos. Now the Arizona Coaching Director for BRUSA, Dos Santos previously played and coached professionally in Brazil with a number of clubs including E.C. Vitoria and Sao Paulo F.C.

This article is comprised of work, which would be done over three to four training sessions. First we look at ball possession in the defensive half, followed by possession in the attacking half. In particular, we look at the movement and rotation of the players as the ball is switched from one side of the field to the other. These drills are practiced using shadow play without opposition. Many variations are practiced using both flanks. This allows the players to get comfortable with their role in the shape of the team depending on the position of the ball. This is followed by a look at the various triangulation combinations used in the attacking half to penetrate and create scoring opportunities. Finally, we take a look at an example of a goal scored by the Brazilian National Team in a game against Holland.

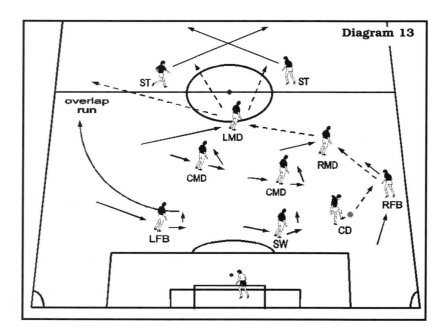

Possession in the Defensive Half

The team is organized into a 4-4-2 formation on a full field. In this example the ball is played from the left to the center defender. Players from the left shift inside to keep the team shape compact for covering and support.

Midfielders Movement

The right midfielder (RMD) moves close to the ball and receives from the right fullback (RFB). He receives the ball with an open body position and looks to switch fields again giving the ball to the left midfielder (LMD) who has moved into a central position. The left midfielder now has many options including playing to the strikers or the overlapping left fullback.

As shown in diagram 14, the center midfielders are in supporting positions which puts the four midfielders in a diamond shape.

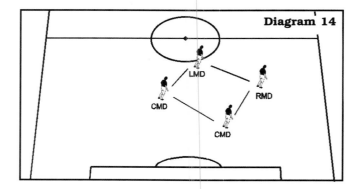

Diagram 15 shows the positioning of the midfielders if the ball comes from the opposite side.

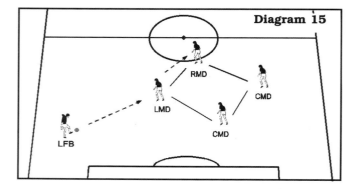

E.C. Vitoria - Brazil

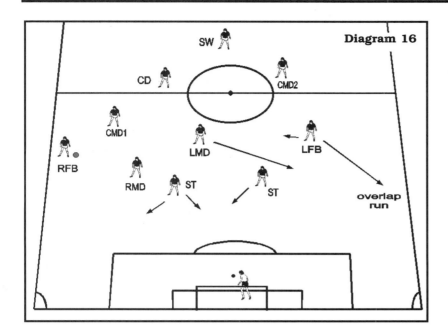

Possession in the Attacking Half

Diagrams 16 and 17 show the movement of players when in possession in the attacking half. Whenever penetration is not possible it is important not to try and force the ball through that area but to switch the ball to the opposite flank by short, quick, diagonal passes and then try and penetrate on that flank. Stress patience and possession but play quickly, not slowly.

Diagram 16 shows the positioning of the players with the ball on the right flank.

As you can see from the movement of players from diagram 16 to 17, the players are fluid in their movement. For instance, as the ball is moved from the right flank to the left, players change from being responsible for supporting the ball to being responsible for marking the opposition's players.

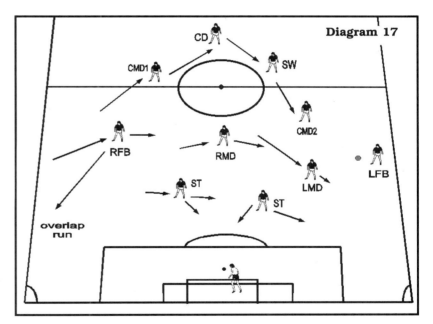

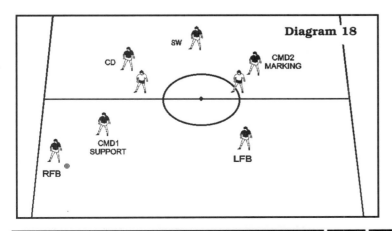

Defender/Midfielder Rotation

Diagrams 18 and 19 are close-ups of diagrams 16 and 17. Here we look at how the players interchange positions depending on the movement of the ball when in possession.

Diagram 18 shows the players positions with the ball on the right flank.

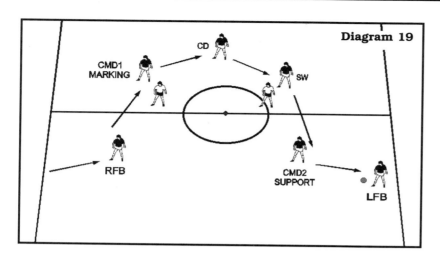

Diagram 19

Defender/Midfielder Rotation – 2

Diagram 19 shows the player movement if the ball is switched to the left flank.

The center midfielder (CMD1) moves from a supporting position to a marking position.

The center defender moves into the sweeper's position.

The sweeper moves to mark the other forward.

The center midfielder (CMD2), who was originally marking the forward, moves to support the left fullback who is in possession of the ball.

Also, the fullbacks slide inside to fill the gap left by the center midfielder who has taken the responsibility of marking the forward. If the ball starts coming back to his flank, the fullback again moves into a wide position.

Once the ball has been switched away from defensive pressure, various passing combinations are practiced, again using shadow play, that are designed to get the ball deep for crossing and shooting opportunities. The following are a number of these combinations.

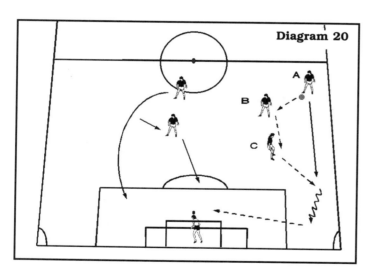

Diagram 20

A passes to B and makes a run down the flank.
B passes to C.
C passes in front of running A.
A takes the ball to the end-line and crosses.

A passes to C and makes a run down the flank.
C lays the ball off with one touch to B.
B passes with one touch into the path of running A.
A takes the ball to the end-line and crosses.

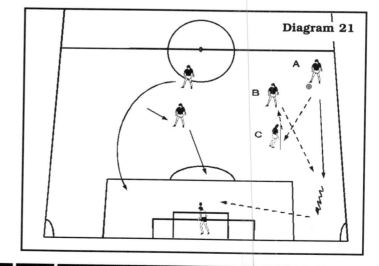

Diagram 21

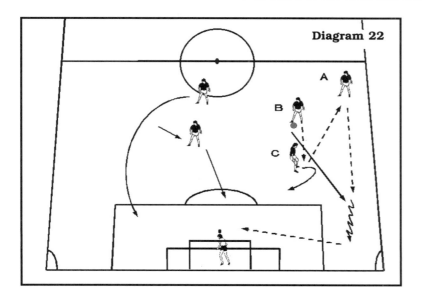

Diagram 22

B passes to C and makes a run into the corner.
C lays off a one-touch pass to A then turns into the penalty area.
A passes down the flank in front of running B.
B takes the ball to the end-line and crosses.

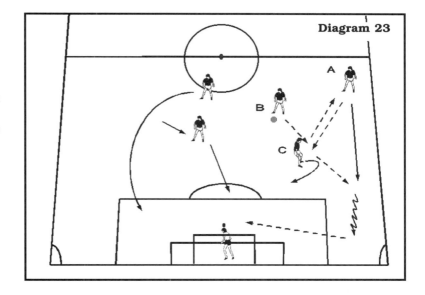

Diagram 23

B passes to C.
C passes to A.
A passes back to C with one touch and makes a run down the flank.
C passes the ball in front of running A then turns into the penalty area.
A takes the ball to the end-line and crosses

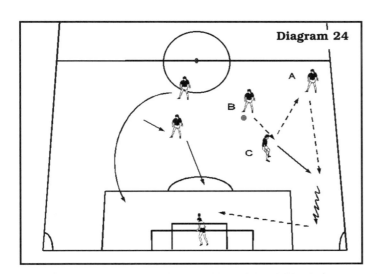

Diagram 24

B passes to C.
C passes to A then makes a run into the corner.
A passes down the flank for running C.
C takes the ball to the end-line and crosses.

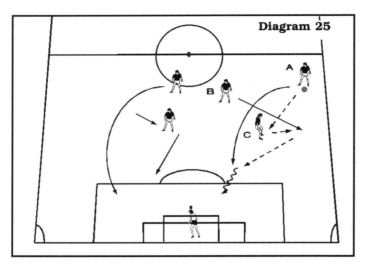

Diagram 25

A passes to C then runs around the inside of him.
C lays off a one touch 'stun pass' for incoming B.
B reverses a pass into the path of running A.
A takes the ball forward and shoots.

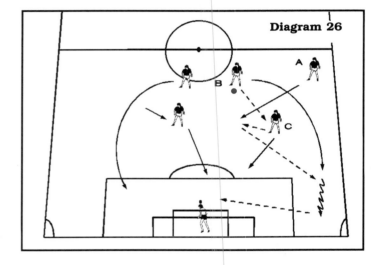

Diagram 26

B passes to C then makes an overlapping run behind C down the flank.
C lays off a 'stun pass' for incoming A.
A reverses a pass into the path of overlapping B.
B takes the ball toward the end-line and crosses.

The following passing combination is from the Holland v Brazil game on August 8, 1996 played in Arena Stadium, Amsterdam. Interestingly, the goalscorer was the center defender, Goncalves, who had made a run from a deep position to enter the penalty area at the far corner and score with a header at the far post.

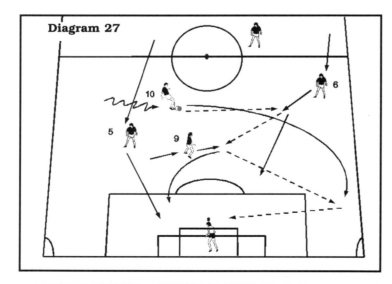

Diagram 27

#6 – Roberto
#9 – Donizete
#10 – Leonardo
#5 – Goncalves

Leonardo brings the ball in from the right side and passes to incoming Roberto.
Leonardo then makes an overlapping run down the left flank.
Roberto passes to the incoming target player/forward, Donizete.
Donizete passes wide to overlapping Leonardo and then makes a run into the goalbox.
Leonardo crosses the ball into the box for the incoming Goncalves to score with a far post header.

Chicago Fire

A complete pre-season practice observed at Myrtle Beach, February 1999.

Warm-Up

After a 15 minute warm-up of jogging and stretching, all 20 players (ten with balls and ten without) were inside a 30 x 30 yard area.

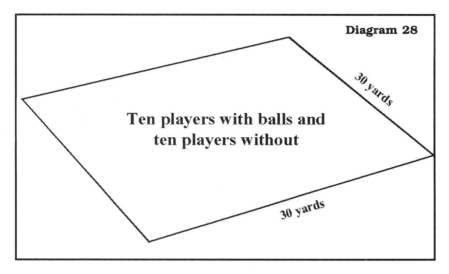

Diagram 28

Ten players with balls and ten players without

1. The players dribble slowly with the ball and pass to a player without the ball. Do for three minutes then stretch for two minutes.

2. Increase the speed of dribble. Do for three minutes then stretch for two minutes.

3. All one touch passing. Do for three minutes then stretch for two minutes.

4. One touch passing – look for short and long passes. Do for three minutes then stretch for two minutes.

Coaching Point

Show for the ball and ask to receive passes.

Conditioned Game

Mark a field as shown in diagram 29 with two 30 yard areas and a 20 yard area in the middle. Use full size goals and goal-keepers. The game is 6 v 6 with two neutral players and four perimeter players that all play for the team in possession. In the 30 yard areas, play 2 v 2. In the middle 20 yard area, play 2 v 2 with the two neutral players playing for the team in possession. The perimeter players are positioned on the flanks as shown.

To start the game, the goalkeeper passes the ball to one of his midfielders or to a flank player. If the ball is passed to a flank player, then he must pass it to one of his midfield players. The two midfield players, along with the two neutral players, have to make at least three passes before they can pass it to one of their forwards. Once the forwards have the ball, they combine with the attacking flank players to create a scoring opportunity. Play for 25 minutes.

Progression

When the ball is passed in to the forwards, the midfielder who passed the ball in can follow his pass and join the forwards to create a 3 v 2 situation in the attacking area.

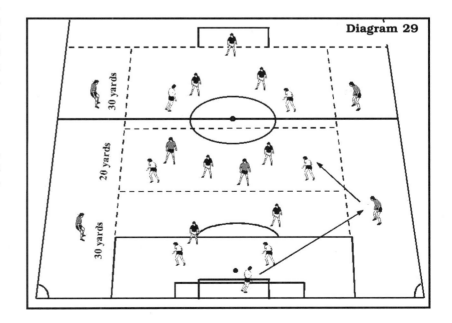

Diagram 29

30 yards
20 yards
30 yards

Conditioned Game

Mark a field as shown in diagram 30. Play 9 v 9 with a perimeter player on each flank. Inside players and perimeter players are all restricted to two-touch.

To make the game competitive, play a series of games. The first team to score two goals wins that game. Then start a new game. Play for 30 minutes. The team that wins the most games is the winning team.

Cool Down

A gentle jog for 5 minutes followed by stretching for 10 – 15 minutes.

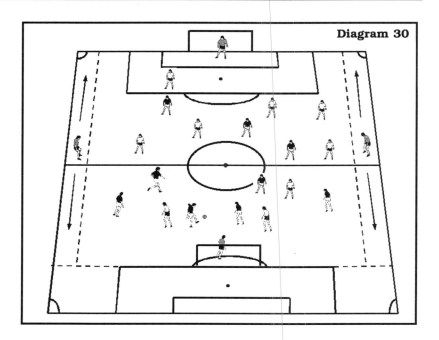

Diagram 30

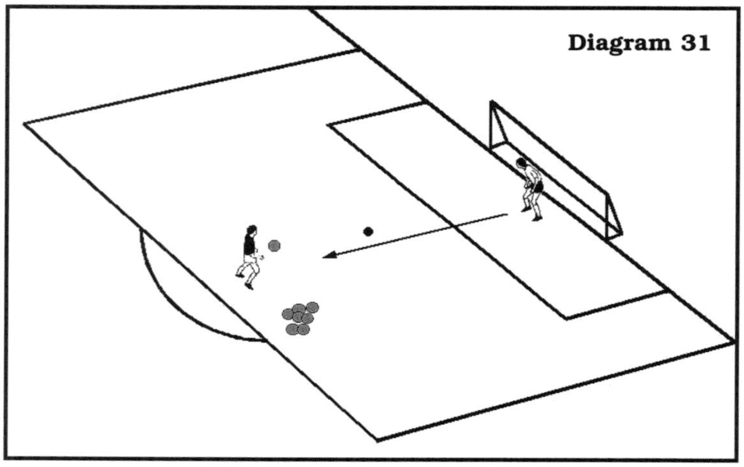

Goalkeeper Conditioning

As the field players do their warm-up, the goalkeepers worked on some conditioning drills. This drill was done after a warm-up of jogging and stretching.

The coach positions himself on the edge of the penalty area. The goalkeeper starts on his goal-line and runs toward the coach. As he approaches, the coach throws a high ball for the goalkeeper to jump and catch. The goalkeeper gives the ball back to the coach and runs back to his goal-line and repeats.

Do three runs from the goal-line, three from the six yard box and three from the penalty spot.

Diagram 31

Newcastle United U17's & 19's

In January I spent time with Newcastle United Youth Team coach, Alan Irvine. Alan played professionally for many years before moving into coaching. Alan coached at Blackburn Rovers before moving to Newcastle United to coach the first team. Alan is now in charge of developing the youth players at Newcastle United. The session below was done over two days and was in preparation for a cup game in which the opposing team sometimes plays with three defenders as opposed to the usual four found in the English game. As a rule, Irvine doesn't organize practices for the youth players to get them ready for a particular game. He feels it is important to concentrate on the longer term development and build training sessions over a period of time to accomplish that goal. The training sessions were focused on switching the ball from flank to flank to try and expose the space that would be available against a three-man defense. The U17's and the U19's trained together for these sessions.

Warm-Up

After 15 minutes of jogging and stretching, the warm-up continues with technical work inside a 20 yard grid. As shown in diagram 32, there are 12 servers with balls around the perimeter and 12 players inside the grid. The players inside the grid move randomly to players outside the grid, receive the ball and pass it back using different techniques. Each technique is done for 45 seconds then the perimeter players switch with the inside players.

Techniques
- One-touch pass
- Two-touch pass
- Headers
- Volleys
- Chest, volley
- Chest, trap, pass
- Thigh, volley
- Experiment with various techniques

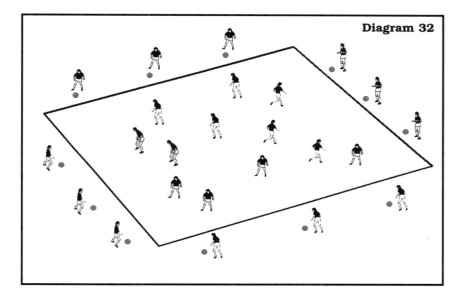

Diagram 32

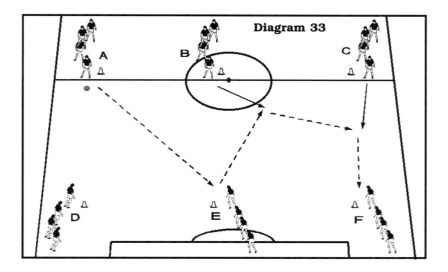

Diagram 33

Unopposed Switching

The players are positioned on the field as shown in diagram 33. The objective of the practice is to get the players to feel comfortable with switching the ball from flank to flank. Different variations are used and practiced.

In this example, the first player in line A passes to line E. Line E passes to line B. Line B passes in the path of the running player from line C who passes to line F. The drill continues with the player in line F passing to line B. The players join the back of the opposite lines after making a pass.

Newcastle United U17's & 19's

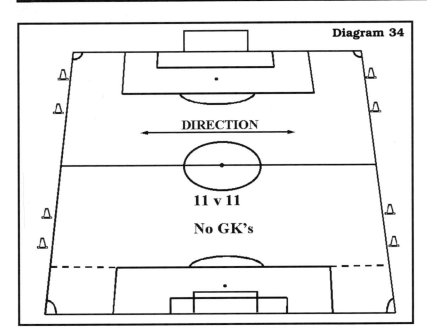

Diagram 34

DIRECTION

11 v 11

No GK's

11 v 11 Switch Game
Practice ended with a game of 11 v 11 on a field marked as shown in diagram 34. Cones are positioned to form two small goals on each sideline. Each team has to defend both of their goals and can score in either of the two goals they are attacking. This arrangement obviously promotes the desired theme of the practice – switching.

At the end of the game the players did a cool down of jogging and stretching.

Vialli Game
The next practice started with the players organized on a half-field as shown in diagram 35. There are two sets of the same drill being done at the same time. Lines A and B play with lines E and F. Lines C and D play with lines G and H. The practice starts with the front player from line E moving forward, showing for the ball and asking for a pass. The first player in line F follows him as a defender. The first player in line B passes to the first player in line A. Player A then passes over the top of player E into his path as he spins. At this point in the practice, player F defends passively. Once player E collects the ball, his objective is to beat player F back to the touch-line. He and player F then join the back of their lines. Players A and B then move into the middle to receive the pass from the next players in lines E and F who step up to the cones. Lines C, D, G and H play at the same time. Play for five minutes then lines A and B swap positions with lines C and D and lines E and F swap with lines G and H. This allows all the players to practice passing with both their left and right feet.

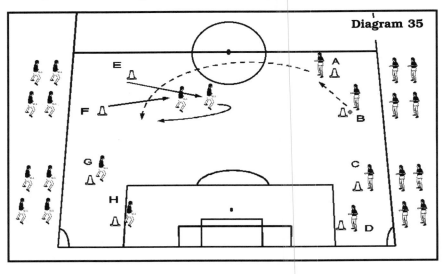

Diagram 35

The drill was set up to practice a 'move' that Gianluca Vialli of Chelsea used against the Newcastle United team in a Premier League game to score a goal earlier in the season. For the goal, Vialli checked forward as if to receive a pass from his teammate. Vialli was tightly marked by a defender. However, as the pass was made, Vialli had spun to receive a long pass instead of the short one he seemed to be asking for, creating the necessary space for him to score a goal.

Of note was the fact that both Vialli and the passer knew that the pass was going to be a long one and not a short one that the defender had expected. To create the same timing and almost telepathic-like thinking between his players, Irvine introduced a 'code word'. Fittingly the code word was 'Vialli'. It worked like this – as the player checked toward the passer he shouted "Vialli" and the passer new he was to play the ball over the top. The next thing to get right was the timing. In the drill in diagram 35, player E, who is coming to receive the pass, shouts 'Vialli" before player A receives the pass from player B. He spins to receive the long pass as player A is about to hit it. By shouting "Vialli" before player A receives the ball, this allows player A to hit the long pass at the exact same time as the player E is spinning to receive it.

Progressions
- The player receiving the pass can either receive it short or long. This keeps the defender on his toes.
- If the pass is played short – combine with the passer to beat the defender.

Half-Field Game
Organize the field as shown in diagram 36 with cones marking out four 5 yard square grids at each corner. The game is 9 v 9 playing from one sideline to the other. Each team places a player in each of the coned grids they are attacking. The objective of the game is to pass the ball to one of your target players in the grid. The player that makes the successful pass changes places with the target player. When the target player receives the ball in the grid he is allowed a 'free' long pass to get the ball back to his defenders. The game continues from there.

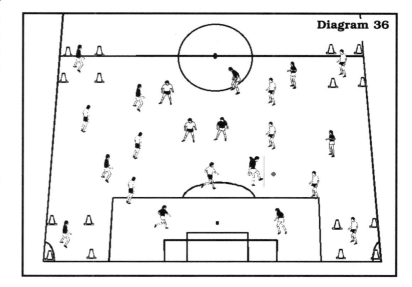

Diagram 36

Coaching Points
- Look to switch and switch quickly
- Look for 'Vialli's'
- Don't force the ball forward and lose possession
- Defend well – close down space and don't allow them time to hit long passes to the target men
- Keep a team shape – play with defenders, midfielders and forwards

Various attacking combinations were practiced that were designed to exploit the space available when the opposition employs a three man defense. The combinations are practiced on both flanks.

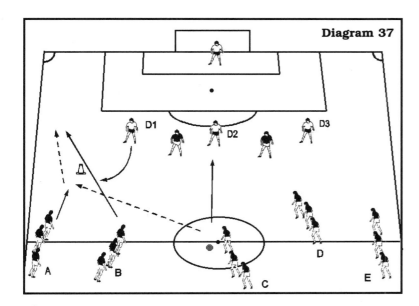

Diagram 37

Attacking Combination – One
C passes wide to A then runs to the edge of the penalty area.
D1 forces A wide.
A passes down the line for B who has made a blind-side run.
D1 chases B and attempts to block the cross.
B crosses into the penalty area for the forwards to finish.

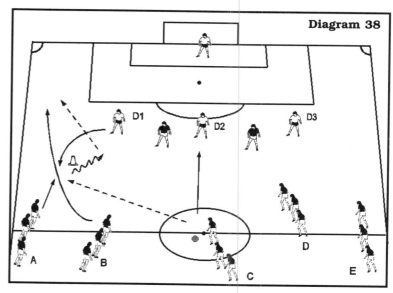

Diagram 38

Attacking Combination – Two

This time the defender forces A inside.

B makes an overlapping run instead of a blind-side run.

As A is forced inside he dribbles then plays a reverse pass down the line for running B.

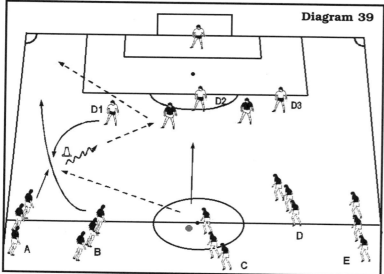

Diagram 39

Attacking Combination – Three

Again D1 forces A inside.

This time, instead of making a reverse pass to overlapping B, A passes to the forward who passes into the corner for B to run on to.

Attacking Combination – Four

If after making his run and receiving the ball, B is not able to cross the ball, he should look to play the ball back to A who is in a supporting position.

If this happens then C should angle his run away from the ball which should make more space for A to attack the goal.

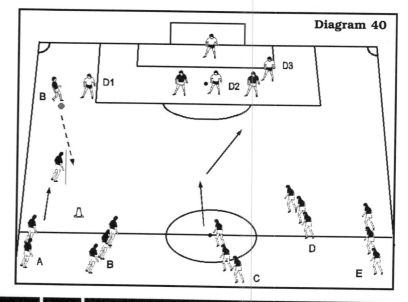

Diagram 40

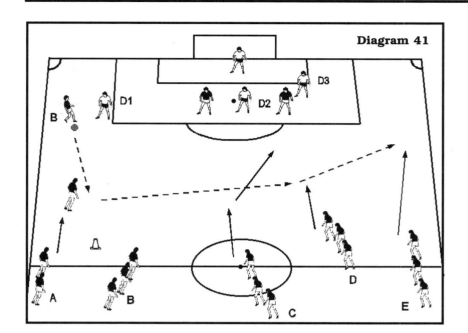

Diagram 41

Attacking Combination – Five

If B plays the ball back to the supporting player A,

A can switch the ball to the other flank using D.

Chicago Fire

A complete pre-season practice observed at Myrtle Beach, February 1999.

Warm-Up

Fifteen minutes of jogging and stretching.

Two-Touch Keep-Away

In a 20 x 20 yard area, play 4 v 4 two-touch keep-away with two neutral players playing for the team in possession. A point is recorded each time a team completes 10 consecutive passes. Play for 15 minutes and keep score.

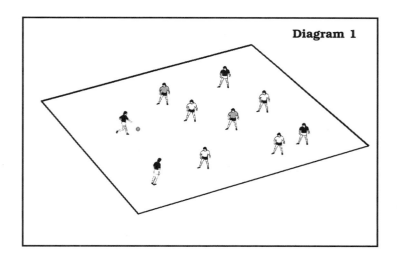

Diagram 1

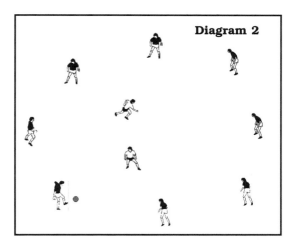

Diagram 2

One-Touch Keep-Away

In a 10 yard area, play one-touch keep-away with eight perimeter players and two defenders in the middle. The player responsible for losing possession changes with the defender responsible for causing the loss of possession.

Small-Sided Game

Play 5 v 5 in a 25 x 35 yard area. Use cones to mark out small goals. No goalkeepers or use of hands. The first team to score two goals wins. Play a series of games for 25 minutes.

Editors Note: After 25 minutes of playing, it came down to one goal to decide the winning team. Both teams showed a tremendous desire to win even though it was just a pre-season practice game. Peter Novak led his team to the final goal which took just over 10 minutes to score.

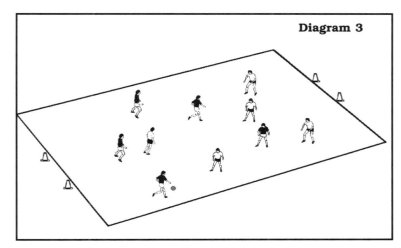

Diagram 3

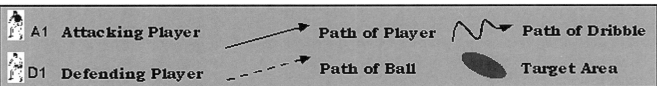

A1 Attacking Player   ⟶ Path of Player   Path of Dribble

D1 Defending Player   ⤏ Path of Ball   Target Area

PSV Eindhoven

Submitted by Dave Clarke, Connecticut Coaching License Coordinator, Coach of Windsor World Class Under 16's and Under 18's and Head Women's Coach, Quinnipiac College.

In April, Dave was extremely fortunate to be able to spend a whole week with PSV Eindhoven and Head Coach Bobby Robson. Below are observations from a day at PSV Eindhoven.

Thursday April 22, 1999
PSV Eindhoven
First Team Squad Practice Session
"De Herdgang" Sports Complex, Eindhoven, Holland

Introduction

PSV Eindhoven started the week in third place, one point behind Vitesse Arnham in the Dutch First Division. Both teams, along with fourth placed Willem II, were seeking to finish second behind champions elect Feyenoord and qualify for next season's UEFA Champions League. A 3 - 3 away draw at Vitesse on Tuesday night (April 20) kept PSV's dream alive, but they now faced a third game in seven days, away to De Graafschap (April 23) and victory was vital if they were to secure the automatic place.

The first team was given Wednesday off and all first team squad players reported for training on Thursday morning at "De Herdgang" (PSV's sports complex).

Twenty players stepped out on to the field at exactly 10:30 am. They were all dressed in the same PSV Nike training gear except for club captain and Belgian international, Luc Nilis. The balls and equipment were already out on the field and the surface was in immaculate condition.

Some players talked to the fans who came to watch the team train. They talked about Tuesday's draw with Vitesse, the upcoming game with De Grafschaap and other general PSV gossip. The players had a smile and a hello for everyone present.

The coaching staff for practice was:

Bobby Robson First Team Coach
Ernie Brandts Assistant Coach

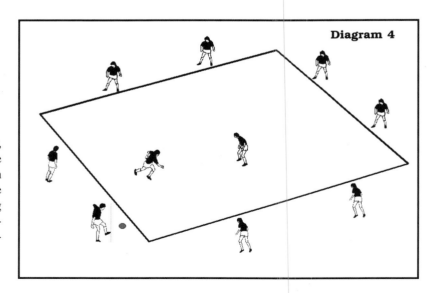

Diagram 4

Warm up (30 minutes)

Bobby Robson called the team together, spoke for a few seconds and then sent the players off to warm up individually, or in small groups. The players did four to five laps each and most did various stretching and loosening exercises. No one was fooling around and the players were all very disciplined in their preparations.

Warm-Up

Two groups of ten players in two 10 x 10 grids played 8 v 2 one-touch keep-away for 10-15 minutes. The two players in the middle only needed to touch the ball to get out. They had to stay in another turn if they were nutmegged with the ball, or if they were split by a pass. The players on the outside could only play one touch and they had to stay on the line to pass and receive. One of the groups varied the game by playing one touch in the air (15 minutes).

PSV Eindhoven

Every PSV team from the U10's to the first team plays this game prior to practice and all seem to enjoy the game. It is their free time within the practice to have fun and express themselves. At first team level it required exceptional technique, quick feet and quickness of thought.

Two groups were divided up into starters and non-starters. Bobby Robson spent 15 minutes watching the non-starters to see who was working hard, to make sure that those players carrying knocks were playing at 100% and to keep an eye on certain players he feels relax when he's not watching.

Small-Sided Game (30 minutes)

In the 18 yard penalty area, two teams (starters v non-starters) played 9 v 9 (diagram 5). The game was free-play with no restrictions. The purpose was to get the ball into a two-yard zone on either end of the penalty area by dribbling or passing to a teammate. Each team defended one zone. Assistant coach Ernie Brandts had a supply of balls to quickly restart the game when needed. Play was always restarted with a throw-in. This game was usually played 11 v 11, but one keeper did some work with Pete Schrijvers and some injured players did a fitness testing session with the team's Sports Physiologist.

Players could not tackle in the end zone to reduce the risk of injury, but tackles were fierce and competitive everywhere else. Not one player wore shin guards which was interesting considering the competitiveness of the game and the importance of the following day's league game to PSV's season. Fortunately, no player got hurt.

The ball was hardly ever out of play for such a crowded area. The ability of the players to pass under extreme pressure and find space where none seemed to exist was tremendous. The game was

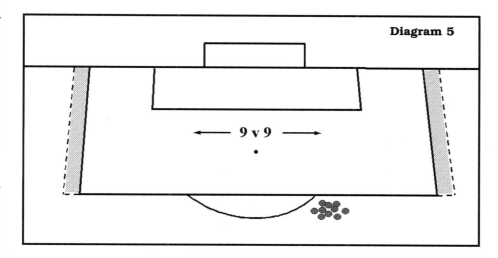

very competitive, everyone wanted to win and all goals were celebrated by the scoring team. When possession was lost, the defending team worked extremely hard to get the ball back. It was a surprisingly tough and tiring game the day before an important league match.

Bobby Robson and Ernie Brandts rarely said anything to the players. They spent most of the session observing them play and making final decisions on the starting line up for the game with De Grafschaap.

After the game, Luc Nilis and Ruud van Nistelrroy (the two starting forwards) worked on individual shooting with one of the goalkeepers. There was no coach with them and they basically had a relaxed, but disciplined session together. They worked on bending balls, half and full volleys, one on ones, heading and finishing low balls. They were very disciplined when they worked together and did not do anything in the practice that they would not probably do a game situation.

Functional Finishing Practice (30 minutes)

The rest of the team worked with Bobby Robson on a half-field functional passing and finishing practice. Players were placed according to the position they played for the team. Nilis and van Nistelrooy were kept out of this practice because Bobby Robson felt that they worked too hard in the finishing games and he wanted the players to conserve their energy for the game with De Graafschap.

PSV Eindhoven

Attacking Combinations

1 has a supply of balls.

1 plays long in the air to 2.

2 controls and plays wide to 3 then continues a forward run into the penalty area.

3 plays down the line for 1.

4 makes an overlapping run around 1.

1 plays the ball to 4.

4 crosses into the penalty area for 5 and 2 to finish. One group worked on the right side of the field while the other group (A players) worked on the left side of the field. Players were rotated to different positions.

Coaching Points

- Players in the group on other side can make late runs into the penalty area
- Players were allowed to decide which player to pass to when they received the ball

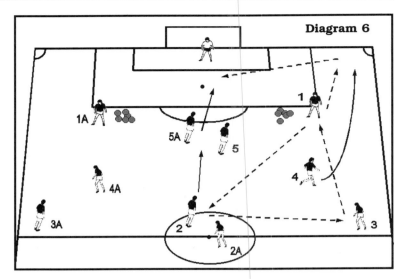

Diagram 6

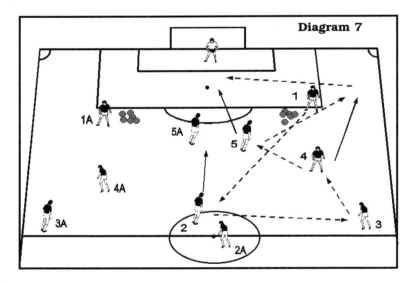

Diagram 7

Variation

1 plays long in the air to 2.

2 controls and plays wide to 3 then continues a forward run into the penalty area.

3 plays to 4.

4 plays a give-and-go with 5.

4 crosses ball into the penalty area for 5 and 2 to finish.

Variation

1 plays long in the air to 2.

2 controls and plays wide to 3 then continues a forward run into the penalty area.

3 plays to 1 then runs down the flank.

1 lays the ball back for 4.

4 plays the ball down the line for 3.

3 crosses into the penalty area for 5 and 2 to finish.

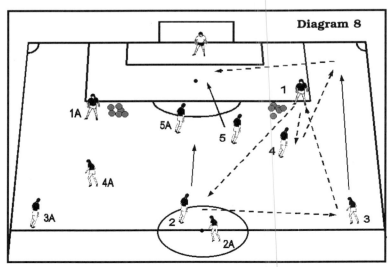

Diagram 8

PSV Eindoven

Variation

1 plays long in the air to 2.
2 controls and plays to 3 then continues a forward run into the penalty area.
3 plays to 4 then runs down the flank.
4 plays to 1 or down the line for 3.
3 crosses into the penalty area for 5 and 2 to finish.

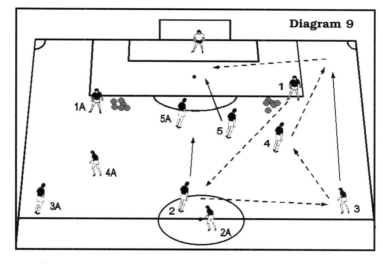

Diagram 9

Observations of this activity

- There was constant movement in the practice and very little standing around.
- The running was done on and off the ball and each execution involved 8 players.
- No defenders were introduced, so the success rate of finishing was high. On another day, defenders would have been introduced to the session.
- The standard of passing, runs off the ball, crossing and finishing was very high.
- Bobby Robson was constantly demanding high standards from his players and he got upset with them if they were not maintained.
- He constantly demanded quality passing, discipline, work rate and quality finishing.

- All shots were followed in by the shooter and the second forward. Rebounds were finished with authority.
- Crosses were varied: driven, bent, near post, far post, flighted, etc.
- Talking was non stop with and without the ball. Players demanded the ball like they were playing in a real game.
- No coaching was done in the session.

Cool Down

Once the practice was finished at noon, Bobby Robson told his players they could go in and shower. There was no team or group cool down and Robson didn't speak to the players to end the practice. Half the players went in while the rest stayed out and did various activities: stretching, extra fitness work, sit ups, and crossing and finishing.

Bobby Robson and I talked for a while together after the practice about the attitude of the players. He said that van Nistelrooy has to be kicked off the field because he will stay out and shoot all day then come game time he will be tired. On this particular day he asked the forward to go inside, but he stayed out and played for a few minutes more. Robson told him to go inside once more and again van Nistelrooy still stayed out. Finally Robson said he would be fined 3000 Gilders if he didn't go in to the dressing room, so the player reluctantly went in. Maybe van Nistelrooy's extra work paid off because the 23 year old was named to the Dutch squad for the upcoming friendly game against Morocco.

The Sports Physiologist continued to work for another 30 minutes with the injured players who were not in contention for playing time in the game against De Grafschaap.

By 12:30 p.m. the whole squad was inside the club house for a team meal which no one other than the playing staff and coaching staff is allowed to attend. Robson said this is a policy that is sacrosanct to the inner workings of the club.

After the team left, Bobby Robson and I had lunch together and we had an in-depth discussion on coaching, coaching education and the game with De Grafschaap.

For an hour after our lunch Mr. Robson dealt with some of the administrative aspects of his job as first team coach of PSV Eindhoven.

- He spoke to a representative of a Portuguese club regarding a scouting report on a player they were interested in signing.
- He returned a call to a foreign player who wanted a trial with PSV.
- He called a soccer reporter to do an interview for Total Sport Magazine.
- He gave an interview to Finnish television regarding Joonas Kolkka, a Finnish national team player at PSV.
- He autographed PSV merchandise for supporters.

Blackburn Rovers F.C.

In January I had the pleasure of spending a day at the Blackburn Rovers training ground in Brockhall Village. As with many of the English Premier League clubs, Blackburn was in the process of building a Soccer Academy on the site which included new fields and an indoor and artificial field as well as dormitories, gymnasium, weight room, classroom, etc. I arrived in the morning and spent the day with coaches Terry Darracott and Ian Miller. The weather was a typical January day, 38 degrees, sun, rain, 25 mph wind and occasional hail.

Morning Session

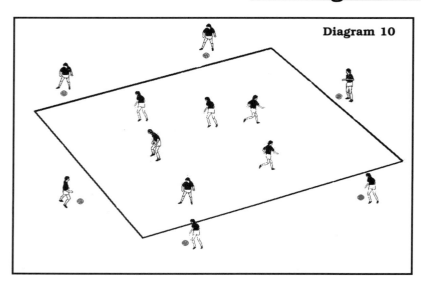

Diagram 10

Warm-Up

The players warmed up and stretched in the gym prior to going outside. Once outside, the 12 players worked in a 15-yard area, positioning six players with balls on the perimeter and six players inside the square. The players inside the grid move to a perimeter player who serves a pass for the inside player to pass back. The inside player then moves to another perimeter player. Various techniques are used such as; volleys, headers, thigh-volley and one-touch passes. Each technique was practiced for 30 seconds then the inside players switched positions with the perimeter players.

Progression

When the inside player returns the pass he runs around the outside of the perimeter player before moving to another perimeter player.

Technique

Using cones, set up three channels about five yards wide and twenty yards long. Position seven players inside the cones as shown in diagram 11. The drill starts with the first player in line (player 1) passing to player 2.

Player 2 receives the ball, turns and passes to player 3 who controls the ball with one touch in the direction of the next channel and passes to player 4.

Player 4 receives the ball, turns and passes to player 5. The drill continues with player 5 passing to player 6 who passes to player 7 who dribbles the ball and joins the end of the line.

When the ball reaches player 5's position, player 8 starts the next pass. Therefore, there could be three

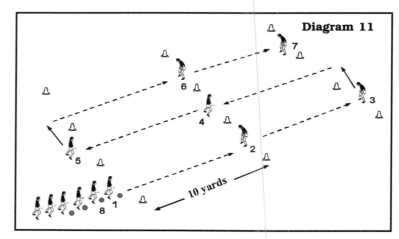

Diagram 11

10 yards

or four balls in circulation at once. After each pass, the players advance a position. For example, player 1 moves to player 2's position, player 2 moves to player 3's position and so on.

Coaching Points

- Firm passes on the ground
- When receiving the pass, the player must 'show' by checking toward the ball
- The middle players must control the ball with an open body position which will allow them to control with one touch and pass with the next touch
- The end players must also control with one touch and pass with the next touch - this makes the players focus on where they should control the ball to enable them to make the next pass
- Try disguising as you control the ball

Blackburn Rovers F.C.

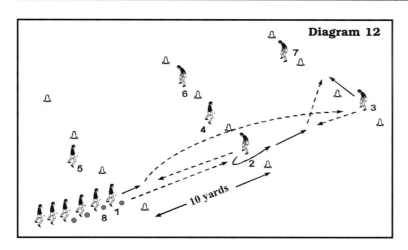

Diagram 12

Progression

This time player 2 passes back with one touch and turns to face player 3.
Player 1 then passes over player 2 to player 3.
Player 3 lays the ball off to player 2 with one touch.
Player 2 passes with one touch into the space in the next channel for player 3 to continue the drill.

Coaching Points

- The set-up pass should be soft
- The quality and pace of the long pass is critical

Variation

Player 1 can either pass to player 2 or directly to player 3.

Small-Sided Game

In a 20 x 20-yard area, play 3 v 3 with six players positioned on the perimeter as shown in diagram 13. The inside players play two-touch, the perimeter players have one touch. Play for two minutes then change.

Coaching Points

- Only pass to perimeter players if you need to
- Show short and long when in possession
- After a pass move quickly to receive the ball back

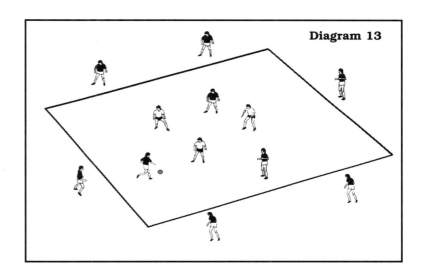

Diagram 13

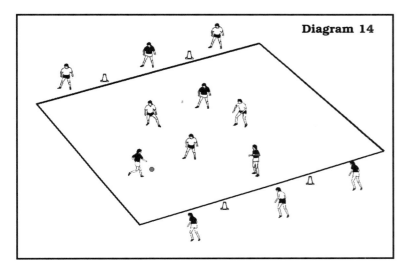

Diagram 14

Progression

Mark two sides of the 20 x 20 yard area into thirds with cones. Split into two teams of six and play 3 v 3 in the middle with the other players positioned on the perimeter between the cones as shown in diagram 14.

As in diagram 13, play two-touch in the middle and one-touch on the perimeter, but you can only pass to the perimeter players that are on your team and the pass must be through his coned area. Play three minutes then change.

Progression

Play unlimited touches for the inside players.

Blackburn Rovers F.C.

Attacking to Goal

In two teams of six, play 3 v 3 in the penalty area with one player from each team at the sides and top of the penalty area. The dark team attacks and the white team defends. The game is started by the ball being passed into the penalty area by a perimeter player. Once inside the penalty area, the dark team attempts to score. The ball can be passed to perimeter players and they cannot be challenged by the other team's perimeter players. The side perimeter players are limited to two-touch and the players at the top of the penalty area are limited to a one-touch shot. After eight attempts, the white team attacks and the dark team defends. Play four rounds of eight attempts with the players alternating positions. Keep score.

Progression

This time both teams attack the goal at the same time.

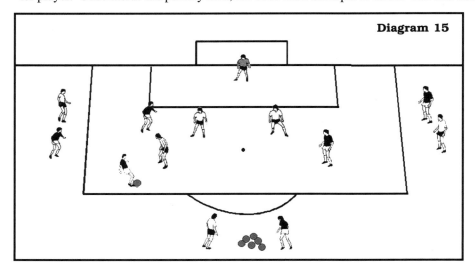

Diagram 15

Afternoon Session

Warm-Up

In pairs 10 yards apart, the players pass back and forth while bouncing on their feet. First, do two-touch passes then one-touch passes. Then player A does one-touch and player B does two-touch passes. Then alternate so that player A does two-touch passes and player B does one-touch passes.

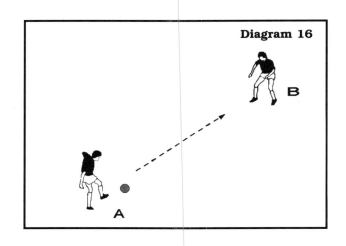

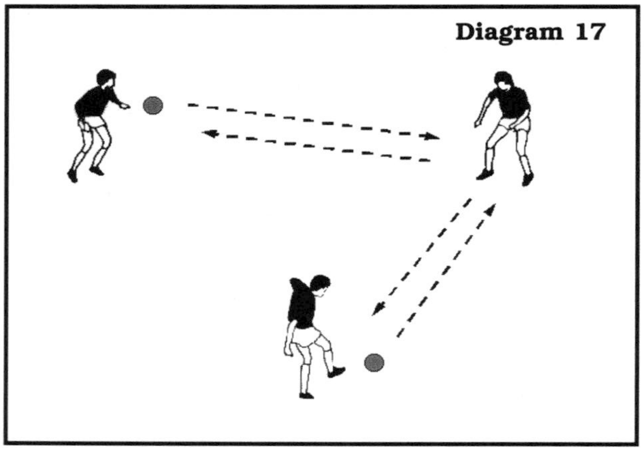

Diagram 16

Warm-Up

In groups of three approximately three yards apart, two players have balls and pass alternatively to the third player who passes back with one touch. One player serves the ball with his hands for the player to volley back, the other player passes on the ground for the player to pass back on the ground. After 30 seconds, the servers alternate from serving in the air to on the ground and vice-versa to give the player a chance to practice with both feet. Then change positions so that each player takes a turn at each position

Diagram 17

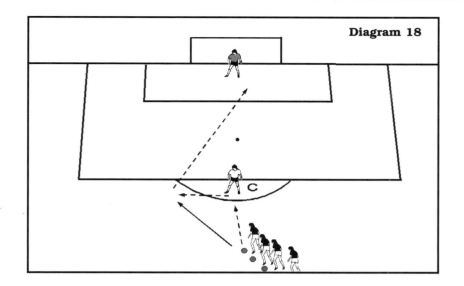

Diagram 18

Shooting

As a warm-up for upcoming shooting drills the players line up 25 yards from goal with a ball, each taking turns to pass the ball to the coach who lays the ball off with one touch for the player to shoot with one touch. The players are told to focus on hitting the target and not on power. If they miss, they have to collect their own ball.

Progression

This time the players line up 30 yards from goal. The players pass the ball to the coach who passes back with one touch. The player then passes down one side of the coach and runs around the other side to shoot with one touch.

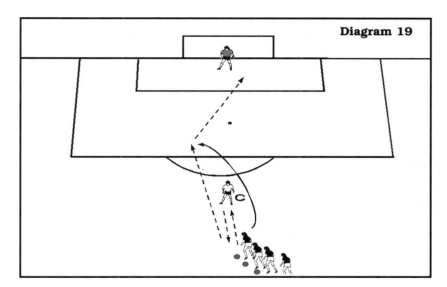

Diagram 19

Diagram 20

Progression

This time, after taking a shot, the player stays and waits for a pass from the next shooter. The next player in line passes to the coach who passes back with one touch. The player then passes to the waiting player (A) who shot before him and plays a give-and-go past the coach and shoots with one touch.

Shooting

Arrange two sets of cones outside the penalty area as shown in diagram 21.
A1 passes to A2 who passes back to A1 with one touch.

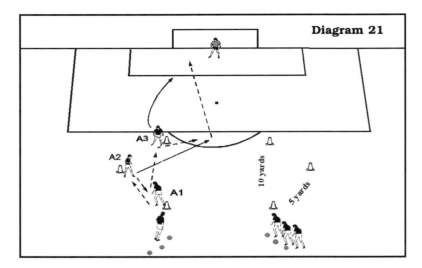

Diagram 21

10 yards

5 yards

A1 then passes with one touch to A3.
A3 lays off a pass for incoming A2 to shoot with one touch.
A3 follows the shot looking for any rebounds.
A1 moves into A2's position. A2 takes A3's position. A3 joins the back of the line. The next player in line moves into A1's position.
Alternate one shot from the left group then one shot from the right group. After 5 minutes, the players change groups so they practice using both feet.

Coaching Points

- All crisp one-touch passes
- Shoot with the nearest foot - don't 'dance' around the ball to use strongest foot

Crossing and Finishing

The players line up in two lines 30 yards from goal with a player on each flank. The ball is passed to one of the players waiting on the flank. The flank player has one touch to prepare then one touch to cross. The front players in line make a crossover run to the near and far posts. Alternate flanks.

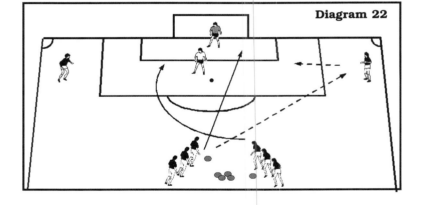

Diagram 22

Coaching Points

- Before the ball is crossed, the defender must choose a player and mark him
- The flank player must look to find the open player and either drive the cross hard to the near post or hit high to the far post
- The near post run must not be in front of the near post
- The far post run must be 5 - 8 yards behind the far post as this makes it difficult for the defender to come that far out to challenge for the header
- Finish in one or two touches
- Time runs into the goalbox so as not to get there too early

Creighton University

The following small-sided games contributed by Doug Fry are used by both the men's and women's programs at Creighton University. They can be used to emphasize both offensive and defensive areas of the game.

Small-Sided Game

Divide the players into teams of four. The format is always 4 v 2. The size of the grid, although rectangular, is dependent on the focus and performance-level of the players and the objective of the coach. The basis of the game/exercise is that each team divides into pairs. A1 and A2 pair while A3 and A4 pair, so do the B's pair--1 and 2, 3 and 4. When A's have possession, one of the B pairs (say B1 and B2) defend their goal (cones about 3 yards apart) while B3 and B4 are passively waiting on the goal-line outside the goal. If the B's win possession, the ball must be passed back to B3 or B4 who now attack A's goal with B1 and B2. During the transition, a pair of A's (A1 and A2) drop back to their goal-line and the other pair, A3 and A4 actively defend. This goes on for about 2 minutes or until a team scores three goals.

The pairs MUST alternate who drops back. If 1 and 2 then next time 3 and 4. You can put in any type of touch restrictions and even allow for the pair that wins possession to quick counter (without passing the ball back to the waiting players). You can also allow for triple value goals if the defending team doesn't drop back before the attacking team scores. You can also allow the defenders to drop off to the sides but only re-enter through their own goal, which would add an element of fitness. There are MANY MANY variations.

Sequence One

The A's have possession and are attacking. The B's are defending with B1 and B2. B3 and B4 have dropped back and are waiting on the goal-line.

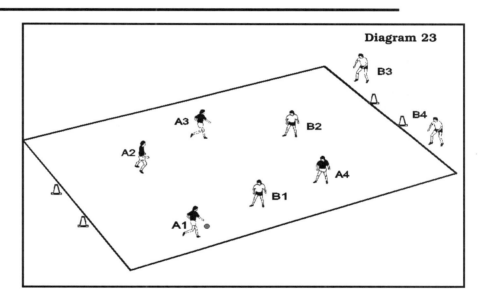

Diagram 23

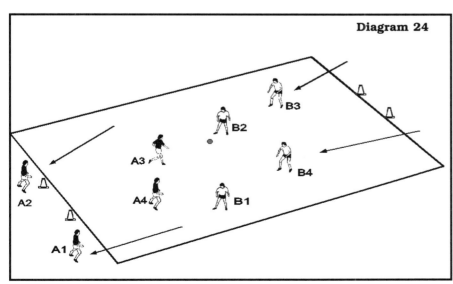

Diagram 24

Sequence Two

After a shot or a loss of possession by the A team, the ball is passed back to either B3 or B4 who bring the ball into play. At the same time, two A players must drop back behind their goal-line. A1 and A2 drop back in diagram 24. This always creates a 4 v 2 situation

D.C. United

A complete pre-season practice with an emphasis on conditioning observed at Myrtle Beach, February 1999.

Warm-Up

Start with a warm-up of jogging and stretching for 20 minutes. Work on various kinds of jogging such as side-to-side, backward, high stepping, etc. Every few minutes stop and stretch the various muscle groups.

Sprints

Mark a 15 yard area and split into two groups. The first group sprints the 15 yards and walks back. As the first group finishes their sprint, the second group starts theirs. As soon as the first group gets back to the starting position, they line up and wait for the coach's signal to sprint again. Continue the sprints for 10 minutes. Use various starting positions such as running on the spot, laying on the ground, facing backwards, etc.

Diagram 25

Pass and Move

For 5 minutes in groups of three, the players pass and move covering the whole area of the field and varying the length of passes.

Keep-Away

Split into two groups of 12 players and play keep-away in a 12-yard area as shown in diagram 25. The player responsible for losing possession changes places with the defender who caused the loss of possession. After 5 minutes, split the 12 players into 6 pairs. Each pair takes a turn in the middle for one minute. Count how many times each pair can steal the ball in the one minute. Keep score to find the winning pair.

Half-Field Ball Conditioning

Split into two groups of 10 players. On one half of the field, stick flag poles in the ground as shown in diagram 26. The first player in line A passes the ball to the end of the flags. He then weaves in and out of the line of flags, catches up with the ball and passes to B.
B passes back with one touch.
A passes to C.
C controls with an open body position and passes to incoming E.
E passes to D with one touch then turns and runs down the line.
D passes down the line for running E.
E crosses for F who finishes with one touch.
All the players advance a position, so A takes B's position, B takes C's position, etc. The drill continues with the next player in line A starting when the ball has been passed by C to E. Do for six minutes, rest for two minutes then change with the group on the other half of the field.

The same drill was being done on the other half of the field with players stepping over flag poles laid on the ground to start the drill.

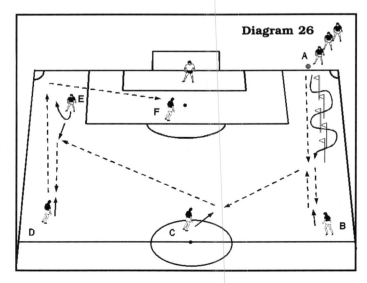

Diagram 26

Wilf Paish - Fitness

Wilf Paish is one of the world's most sought after fitness experts. For over 40 years Wilf has been involved with world class athletes. His resume reads like a who's who of national champions, Olympic medallists and world record holders. As a track and field coach for the Great Britain Olympic Team from 1964 – 1984, Wilf helped produce several Olympic Medallists, world record holders and many international track and field stars. In soccer, Wilf has worked with many English Premier League clubs including Liverpool, Leeds United and Sheffield Wednesday.

Skill will always be the predominant factor when trying to determine how good a player is. However, skill is not the only factor. Players can make up for lack of skill and improve their level of performance, but only to a limited extent, through carefully planned conditioning training.

The trainer/coach MUST prioritize and keep everything in perspective and sequence. Many of the training components have a cross-component effect, i.e. development of strength should help power and thus SPEED. However, qualities such as speed and power regress very quickly hence there must be regular stimulation, at least once a week, throughout the year.

The areas that need careful consideration are speed and the related component of power/strength - speed endurance, skill endurance and strength endurance. ALL MUST BE MADE SPECIFIC TO SOCCER.

SPEED IS WITHOUT DOUBT THE MOST IMPORTANT SINGLE FACTOR TO TRAIN. While it is to a large extent genetic, it can be improved by carefully planned and regular training. It needs three short sessions each week in pre and early season and two sessions each week thereafter. Since it is a component which is sadly affected by lack of the appropriate energy, it must be trained as the first component each day. The plus is that the players will recover very quickly from the training, hence it is possible to follow it with skill or any other training after a short rehydration recovery break. A total speed session should not take longer than 30 minutes even allowing for the recovery necessary to replenish the alactic energy system between bouts of activity.

Below are four typical speed sessions.

Session One

In groups of four working as two pairs, sprint to catch a ball pushed-passed over 15 yards by a partner. A group of four will permit enough recovery. A fifteen minute period broken down into five one-minute sessions with three minutes recovery break between each session. Player's times will improve rapidly when sprinting to catch a ball. In diagram 27, player 1 passes the ball for player 2 to chase. Next, player 3 passes for player 4 to chase. Player 4 continues the drill by passing for player 1 to chase.

Session Two

Handicap 30 yard sprints. In groups of five, the winner is penalized by a one yard handicap which is never redeemed. Do three sets of 5 x 30 yards with two minutes recovery between each 30 yard sprint. Three minutes recovery between each set of five sprints.

Session Three

40 yards...60 yards...80 yards x 3...Three minutes recovery after each sprint followed by five minutes recovery after each set of three sprints. Place in competition and motivate.

Diagram 27

Session Four

Ten x diagonal pitch sprints. Three minutes recovery after each sprint.

Strength Training

Strength...link in with strength endurance. Place in pairs and give 30 seconds activity and 30 seconds recovery. Use a circuit system. Have enough items to permit the use of the group. A group of 20 needs 10 exercise stations. Go arm, trunk, leg rotation. If not enough equipment, use circuit exercises such as sit-ups, etc. to fill out.

This MUST be linked in with power training. That is plyometrics. Any form of hopping and bounding will do. The use of the muscles in an "explosive" way must be encouraged. The jumps decathlon competition, occasionally measured, is good. Medicine ball work on the legs also helps.

Speed Endurance

Must be done at the end of the training day since it promotes general fatigue. Below are four typical sessions.

Session One

Using a standard field, sprint a diagonal, a triangle, a small figure of 8, a large figure of 8 as shown in diagrams 28 - 31. First start with the shortest run - the diagonal, working through all four runs to the longest run - the large figure of 8, then work back to the diagonal run again. Allow three to five minutes recovery time between each run. This is most important work. Players will not like it because it is hard, but so is a long hard game of soccer.

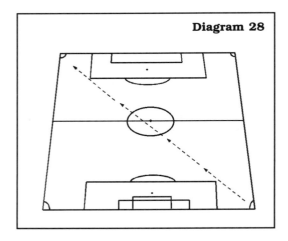

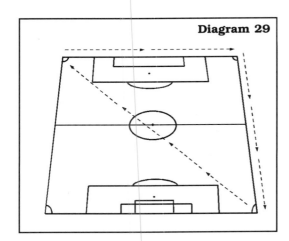

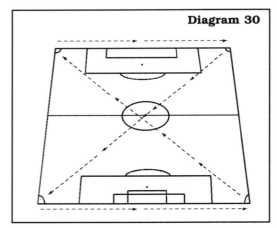

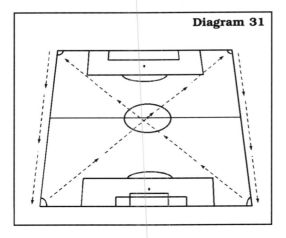

Session Two

Starting from the 125-yard marker, sprint then walk back to recover. Next start from the 150-yard marker, sprint then walk back to recover. Then start from the 175-yard marker, then the 200-yard marker and finish with the last sprint from the 225-yard marker.

Session Three

As in session two but this time start from the longest run, the 225-yard marker, working down to the last sprint being the 125-yard marker.

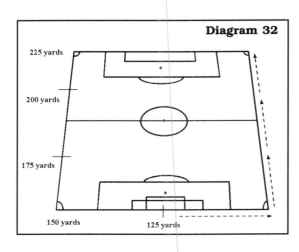

Wilf Paish - Fitness

Session Four

5 x "U" pitch with 8 minutes recovery between each run. Keep all runs under 45 seconds. See diagram 33.

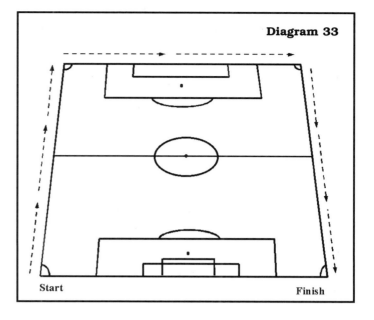

Diagram 33

Start   Finish

Skill Endurance

Use the following three shuttle relays.

Out and Back

Set five cones at 10-yard intervals as shown in diagram 34. Two players, each with a ball, start at A. Player 1 passes his ball and sprints after it to stop it at B. He then turns back and sprints back to A.
Player 2 then passes his ball and sprints after it to stop it at C. He then turns, sprints back to B, passes player 1's ball back to him and continues on back to A.
Player 1 then passes his ball and sprints after it to stop it at D. He then turns, sprints back to C, passes player 2's ball back to him and continues back to A.
The drill continues with player 2 passing his ball to E.

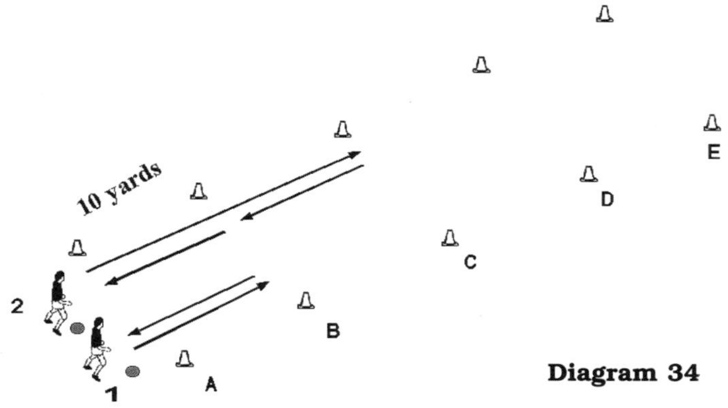

Diagram 34

Petal

The players line up at cone A. Balls are placed at cone A and the center cone X. The first player dribbles the ball to X, changes balls and dribbles around cone B and back to X. Again he changes balls and continues round cone C, back to X, round D, back to X and finally to A always changing balls at X. When he gets back to cone A, he passes the ball to the next player in line.

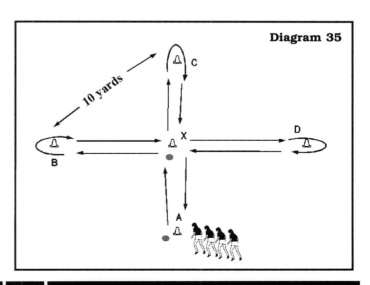

Diagram 35

Wilf Paish - Fitness

Zig Zag

The players line up at cone A. The first player passes the ball to cone B and sprints after it (he should pass the ball at a pace that he can catch up with it at cone B by sprinting 100%). He then passes the ball to cone X and sprints after it. Starting at cone X he dribbles in and out of the line of cones to cone Y and back again to cone X. He then passes the ball to cone C and sprints after it. He then passes the ball to cone D and sprints after it. On reaching cone D, he passes the ball to the next player in line at cone A.

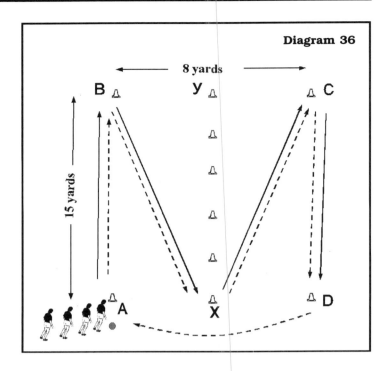

Diagram 36

Weekly Training Schedule

- Day One—Speed work….Normal team session….Strength work in gym
- Day Two—Normal team session….Skill endurance
- Day Three—Normal team session….Speed endurance
- Day Four—Speed work….Normal team session….Power work (plyomentrics/bounding)
- Day Five—Speed work….Normal team session….Strength work in gym

During pre-season, each day can be ended with a 20-30 minute sustained run.

Sunderland F.C.

Sunderland F.C. won promotion from the First Division to the English Premier League last season in convincing style. They finished as clear champions of the First Division losing only three league games from the 46 they played. In January I spent the morning observing the Reserves and the U19 team train.

U19's Warm-Up

All the players move around in a 30 x 30 yard area. Three players start with balls. The players continued to move inside the square passing the balls to each other. The players without balls should look for opportunities to call and ask for passes from the players in possession of the ball.

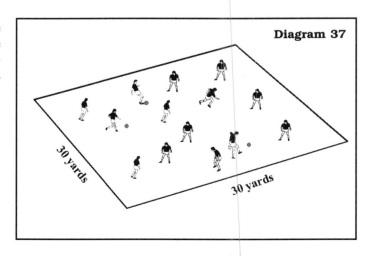

Diagram 37

Receiving Techniques

- Receive with a fake
- Receive with inside of foot
- Receive with outside of foot
- Receive with an open body position
- Receive with outside of foot, shield and turn
- Receive then turn

Sunderland F.C.

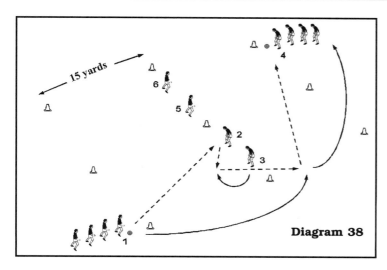

Diagram 38

One-Touch Passing Drill

Player 1 passes to player 2.

Player 2 lays off a 'stun pass' to player 3 who has moved to face player 2.

Player 3 opens his body position when controlling the ball and passes in the path of running player 1.

Player 1 passes across to the first person in the opposite line and joins the back of that line.

Both sides play at the same time, i.e. player 4 passes to player 5 at the same time as player 1 passes to player 2.

All passes are one-touch.

Change players 2 and 3 every few minutes so each player has a turn.

Variation

Place two players at the position of player X in diagram 39. This time, instead of player 3 passing to player 1, he passes to player X.

Player X lays off a 'stun pass' to running player 1.

Player 1 passes to the first person in the opposite line to continue the drill.

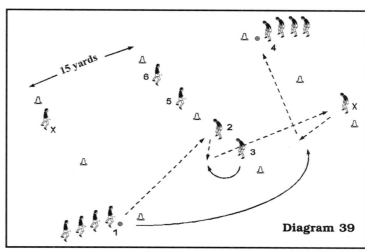

Diagram 39

The players then did 30 minutes of conditioning work following a circuit of different stations including fast footwork drills over cones and flags laid on the ground, short sprints, plyometric jumps and heading a ball hanging from a rope.

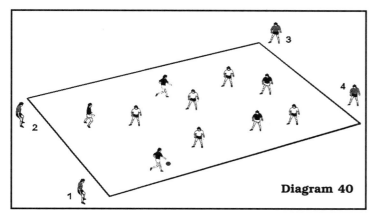

Diagram 40

Small-Sided Games

Practice ended for the U19's with a series of small-sided games in a 40 x 30-yard area. The first game was a simple 7 v 7 keep-away. One point was awarded for five consecutive passes.

The next game was 5 v 5 keep-away with a neutral player placed at each corner of the playing area playing for the team in possession as shown in diagram 40. If the ball was passed to a corner player, he would look to switch the ball to another corner player who would then put the ball back into play. For instance, if the ball was passed to player 3, he would switch it to either player 2 or player 4.

The final game was 7 v 7 directional with each team defending one of the 30-yard lines. To score, the ball needed to be passed over the opposition's end-line to a teammate who would need to have control of the ball.

Sunderland F.C.

The Reserves had a short session, as they were due to play a game the next day.

Two-Touch Passing Drill

In a 20 x 20-yard area, position players at each corner. Start with two balls at opposite corners and pass round the square at the same time using two touches. Follow your pass and join the next line. After a few minutes change the direction of the passes.

Coaching Point

Receive the ball with an open body position to put you in a position to make the next pass.

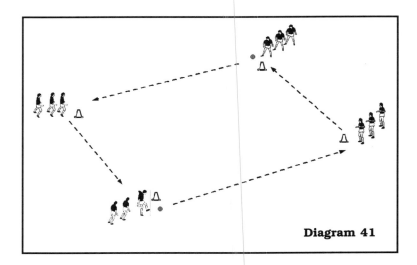

Diagram 41

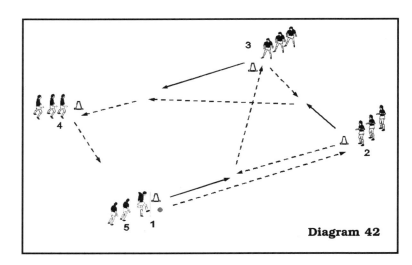

Diagram 42

One-Touch Passing Drill

The same organization as diagram 41.
Player 1 passes to player 2.
Player 2 passes back to incoming player 1.
Player 1 passes to player 3.
Player 3 passes to incoming player 2.
Player 2 passes to running player 3.
Player 3 passes to player 4.
The drill continues with player 4 passing to player 5. All players follow their pass and join the back of the next line.

Coaching Points

• All one-touch passes
• Think about the weight of the passes

Line Passing Drill

Player 1 passes to player 3.
Player 2 steps forward allows the ball to run through his legs and turns to receive a one-touch pass from player 3.
Player 2 passes back with one touch to player 3, turns and joins the back of the opposite line.
Player 3 continues the drill by passing to player 4. Therefore, player 1 steps forward and allows the ball to run through his legs.

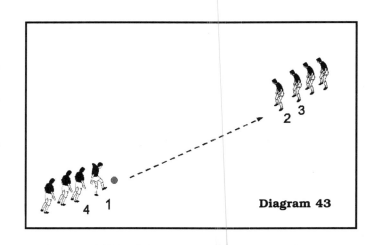

Diagram 43

Sunderland F.C.

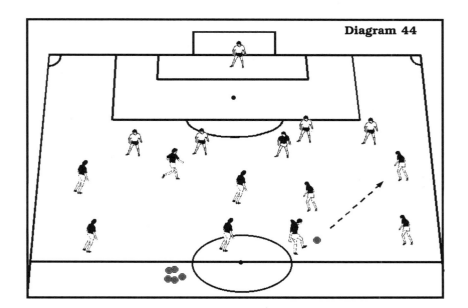

Diagram 44

Attacking Combinations

Practice ended with 15 minutes of ten field players in their regular playing positions playing against a 'flat back four' defense on half a field. Various combinations were practiced with a focus on getting the ball wide and using overlaps.

If the defenders won possession of the ball, they played a long pass to the attacking team's defenders on the half-line and play started again.

November/December 1999 Issue

193

Kansas City Wizards

This practice was observed in Kansas City on July 28, 1999 in the middle of a heat wave with days that were consistently in the high 90's and 100's. Because of this, the practice was shortened to just over an hour in length. Following a run of games where too many goals had been conceded, coach Bob Gansler, who had recently taken the Wizard's head coaching job, was focusing on improving the team's defense. Both Head Coach Bob Gansler and Assistant Coach Ken Fogarty worked with the players. Ken also spent time with me explaining the practice and what they were trying to accomplish. I was particularly impressed with Bob Gansler as he stopped the practice to put across certain coaching points. Gansler also took time during practice to talk individually to certain players to get his message across. At the end of practice, the players watched a videotape of a recent game.

Warm-Up
Five minutes of jogging and stretching.

This was followed by a similar drill done by Manchester United that appeared in the July/August 1999 issue. The players line up in pairs as shown in diagram 1. The dark players dribble the ball towards the end-line while the white players retreat in a 'jockeying' position. After reaching the end-line, the white players dribble the ball back to the half-line with the dark players retreating in a 'jockeying' position. Then stretch and repeat.

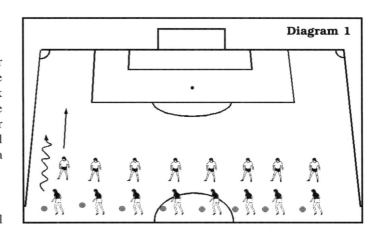

Diagram 1

Progression
As before, however, this time the player dribbling the ball attempts to go past the retreating player.

Progression
As before, the dark players advance while the white players retreat. This time they juggle the ball keeping it in the air between them to the end-line. They then return, juggling to the half-line with the white players advancing and the dark players retreating.

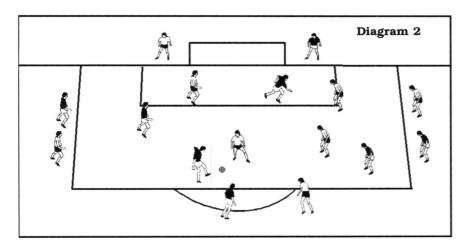

Diagram 2

Possession Game
Inside the penalty area, play 4 v 4 two-touch possession. On the perimeter are four players from each team. The players inside the penalty area can pass to the perimeter players on their team if they choose. When a perimeter player receives a pass, he enters the field and changes places with the player that passed him the ball.

Play for four minutes then stretch.

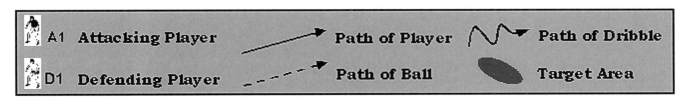

Kansas City Wizards

Half-Field Defending

The starting back four defenders and four midfielders play against eight attackers. The ball always starts with the attacking team at the half-line. The attacking team attempts to score. If the defending team wins possession, they make two or three passes, and then hit a long pass to the player on the attacking team on the half-line. This player continues the game by passing the ball back into play. Play for 25 minutes.

Coaching Points

- Work on defending diagonal runs
- Communication - especially from the goalkeeper
- After a long clearance, the midfielders must pressure the ball so as not to allow an immediate penetrating pass
- Push out after a clearance
- Individual defending techniques
- Cover and balance

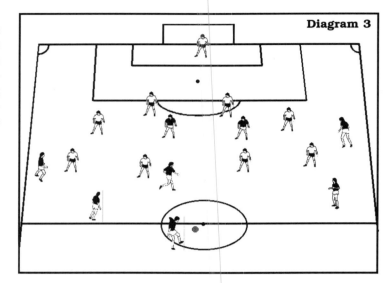

Diagram 3

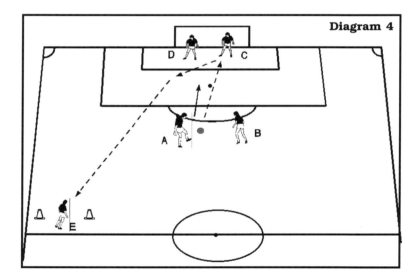

Diagram 4

While the field players worked on one half of the field, the goalkeepers worked on the other half with Wizards goalkeeper coach, Alan Meyer.

Goalkeeper - Distribution

Four goalkeepers are positioned as in diagram 4 with C and D inside the goal and A and B 35 yards from the goal. A passes to C and follows his pass to pressure C. C controls the ball with one touch, then serves the ball to E attempting to get the ball between the cones. After each attempt A, B, C and D rotate positions.

Goalkeeper - Distribution

Two goalkeepers are positioned either side of the penalty area as shown. Cones are placed ten yards from the sides of the penalty area and a 'dummy wall' is placed in the center of the penalty area. The game is played like a game of tennis with the objective to pass the ball over the wall and land it in the 10 yard deep area over the side line of the penalty area to the cones. When receiving the ball, the goalkeeper must control the ball with one touch while keeping it in the 10 yard area and then pass it back with his next touch. Points are scored for your opponent if passes land outside the 10 yard deep area or they don't go over the wall or if the ball isn't kept in the 10 yard deep area when controlled.

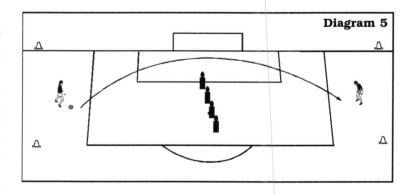

Diagram 5

New England Revolution - Fitness Testing

Vern Gambetta, head of Gambetta Sports Training Systems, has served as the conditioning consultant to the U.S. Men's National Team and the New England Revolution. Vern has also worked with other prominent organizations such as the Chicago Bulls, Chicago White Sox, Women's National Soccer Team, Tampa Bay Mutiny and the North Carolina Women's Soccer Team. Vern is recognized internationally as an expert in training and conditioning for sports. He is a popular speaker and writer on conditioning topics having lectured and conducted clinics in Canada, Japan, Australia and Europe. The following article is a test battery that was used to test the New England Revolution players in 1998.

The testing was done during training camp in Pensacola, Florida. Selected tests were repeated in Boston in April. The jump tests were done early at the MLS pre-season camp in Orlando to familiarize the players and coaches with the tests and then repeated during training camp. The jump tests are primarily designed to indicate the state of the player's nervous system. The other tests are designed to identify the underlying athletic components of soccer performance as an aid to developing more specific directed training programs. Since I was a consultant who did not work with the team on a day-to-day basis, the tests were used to give recommendations to the coaches who would implement the training recommendations in daily and weekly training sessions. The lack of daily contact did not allow me to follow-up on the recommendations to the degree that I would have liked. My goal was to use the testing to design individual training programs as well as to make training more specific to the physiological and biomechanical demands of the game.

It is important to remember that testing is the highest form of training stress outside of the actual game. Testing is important to determine the individual player's athletic qualities relative to the demands of their position and the game. I am not interested in comparing a player against some arbitrary norms. I am interested in intra individual comparison, comparing them against themselves. We must be careful not to draw too many conclusions from one series of tests. Only after several tests conducted periodically throughout the training year can an in-depth profile of each player be determined. In most instances, the tests indicated deficiencies that were already identified through observation of training and game performance. The tests give specific numbers to compare for improvement and motivation, but remember, the ultimate test is the match itself.

The Tests

All tests were electronically timed to ensure accuracy.

Ten Meter Start
Use a standing start with the right foot forward and then the left. This tests the ability to accelerate. A deficiency here indicates a lack of strength and/or poor starting technique. It would be best if there was very little difference between the two times. That would indicate symmetry between legs, which is desirable in soccer.

Twenty Meter Flying Start
Begin running 20 meters before the starting line to insure that you are at top speed during the twenty meter test distance. This indicates top end speed. This is also used to indicate closing speed as expressed in meters/per second. This is how much distance a player can cover in a particular time. A deficiency here indicates a lack of speed due to lack of power (indicated on repetitive jump test) or poor acceleration technique.

Illinois Agility Test
(See diagram 6) Start lying prone by cone 1, get up and sprint to cone 2, go around cone 2, sprint diagonally to middle end cone, weave in and out of the middle cones and then back, sprint to the corner cone, turn around corner and sprint to the finish. This tests the ability to change direction and control the center of gravity. It also indicates body aware-ness, body control and footwork. A deficiency here indicates a lack of functional core and leg strength. This was the agility test that the U.S. men's national team used, therefore I also chose to use it as basis of comparison for the players in the national team pool. Any score under 15 seconds is considered good.

Fifty Yard "Ajax" Shuttle
(See diagram 7) Mark two lines 10 yards apart. The player begins at line A, then runs and touches line B, plants and returns to line A. Repeat this five times for a total of 50 yards. Indicates the ability to start/stop/restart. A deficiency here indicates a lack of functional leg strength and core strength. A score under 10 seconds is considered good.

Bangsbo "Intermittent Recovery" Beep Test
A series of sprints over a 20 yard distance. Indicates specific endurance for soccer in terms of the utilization of oxygen. A deficiency here indicates a lack of overall work capacity. 1,000 meters is considered the minimum standard to be able to play 90 minutes at the highest levels. For further information on the Bansbo Beep Test visit www.soccerfitness.com or Email jbansbo@aki.ku.dk

The following jump tests are performed on an electronic mat.

Jump Test - Squat Jump (SJ)

Start in a stationary squat position with hands on hips and thighs parallel to the floor. Jump as high as possible. This tests the contractile properties of the muscles. Related to basic strength. This relates to the standing start.

Jump Test - Counter Movement Jump (CMJ)

Start upright and quickly squat down and jump as high as possible. This tests the elastic properties of muscle and basic explosive power. Performance on this test relates to the Twenty Meter Fly. It would be best to see a significant difference between height on squat jump and counter movement jump.

Jump Test - Repetitive Jump (RJ)

Perform as many counter movement jumps as possible in fifteen seconds. Power and power endurance. Performance on this test also relates to the Twenty-Meter Fly.

Jump Test - Squat Jump (SJ)

Start in a stationary squat position with the thighs parallel to the floor. This tests the contractile properties of the muscles. Related to basic strength. This relates to the standing start.

Illinois Agility Test

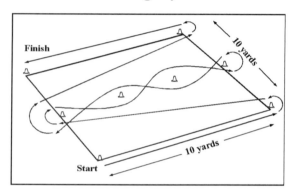

Fifty Yard "Ajax" Shuttle

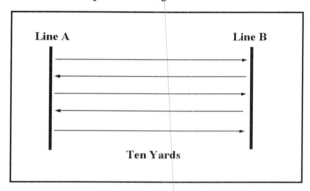

Results and Recommendations

The following are examples of specific training recommendations of two New England Revolution players based on test results. The Power Rating is derived from a formula measuring the contact time on the electronic mat when measuring the Squat Jump, Counter Movement Jump, and the Repetitive Jump.

Player #1

Ten Meter Left	Best: 1.83 sec	Average: 1.86 sec	
Ten Meter Right	Best: 1.80 sec	Average: 1.80 sec	
20 Meter Fly	Best: 2.45 sec	Average: 2.48 sec	Maximum Velocity m/s: 8.16
Illinois Agility	Best: 16.00 sec	Average: 16.05 sec	
Ajax Shuttle	Best: 10.73 sec	Average: 10.79 sec	

Beep Test   Speed/Level: 21/4   Distance: 920 meters

Squat Jump   Height: .464 meters

Counter Movement Jump   Height: .484 meters

Repetitive Jump   Number of Jumps: 15   Average Height: .414 meters   Power: 31.16

Recommendations - Acceleration work two times a week, all short burst with an emphasis on good technique. He tends to take too long a first step. Work agility on the same day - here the emphasis should be on quick change of direction and footwork. He should be doing some agility work each day! His 15 second repetitive jump test indicates good power, in fact, his jump test indicate good power potential but it does not show up in the speed & agility tests. I also think it is reflected on the field in his inability to gain a step on the opposition.

Player #2

Ten Meter left   Best: 1.72 sec   Average: 1.77 sec

Ten Meter Right   Best: 1.84 sec   Average: 1.83 sec

20 Meter Fly   Best: 2.35 sec   Average: 2.36 sec   Maximum Velocity m/s: 8.51

Illinois Agility   Best: 14.60 sec   Average: 14.65 sec

Ajax Shuttle   Best: 10.00 sec   Average: 10.05 sec

Beep test   Speed/Level: 21/6   Distance: 1000 meters

Squat Jump   Height: .383 meters

Counter Movement Jump   Height: .394 meters

Repetitive Jump   Number of Jumps: 14   Average Height: .445 meters Power: 26.73

Recommendations - Needs work on acceleration. Emphasize correct mechanics! Agility is good. Endurance is just barely acceptable for a player at this level. Jump tests indicate that he needs to emphasize a plyometrics program two times a week. Poor jump results are reflected in his lack of ability to accelerate. The emphasis should be on standing jumps and hurdle jumps. Strength training with emphasis on legs and trunk two times a week.

F.C. Petrolul Ploiesti - Romania

WORLD CLASS COACHING has published a number of articles from F.C. Petrolul Ploiesti who plays in Division One of the Romanian Football League. This article from coach Constantin Moldoveanu shows three different patterns they use when practicing 'fast breaks'. These patterns are initially practiced unopposed until the players are comfortable with them and can repeat them successfully at speed. Defenders are then introduced to make the practice more game-realistic. Also, a time restriction can be in effect to make sure they are practiced at full speed. All the combinations start with the goal-keeper in possession but they can easily be adapted to start with a defender in possession. Practice using both flanks.

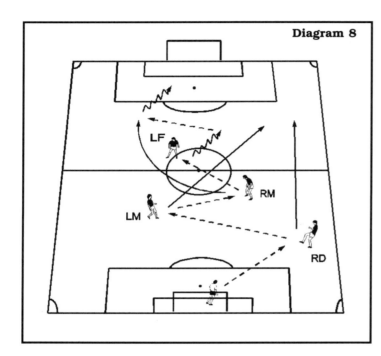

Diagram 8

Fast Break One

The goalkeeper distributes by passing or throwing to the right defender.

The right defender passes firmly to the left midfielder and makes a run up the flank.

The left midfielder passes to the right midfielder and makes a diagonal run.

The right midfielder passes into the left forward's feet and makes an overlapping run past the left forward.

The forward dribbles the ball across the field then cuts a pass back in the direction of the overlapping right midfielder.

The right midfielder then has the option to shoot or cross.

Note

It is important to note that in order to take the opponents' defenders away, the runs without the ball of the RD, LM and the run with the ball of the LF are all away from the run of the RM who should receive the ball in space and in a goal scoring situation.

Coaching Points

- Firm passes
- One or two touches

Fast Break Two

The goalkeeper passes the ball to the center defender.

The center defender passes to the right defender.

The right defender passes to the left midfielder and then makes a run down the flank.

The left midfielder passes into the path of the running right defender.

The right defender then has the option to cross, dribble or shoot.

Note

Again, the runs without the ball (LF and RM) are away from the final pass to RD giving him time and space to cross, dribble or shoot.

Coaching Points

- Timing of runs
- Firm accurate passes

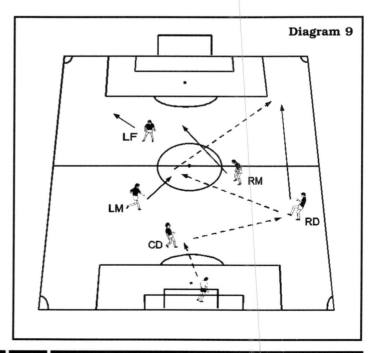

Diagram 9

F.C. Petrolul Ploiesti - Romania

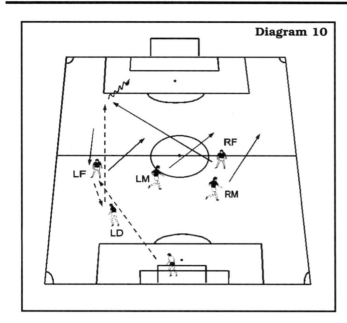

Diagram 10

Fast Break Three
The goalkeeper throws a long pass to the left forward who has checked back to receive the ball.

The left forward trails a pass to the left defender and makes a diagonal run across the field.

The left defender plays a long pass toward the corner for the right forward who has made a diagonal run from the left side of the field.

Notes
Again the runs of players without the ball are designed to take the opponents' defenders away from the where the RF will receive the ball.

Coaching Points
As in the previous two patterns.

Interview with Tony DiCicco

Tony DiCicco, coach of the U.S. Women's National Team and newly crowned 1999 World Cup Champions, shares some thoughts and a possession practice with WORLD CLASS COACHING.

Firstly, congratulations on winning the World Cup. It was a tremendous achievement.

Thank you very much. It was obviously exactly what we were after and the scope of the event went beyond our expectations.

What would you say were the main factors that led to your team's success, not just in the World Cup but in the games building up to the World Cup?

Number one was the talent on the team. We are a very talented team. We have players that are very experienced and capable of winning the big games. Secondly, our preparation, along with China, was probably the best of all the teams. Because we don't have a domestic league, our players weren't being pulled back and forth from their club teams as we see in many other countries and certainly in the men's side of the game. We were able to bring them into a residency situation in Florida, train day in and day out and play international games and tournaments to replicate a league season like a professional team. Finally, I think the closeness of the team was a major factor. The players were all very supportive. For instance, I had Olympic gold medallists that sat on the bench but supported the players on the field. I think that kind of closeness gets you through the tough games and the penalty shootouts, etc.

How was the build up to the games?

My philosophy in coaching is 'less is more' just before an event. I find that if you try to do that extra training session or fit in the extra practice, you tend to do too much. So as long as your preparation is good, then right before the event I feel that 'less is more' is good. We finished our preparation June 6 in Portland and I gave everyone the next week off before we went into training for our first World Cup game in New Jersey. In preparation for our first game in New Jersey, I thought the team was well rested and enthusiastic to go out and train. Also, we had always realized that to win the World Cup, we would have to be together for a four-week period, and by giving them that week off just before the training for our first game, it fitted into that four-week cycle. If we had trained that week, we would have been together for over 5 weeks, which we felt was too long.

What about the playing formations that you used?

We pretty much used the 4-3-3 all the way through 1999. One midfielder would be a defensive/holding midfielder and two of the forwards would play wide, almost like traditional wingers. The reason we went to this system was twofold. Firstly, I wanted to keep a three-front. The reason was that all the other countries played a two-front so we wanted to do something that other teams would have to adjust to. The other reason was we wanted to protect the center of our defense a little more. In the past, we have played with only three defenders. However, I felt it was important to protect the space in front of our center back and behind our two

Interview with Tony DiCicco

attacking central midfielders. This also allowed our outside backs to push forward, and as you saw, both Chastain and Fawcett scored goals in the World Cup.

What did you work on the most with your team during practices?

Generally, we did a lot of possession work. However, I wasn't pleased with our possession play so we obviously need to keep working at it. We do a lot of possession work where the players have to deal with tight spaces, the pressure of an opponent, and keeping the ball. It's technical work that is also tactical work – how quickly a player can solve pressure and get the ball to a teammate who can now start to generate an attack. We also spent quite a bit of time on defense such as closing and pressurizing quickly because the teams we come up against, if you give them time and space, they are going to exploit it. We always spend time, though not considerable time, on set pieces. I like to say we 'imprint' set pieces. We don't train until we are doing it successfully every time, because the next time you do it in a game or practice, it could be a disaster. So we 'imprint' the set piece

so the players know what we are looking for and that's it. Finally, we are always looking to enhance our goalbox organization, the quality of runs into the penalty area, our finishing, etc.

How long would a typical training session be?

Typically between 75 and 90 minutes. At the end of practice, the players will have about 15 minutes to work on their own and do some shooting, crossing, etc.

Do you use video analysis?

We videotape all our games. Occasionally, we will videotape a practice, but our video capability isn't really good enough to warrant taping all the practices. Our games are edited using a sophisticated editing system where we can edit the game to about 20 minutes in length. This will be in sections, such as, negative defending, positive defending, positive attacks, goals, etc. This then becomes a key-coaching tool at team meetings.

Women's World Cup Team - Possession

Small-Sided Game

After an individual warm-up of jogging and stretching, the formal warm-up will begin with the whole squad playing 8 v 8 plus two players who play for the team in possession. We would use a 20 x 40 yard area or play in the goalbox as shown in diagram 11. To start with, the players must play two-touch. The objective is to improve the first touch because you have to have a good first touch that allows you to keep playing. Secondly, your first touch should eliminate pressure. There will be a lot of mistakes made but the tight space will replicate some of the demands you will find in a game.

Progression

Play free soccer. Now we are looking at the decision making - when to play one-touch, when to keep the ball and relieve pressure individually, when to switch play to the other end of the grid, etc.

Progression

We end with a game called 'Twenty Five'. Each team counts their passes (don't have to be consecutive) and the first team to 25 passes wins the game. It usually takes four or five possessions to get to 25 passes.

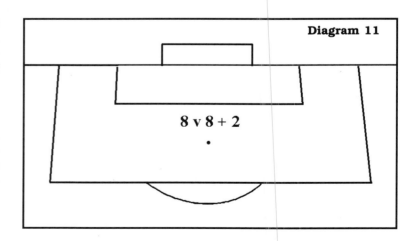

Diagram 11

8 v 8 + 2

Women's World Cup Team - Possession

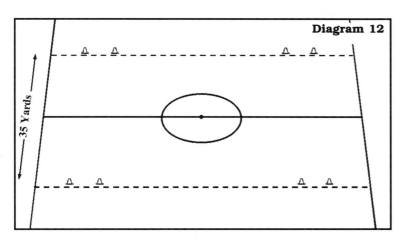

Diagram 12

Change Of Point Game

Mark a field 35 yards deep using the full width of the field. We typically use the middle third of the field as shown in diagram 12. Place small 3 yard goals (or cones) 10 yards in from each touch-line. We occasionally use full size goals but mostly the small goals. Play the same 8 v 8 plus two players playing for the team in possession. The objective of the game is to keep possession and look to change the point of attack to create scoring opportunities. What I am looking for in this game is 'initial penetration to look for scoring opportunities and then assessment'. If the scoring opportunity is on, then we should go for it. If not, we should look for a central player who can then find another player on the other side of the field and see if we can create a scoring opportunity there. If we can't create a chance there, we will look to switch it again. I am looking for the team to play a little east to west if we can't go forward because of our player personnel. If I can get Mia Hamm or Tiffany Millbret or Cindy Parlow or Kristine Lilly or Shannon McMillan, etc. a little more time and space, then they have the ability to run at the defender and beat them, causing the defense to make dramatic adjustments.

Progression

A 20 yard channel is marked in the middle of the field. In this channel, players can only play one-touch. The 'one-touch channel' is designed to keep any switches moving quickly.

Coaching Points

- Read the defense
- How organized are the defenders
- Will one change of point be enough to break down the cohesiveness of the defense

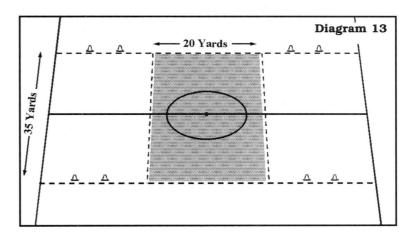

Diagram 13

← 20 Yards →

Full-Field Game

We now progress the practice into an 8 v 8 game using full size goals positioned on the top of each penalty area and goalkeepers. This gives us the opportunity to coach the players within the game. We will often have the first team players play against the reserves. This way we can ask the reserves to play a certain way. For instance, if we feel our upcoming opponents will look to push their defense up and pressure us, we can ask the reserves to play that way giving us the opportunity for our players to attempt to solve that style of play, and also, we as coaches can see how best to solve that situation. The same situation applies for other situations we may come across, such as, a 'Bunker' defense, where the other team sits with 11 players behind the ball and looks to crowd the defensive third and counter-attack.

Coaching Points

- Coach all previous coaching points
- Offside is in effect

Diagram 14

Submitted by Vinicius Dos Santos. The following practices were observed at the Clube Pequeninos Do Jockey, Sao Paulo, Brazil in the summer of 1998. Clube Pequeninos Do Jockey is a major youth soccer development program similar to the Tahuichi program in Bolivia. Pequeninos has relationships with many Brazilian, South American and even European Clubs. Their main function is to search and develop new talent for its clubs. Many professional players started their careers at Pequeninos including Ze Roberto of Bayer Leverkussen and the Brazilian National Team. Pequeninos is basically an inner city program. They have around 2,000 players aged 5 - 20 and almost 100 coaches. The following practices were done with the U14 age group

Technical/Tactical Circuit

Position cones as shown in diagram 15. Have a supply of balls at the center of the field at A. Depending on the number of players, have 3 or 4 players at each cone.

Midfielder A passes a long driven ball in the air to center defender B and then starts moving wide to receive a pass later.

Center defender B controls and passes wide to defender C, then runs the length of the field to the edge of the penalty area.

Defender C controls and passes to incoming D (can be defenders, midfielders or forwards). He then makes an overlapping run down the flank.

Player D receives the ball, turns and weaves in and out of the flags and passes to midfielder A who has made his way from his starting position. Player D then makes a curved run to the far post area.

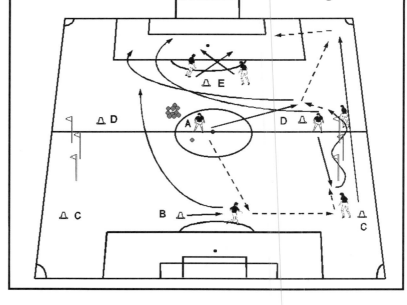

Diagram 15

Midfielder A then passes toward the corner for overlapping defender C and then makes a curved run to the far post area.

Defender C then crosses the ball into the penalty area.

The two forwards at E make criss-cross runs from outside the penalty area.

The players in the penalty area attempt to finish with one touch if possible.

Restart again going in the opposite direction.

Coaching Points

- Play at a fast game pace
- Time runs into the penalty area
- Firm 'crisp' passes
- A good first touch to allow for a quick accurate pass

Progression

Add defenders in the penalty area.

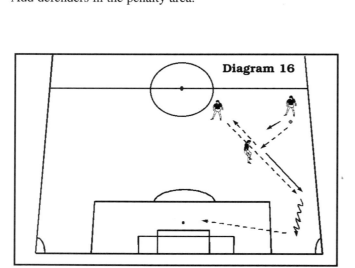

Diagram 16

Variations

Vary the triangulations between A, C and D. Diagrams 16, 17, 18 and 19 are possible combinations. There were also many possible combinations in the E.C. Vitoria article from the July/August issue that could be adapted for this practice.

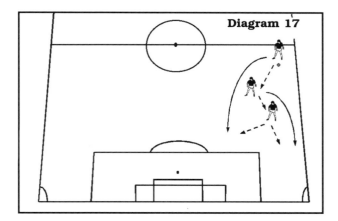

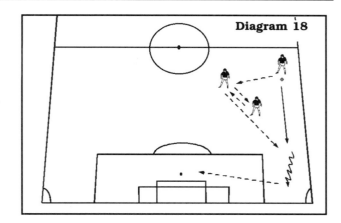

The following practice, also observed at the Clube Peneninos Do Jockey, is the first in a series of practices designed to imprint the principals of 'Brazilian' soccer into their young players. In this issue, we look at player rotation when bringing the ball out from the back. In future issues, we will build on this theme with sessions on Midfield Play, Attacking Play and finally a practice on how to piece everything together.

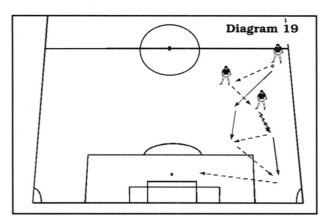

Building from a Defensive Back Four

Mark a field approximately 50 x 50 yards with full size goals as shown in diagram 20. Organize into three groups of four players with one group playing at a time. Using shadow play without any opposition, the players practice bringing the ball out from the defensive third and converting that possession into an attack. Special attention is given to forward runs of the defenders. Many different combinations can be practiced. In this example, the ball is switched involving the goalkeeper. The right defender, A, starts the switch by passing to the goalkeeper.

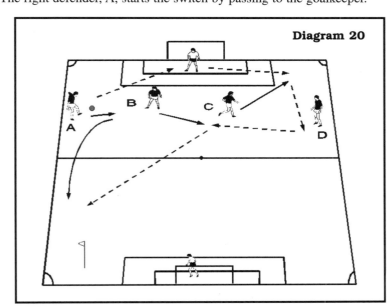

The goalkeeper controls the ball with an open body position and passes to the opposite flank for the center defender, C, who is running back to receive the ball.

C passes down the line to the left defender, D.

D passes inside to the sweeper, B, who has moved from his deep position to make himself available for the pass.

B controls the ball with an open body position and switches the ball again to right defender A who has made the run from his original starting position.

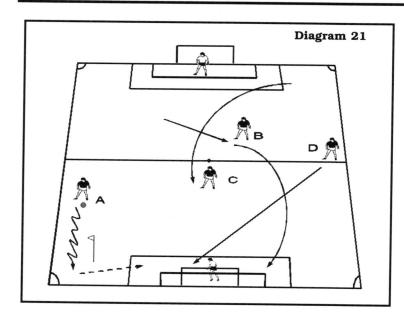

Diagram 21

Building From a Defensive Back Four

Diagram 21 shows the forward runs of all four players. Right defender A dribbles the ball past the flag and crosses for incoming B and D. The center defender, C, holds his run outside the goal-box for any rebounds.

Following an attempt on goal, all the players retreat backwards as quickly as possible but keep facing the goal so they can see what the goal-keeper is doing. The goalkeeper punts the ball and the player receiving has to control the ball before it bounces. Once he has control of the ball, he passes it wide to a defender who passes it back to the goalkeeper that just punted it and the drill starts again going in the opposite direction.

Coaching Points
* Timing of runs
* Start from alternate flanks
* Try different combinations

Nottingham Forest - U11 Youth Team

Contributed by Nottingham Forest youth team coach, Peter Cooper. Peter has experience coaching youth players of different ages at a number of English Premier League clubs including Leeds United and now Nottingham Forest. This article focuses on defending individually, in twos and threes, and as a team.

Warm-Up
The players line up in pairs facing each other three yards apart. The ball is passed back and forth with firm, hard passes. The players should test each other by hitting quick, firm passes.

Coaching Points
* Accurate firm passes
* Be on your toes ready to receive a pass
* Concentrate on a good first touch
* Avoid easy slow passes

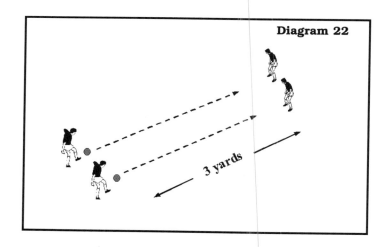

Diagram 22

3 yards

Nottingham Forest - U11 Youth Team

Closing and Pressure

Keep in pairs as in the warm-up. This time move five yards apart. The 'A' players pass the ball to the 'B' players who control and stop the ball. As soon as player A has passed the ball, he closes down player B. Player B then leaves the ball for player A and jogs to the opposite end where player A came from and player A continues the drill by passing to player B again. Alternate after 3 or 4 attempts.

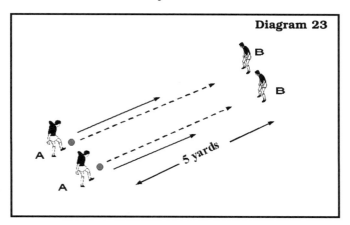

Diagram 23

5 yards

Coaching Points

- Close down the first 3 - 4 yards very quickly then slowly creep forward toward the player
- Put the brakes on 1 - 2 yards from the player
- Pressure with a sideways stance
- Keep your eye on the ball

Progression

Allow the receiving player to perform a fake or dummy just a little distance either side of the defender.

Coaching Points

- Can you 'nick' the ball away
- Change your body stance according to the position of the ball

One v One Shielding

The players continue to be organized in pairs. (Change partners from previous drills if desired.) One player has possession of the ball and attempts to keep the ball from his partner for a period of time (30 - 60 seconds). Alternate the player starting with the ball.

Coaching Points

- The ball should be positioned at the furthest point away from your partner
- Position your body between the ball and partner
- Be strong and concentrate

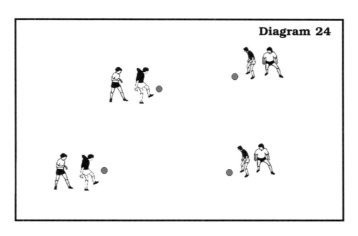

Diagram 24

Small-Sided Game

The players continue to be organized in pairs. (Change partners from previous drills if desired.) Mark a field of 40 x 30 yards

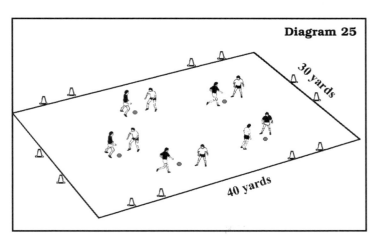

Diagram 25

30 yards

40 yards

with six small goals (cones) around the perimeter. One player has possession of the ball and attempts to dribble through any of the small goals around the perimeter. The partner defends. Once a goal is scored, the player must score his next goal by dribbling through a different goal. The game can be made competitive by playing for one minute and keeping score.

Coaching Points

- Show good ball control when dribbling
- Keep your head up
- Change of pace coupled with a change of direction
- Defenders should set themselves and be aware of their positioning in the grid
- Body shape of defender

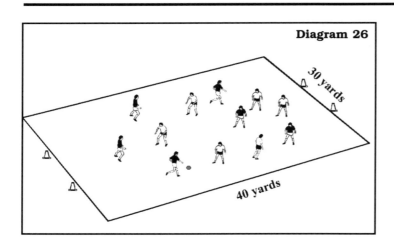

Diagram 26

Small-Sided Game

Use the same 40 x 30 yard area, this time with goals at both ends. Play 6 v 6 with man-for-man marking. (Each player has a partner on the other team that they are responsible for marking for the whole game.) Players can go and challenge any other player, but if the partner that they are supposed to be marking scores, they do five push-ups.

Progression

All the players on a team need to be in the attacking half when that team scores.

Progression

One player has to hold back and give his team instructions.

The following three drills are a progression of a practice session to improve defending in pairs, threes and as a team.

Defending In Pairs

The goalkeeper serves to the dark players who attack the goal in pairs. The first two white players in line move up to defend.

Coaching Points

- Pressure and cover
- Block shots
- Goalkeeper and back defender should talk

Progression

Add another defender to make a 3 v 2 situation.

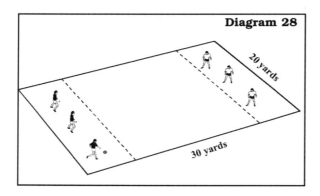

Diagram 27

Defending In Threes

Mark a field of 30 x 20 yards with 5 yard end zones at each end. The white team serves the ball in the air or on the ground to the dark team. The dark team then attempts to cross into the white team's end zone with the ball under control.

Coaching Points

- Pressure, cover and balance
- Communication
- Blocks
- Get in line

Diagram 28

Team Defending

Mark a field 40 x 20 with two 10 yard end zones. Use goals and goalkeepers, three defenders in each end zone, and four attackers in the middle area. The goalkeeper of the white team serves a ball to one of the dark team players who plays it with one touch, if possible, to the gray attackers who then attack the three dark defenders.

Coaching Points

- Previous coaching points
- Stay on your feet
- Narrow angles

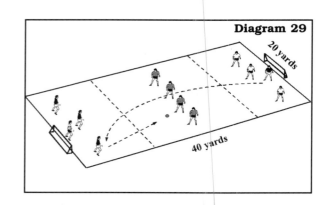

Diagram 29

Newcastle United Youth Teams

I observed the following practices of the Newcastle United U13 and U15 teams during my visit to England in February. The practices were held in the evening on an artificial surface. The temperature was just a few degrees above freezing but the players were dressed accordingly and never showed a hint of being cold. In fact, the practice was performed at a quick tempo so the players were always on the move and obviously kept warm that way.

Warm-Up

The players form a 12 yard circle with two players in the center with balls. The center players play a firm pass to an outside player, follows the pass and pressures the outside player as he receives the ball. When the outside player receives the ball, he controls it with one touch across his body and then moves into the center of the circle changing places with the player that passed him the ball.

Coaching Points

- Work on receiving the ball with both feet
- Receive with one foot and pass with the other foot
- Firm passes

Progression

Enlarge the circle to 30 yards. Now the inside players should 'ping' hard passes to the outside players to test their controlling first touch.

One-Touch Lay-Offs and Passing

Organize the players in a 40 x 30 yard area as shown in diagram 31. Three of the perimeter players have balls.

A passes to B who lays the ball off with one touch to C.

C passes with one touch, if possible, to D.

C then asks for a pass from another perimeter player with a ball and the drill continues.

Therefore, both center players practice receiving the long pass on alternate plays. Play for two minutes, then change players so that all the players take a turn in the center.

Diagram 30

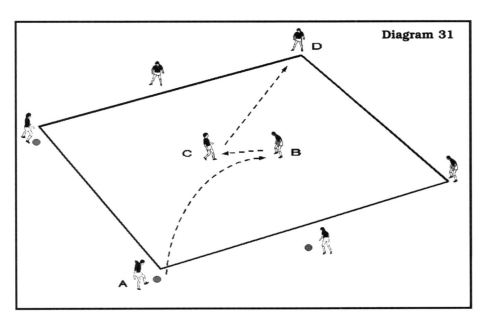

Diagram 31

Coaching Points

- Vary the pass into the center - low, high, hard passes, etc.
- Work on different receiving techniques - head, chest, different parts of the foot, etc.
- Lay-offs should be in the space in front of the receiving player so that he can make a one-touch pass to the perimeter player.
- The player receiving the lay-off should be alert and ready to adjust his position according to where the lay-off is.

Progression

Add a defender to put slight pressure on the player receiving the lay-off.

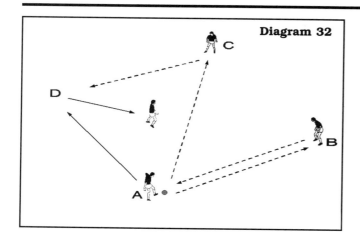

Diagram 32

One-Touch Passing

Organize the players in 10-yard areas with a player on each corner as shown in diagram 32.

A passes to B.

B passes straight back with one touch.

D moves into the center to defend.

A has the option of playing a give-and-go with C (as in diagram 32) or receiving the pass from B on his back foot and moving into D's position (diagram 33). D then takes A's position.

A passes the ball to C who then continues the drill by passing to B.

Variation

Diagram 33 shows player A receiving the ball on his back foot and dribbling to D's position.

Coaching Points

- Quality firm passes
- Use one touch whenever possible
- A decides which option, depending on the position of D

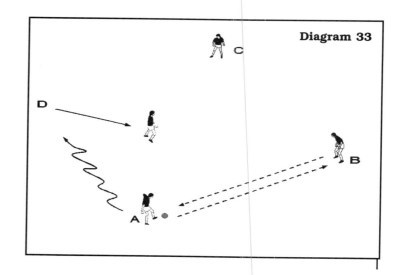

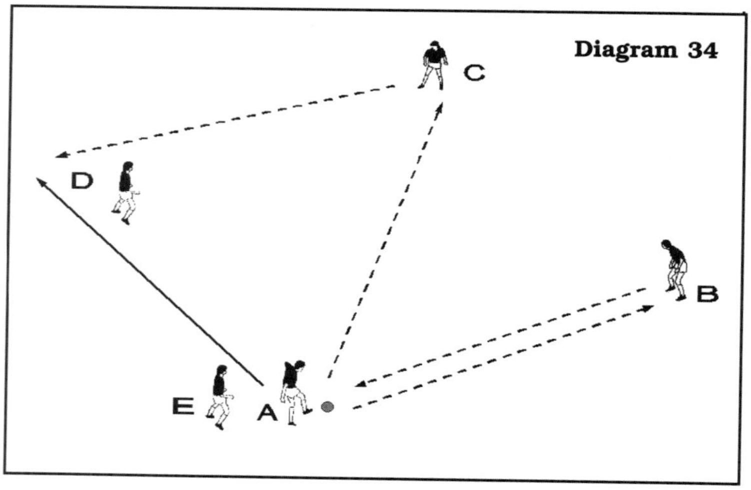

Diagram 33

One Touch Passing

Organize the players in groups of five in 10 yard areas with two players on one corner and one player on each of the other corners.

A passes to B.

B passes straight back to A.

A passes to C then runs to D's position to receive the return pass from C.

The drill continues with A passing the ball back to C who passes to E and runs to B's position to receive the return pass from E.

Diagram 34

Coaching Points

- One touch passes whenever possible
- Focus on the weight of the passes

Practice ended with a small sided-game. The coaches looked for the players to put into the game the things they had been working on during practice. However, it is worth noting that the coaches allowed the players to play without many stoppages to get across any coaching points. Mostly the coaches kept encouraging the players and complimenting them whenever they excelled.

Neil Turnbull, the coach of the Canadian Women's National Team, outlined his thoughts and recommendations on coaching young girls at a recent Bryst International coaching seminar.

National Women's Team Training Priorities For Youth Players

Since 1996 and earlier, I have had the opportunity to view the top U15, U17, U19 and U20 players in this country, as well as work with the U11 and U13 age groups. The following are several observations, comments and recommendations. (Please note that not all will be applicable to the younger age groups.)

Mental Toughness

Players need to know that it is ok to compete – players need to understand the importance of every ball possession. Each ball possession should be of utmost importance. If a player has possession of the ball, they need to fight to keep it, and if they lose possession of the ball, they need to fight to win it back. Too often a player will give up the ball either by dispossession or a poor pass and a goal is scored as a result. Players must be shown and learn the importance of ball possession.

One v One Play

The basic element for the game of soccer; players must understand and be strong and capable in this area – when in possession and when not in possession of the ball.

Technical Abilities – All Areas

- First touch – learn to play with head up
- Power/technique – ability to hit balls over 40 yards with both feet… in the air and above head height
- Ability to receive and control passes that are played over 40 yards
- Shooting/finishing – be consistent and take opportunities… players should only be satisfied with a goal
- Finishing from crosses – one-touch volleys, half volleys and headers
- Arial Balls – heading, heading the ball forwards and not letting the ball hit the ground

Possession

Although the female players are making great strides forward in the game, the technical and technical/tactical habits must be hammered home. Too often the ball is given away.

Each practice should incorporate possession training or possession under pressure training. Introduce combination plays – give-and-go's, takeovers, overlaps, third player runs, etc. Play small-sided games with an emphasis on possession under pressure.

Decision Making

A. Movement off the ball – both in attack and defending situations
B. Understanding what is dangerous and non-dangerous space while in attack
   Willingness and ability to go at and past defenders in one v one situations
   Greater emphasis placed on creative play in the attacking third – combination play
C. Understanding what is dangerous and non-dangerous space while in defense
   How to defend the player with the ball
   How to defend the player without the ball
   Willingness and ability to win the one v one battles
   Willingness and ability to adjust to the flow of the game – starting position

Speed of Play

- Players too often play at one speed – There must be a change of pace – explosive power
- Players must perform basic explosive combination plays (give-and-go's, overlaps, takeover runs)
- Players must train at speed

Goalkeeping

The standard for goalkeepers is certainly improving, but the emphasis needs to focus on:

- Goalkeepers must be able to take their own goal kicks and the distance must increase to reach the center circle
- Goalkeepers must improve on the balls crossed into the penalty area. In most cases, high balls are not caught at the highest point possible. Also, they must attack the ball from the cross.
- When the ball enters the goalkeepers' middle of the defending third, they need to start one or two yards closer to their own goal line – not necessarily the traditional starting position of the male goalkeeper.
- Goalkeepers must learn to hold on to shots, and not allow the ball to drop to the ground.

Fitness Level and Lifestyle – Year Round

Players should understand that a basic foundation of fitness is required. A greater emphasis needs to be placed on an aerobic base, speed and power training, as well as strength training. Players must learn to balance soccer, school, work and social life. There is a need for players to better understand the GAME, watch tapes or live games on the television and read from text.

The following practical session on improving Possession/Possession Under Pressure was presented by Neil Turnbull, coach of the Canadian Women's National Team at a recent Bryst International Coaches Seminar.

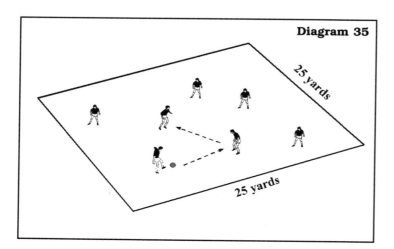

Diagram 35

Possession Warm-Up

Organize six or seven players in a 25 x 25-yard area. Using one ball, the players pass and move staying inside the area.

Coaching Points

- Head up
- Early communication
- Movement

Progression/Variation

Play with two balls - pass one ball and then look for the other.

Possession Warm-Up

In the same 25 x 25 yard area, have four pairs of players with each pair wearing different colored jerseys. Play 6 v 2. In diagram 36, the six players are keeping the ball from the two white players. The pair that is responsible for losing possession then become defenders.

Coaching Points

- As in previous warm-up
- Support angles and distance
- Prepare body to receive a pass - open body position
- Speed of thought
- Transition

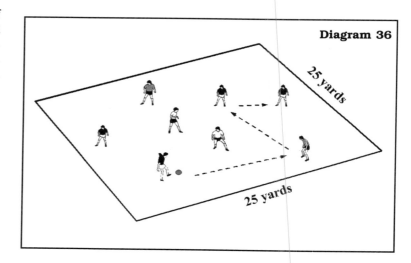

Diagram 36

Diagram 37

Progression

As above, but this time two target players on the outside and 4 v 2 inside. The team of four attempts to keep possession and play to a target player. Target players are limited to two-touch. Once successful, the target player passes back to the team of four who now attempts to pass to the other target player making the game directional.

Coaching Points

- As in the previous two warm-ups
- Thought - possession with the idea to go forward

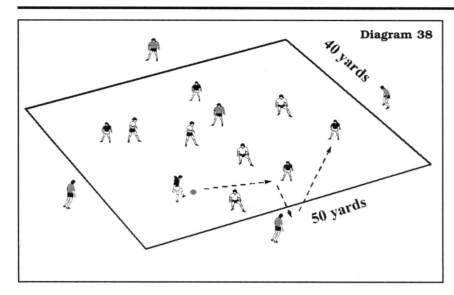

Diagram 38

40 yards

50 yards

Possession Under Pressure

Two teams of five play possession in a 50 x 40-yard area. The third team of five positions four players on the perimeter and one player inside. These players all play for the team in possession.

Coaching Points

Apply the coaching points from the previous two warm-ups.

Progression

Two perimeter players on opposite sides act as targets only. The team in possession must now play directional to the targets. Now the emphasis can be placed on possession under pressure with the idea to go forward.

For further information on Bryst International Coaching Seminars contact Gary Miller at 905-898-8141.

"If You Like Our Book You'll Love Our Newsletter"

"Join the thousands of coaches from 27 countries worldwide and subscribe to our bi-monthly newsletter".

Visit our website at
www.worldclasscoaching.com
or call out toll free number to order your subscription or for further information.

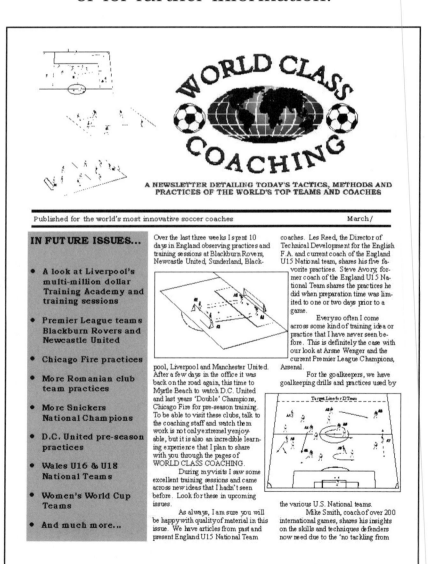

REEDSWAIN BOOKS

#291 Soccer Fitness Training • $12.95
by Enrico Arcelli and Ferretto Ferretti

#169 Coaching Advanced Soccer Players • $12.95
by Richard Bate

#225 The Sweeper • $9.95
by Richard Bate

#793 Coaching the 5-3-2 with a Sweeper • $14.95
by Fascetti and Scaia

#264 Coaching Soccer 6 to 10 year Olds • $14.95
by Giuliano Rusca

#167 Soccer Training Games, Drills and Fitness Practices
by Malcolm Cook
$14.95

#792 120 Competitive Games and Exercises for Soccer
by Nicola Pica
$14.95

#256 The Creative Dribbler • $14.95
by Peter Schreiner

#262 Psychology of Soccer • $12.95
by Massimo Cabrini

#905 Soccer Strategies: Defensive and Attacking Tactics
by Robyn Jones
$12.95

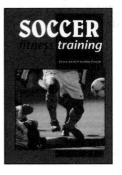
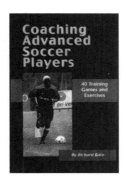

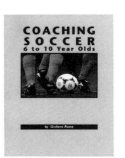

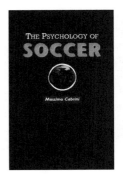

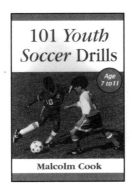
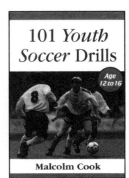

#254 101 Youth Soccer Drills Ages 7-11 • $14.95
by Malcolm Cook

#255 101 Youth Soccer Drills Ages 12-16 • $14.95
by Malcolm Cook

REEDSWAIN BOOKS

#788 Zone Play: A Tactical and Technical Handbook
Pereni and Di Cesare
$14.95

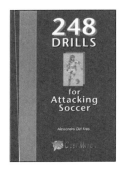

#794 248 Drills for Attacking Soccer • $14.95
by Allessandro Del Freo

#154 Coaching Soccer • $14.95
by Bert van Lingen

#177 Principles of Brazilian Soccer
by Jose' Thadeu Goncalves
$16.95

#175 The Coaching Philosophies of Louis van Gaal and the Ajax Coaches
by Kormelink and Seeverens
$14.95

#244 Coaching the 4-4-2 • $14.95
by Marziali and Mora

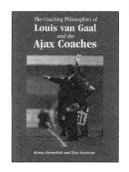

#789 Soccer Scouting Guide • $12.95
by Joe Bertuzzi

#284 The Dutch Coaching Notebook • $14.95

#785 Complete Book of Soccer Restart Plays
by Mario Bonfanti and Angelo Pereni
$14.95

#261 Match Analysis and Game Preparation • $12.95
by Kormelink and Seeverens

#765 Attacking Schemes and Training Exercises
by Fascetti and Scaia
$14.95

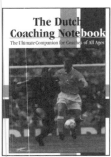

#185 Conditioning for Soccer • $19.95
Dr. Raymond Verheijen

#786 Soccer Nutrition • $10.95
by Enrico Arcelli

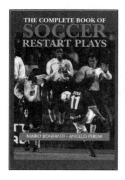

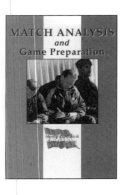